Streams of Cultural Capital

Mestizo Spaces

Espaces Métissés

V. Y. Mudimbe
EDITOR

Bogumil Jewsiewicki
ASSOCIATE EDITOR

CONTRIBUTORS

Arjun Appadurai

Xiaomei Chen

Hans Ulrich Gumbrecht

Biodun Jeyifo

Bruce Kapferer

Judith Kapferer

Anne Knudsen

Mary N. Layoun

Jean-François Lyotard

David Palumbo-Liu

Brad Prager

Michael Richardson

Carlos Rincón

Irmela Schneider

Robert Weimann

Streams of Cultural Capital

Transnational Cultural Studies

Edited by
David Palumbo-Liu *and*
Hans Ulrich Gumbrecht

STANFORD UNIVERSITY PRESS   *Stanford, California 1997*

Stanford University Press
Stanford, California

© 1993 by ANMA Libri and the
Department of French and Italian,
Stanford University
New Introduction and Epilogue © 1997
by the Board of Trustees of the
Leland Stanford Junior University

Originally published in the
Spring-Fall 1993 issue of *SLR*
(*Stanford Literary Review*),
Volume 10, Numbers 1–2.

Reprinted, with a new Introduction and
Epilogue, in 1997 by Stanford University Press.

LC 97-67436
ISBN 0-8047-3036-9 (cl.)
ISBN 0-8047-3037-7 (pbk.)

⊚ This book is printed on acid-free, recycled paper.

Printed in the United States of America

Original printing 1997
Last figure below indicates year of this printing:
06   05   04   03   02   01   00   99   98   97

Preface

This volume originally appeared in 1993 as a special issue of *Stanford Literature Review*. Because of a number of inquiries about that volume, which had a small print run, the formation of the Mestizo Spaces / Espaces métissés series, and the interest expressed by the series editors and Stanford University Press, we decided it would be worthwhile to reprint these essays. We have written new essays to introduce and comment on the topic of the anthology; these recast our sense of the particular contribution of this volume and recontextualize it within current debates.

We wish to thank Helen Tartar of Stanford University Press for her interest in the project, as well as the series editors for their support.

D.P.-L. and H.U.G.

Contents

Contributors

ARJUN APPADURAI is professor of anthropology and South Asian languages and civilizations at the University of Chicago, where he was previously director of the Chicago Humanities Institute. His many publications include *Modernity at Large: Cultural Dimensions of Globalization*. He is the director of the Globalization Project at the University of Chicago and is currently researching the relation between ethnic violence and images of territory in modern nation-states.

XIAOMEI CHEN, associate professor of Chinese and comparative literature at Ohio State University, is the author of *Occidentalism: A Theory of Counter-Discourse in Post-Mao China*. She is currently working on a book entitled *Acting the Right Part: The Politics of Drama in the Age of Mao*.

HANS ULRICH GUMBRECHT is Albert Guérard Professor of Literature in the departments of comparative literature and French and Italian at Stanford University. His main fields of research include medieval culture and "literature," the culture of European Enlightenment and the bourgeois revolutions, media history and the cultural history of the body, the history of literary scholarship, and literary/cultural theory. Among his publications in English are *Making Sense in Life and Literature, Materialities of Communication*, co-edited with Ludwig Pfeiffer, *A History of Spanish Literature* (forthcoming; published in German in 1990), and *1926* (forthcoming).

BIODUN JEYIFO, professor of English at Cornell University, specializes in African, African-American, and postcolonial literatures and cultural production. Among his books are *The Yoruba Popular Travelling Theatre of Nigeria*, *The Truthful Lie*, and *Wole Soyinka: History and Mythopoesis* (forthcoming).

BRUCE KAPFERER is professor of anthropology at University College, London, and foundation professor of anthropology and archaeology at James Cook University, Australia. He is the author of *The Feast of the Sorcerer*.

JUDITH KAPFERER teaches in sociology of education and Australian studies at Flinders University, South Australia. A graduate of Sydney University, Manchester University, and Flinders University, she has published on education, sociology, and cultural studies. She is the author of *Being All Equal*.

ANNE KNUDSEN writes about European Union minority policies, cultural-political and ethnic movements, and other minority issues in the Danish political weekly *Weekendavisen*. She has published several books in Danish about modern European history, European cultural conflicts, and European Union language policies. Her latest book, *All Is Well, Send More Money*, a critique of Danish culture, topped the Danish bestseller list for three weeks in 1996.

MARY N. LAYOUN is associate professor of comparative literature at the University of Wisconsin, Madison. Author of *Travels of a Genre: The Modern Novel and Ideology*, she teaches and writes about modern literatures and cultures, nationalism and gender, political culture, fascism, disciplinary histories, and institutional politics.

JEAN-FRANÇOIS LYOTARD is professor emeritus of philosophy at the University of Paris—VIII. He is the author of some eighty articles and thirty books published in Europe, America, and Japan, the most recent of which is *Signe Malraux*.

DAVID PALUMBO-LIU is associate professor of comparative literature at Stanford University. His research interests include ethnic and cultural studies, with specific work in Asian American studies. Editor of *The*

Ethnic Canon: Histories, Institutions, Interventions (1995), he is completing a book entitled *Asian America: Body, Psyche, Space*, which explores the nexus of Asia and America in twentieth-century America.

BRAD PRAGER is a Sage Fellow in the department of German studies at Cornell University. His research interests include German Romanticism and the Frankfurt School.

MICHAEL RICHARDSON is a Sage Fellow in the department of German studies at Cornell University. His research interests include the Frankfurt School and the political theater of the Weimar Republic.

CARLOS RINCÓN is professor of Lateinamerikanistik at the Zentralinstitut Lateinamerika, Freie Universität Berlin. His publications include *El cambio de la noción de literatura*; *Mapas y Pliegues: Ensayos de carrogradia cultural y de lectura del Neobarroco*, for which he was awarded the 1995 Colombian National Culture Prize for essays; and *Surrealismo y el Nuevo Mundo*, for which he received the 1996 Luis Cardoza y Aragon International Prize.

IRMELA SCHNEIDER is professor of German literature at the Technische Universität, Berlin, and research project leader in the Sonderforschungsbereich "Bildschirmmedien" (special collaborative research department "television screen media") at the University of Siegen. She has published several books and essays on the history of German television as well as on the theory of film and television.

ROBERT WEIMANN, professor of dramatic theory at the University of California, Irvine, is currently editing a volume of essays on representation, colonialism, and modernity for publication in Germany. His most recent English-language publication is *Authority and Representation in Early Modern Discourse*. He is also at work on a book on authority, text, and performance in Shakespeare.

Streams of Cultural Capital

Looting in Koreatown during the 1992 Los Angeles riots.
Photo by Jean-Marc Giboux, courtesy of Gamma Liaison, New York.

Introduction: Unhabituated Habituses

DAVID PALUMBO-LIU

A color photograph printed in the May 11, 1992, issue of *Newsweek*: a young Korean American male in the foreground looks askance toward the left of the frame while holding a semi-automatic handgun upright. He is wearing a Malcolm X T-shirt with the caption, "By any means necessary . . ." Depicted beneath that caption on the black and white shirt is a print of a photograph of a black man in a suit and tie holding an automatic rifle, looking down to the right of the frame, out a window. In the background of the magazine photograph, two red fire engines spray jets of water on a smoldering building; a street sign tells us this is Olympic Boulevard. *Newsweek*'s caption: "This is not America."

How to decipher this intensely overdetermined set of signifiers? The pose seems (too deliberately) to answer, to throw into irony, the figure of Malcolm X — reverse angles of vision, of perspective, and of object — Malcolm X guards against the attack of the State; the young Korean American stands in for a police force that withdrew its protection of his property to guard white property against (predominantly) black and Latino looters and burners.[1] Traffic signals go through their mechani-

---

[1] Peter Goldman asserts that this photograph of Malcolm X, published in *Ebony* magazine, was part of a series of staged photographs Malcolm X set up to deter assaults by both white racists and his black enemies. See *The Death and Life of Malcolm X* (New York: Harper and Row, 1973) 155-56. Goldman's text reproduces the photo on an insert following page 170.

Malcolm X's best-known pronouncement on blacks arming themselves — his

1

cal rhythms but are eminently dysfunctional, their signals scrambled by the historical moment, by a rebellion that has superseded, taken authority (albeit only momentarily) over that section of the city. How has an icon of Black Power come to sanction and even prescribe counterviolence against blacks and others? How has Asian property come to stand in for white property? What, exactly, is the absent referent ("America") beyond the frame of the photograph? And how can the simple declarative summary statement of *Newsweek*'s caption be read? But most compelling and confusing in this frame is the particular semiotic double inscription upon that T-shirt and the body that displays it, the body and the shirt that augments the representation of that multiply significant body (Asian, American, male, merchant, vigilante, etc.) — and their particular *materializations* in the historical moment. When did that man purchase that shirt, from whom? And why? What sense of its significance informed its production and its presence on that body, and what sense is projected in its current and temporally specific incarnation? What has it been transformed into, and what can/will it become? On June 5, 1992, I saw this color photograph of a moment, produced in a popular American weekly, already made into a two-tone stencil and spray-painted repeatedly onto the pavement of the University of California campus at Irvine. Who did that, and what and *how* does it signify?[2]

Another example, this time with an inter-national perspective. Writing on the burgeoning practice of transforming prison labor and inserting it into the wider markets of the nation and beyond, Christian Parenti points out that the California Department of Corrections has

---

speech "The Ballot or the Bullet" — holds that such acts are necessary for self-defense against racist attacks in an era when the police refuse to grant blacks equal protection. This then ironically coincides with the reason Korean-Americans took to the streets with handguns — to protect themselves when the police refused to. The context of the speech does not completely coincide with the caption chosen for the T-shirt, which uses a general statement regarding the liberation of blacks to endorse specifically violent means. Goldman recounts a conversation between Malcolm X and a black reporter: "I'm for the freedom of the 22 million Afro-Americans by any means necessary. By any means necessary. I'm for a society in which our people are recognized and respected as human beings, and I believe that we have the right to resort to any means necessary to bring that about" (222).
[2] In "LA, Asians, and Perverse Ventriloquisms: On the Function of Asian America in the Recent American Imaginary" (*Public Culture* 13 [1994] 365-84), I explore the particular semiotics and ideological functions of this photograph.

inmates manufacturing a line of designer jeans called "Gangsta Blues": "In an odd twist, the much-deplored hip-hop culture of African-American and Latino youths is now being appropriated, glamorized, and sold back to the public by the very criminal justice system that claims to wage war on the insidious threat of gangsta culture."[3] Parenti goes on to note that the Department is trying to break into the niche market for U.S. designer jeans in Japan.

Thus we have incarcerated blacks and Latinos manufacturing their "lifestyle" apparel stripped of its material inscriptions in the socioeconomic structure of a ghettoized underclass and the state's disciplinary practices, in the political economies of a prison system facing the imperatives of privatization that include state legislation to continually hyperproduce criminals so as to justify the financing of more and more prisons and their accompanying technologies, *and* the imbrication of this new forced labor source within international markets. These apparatuses are seemingly made invisible in a process of commodification that presses the concepts of alienated labor and the fetishization of commodities and human relationships to new limits, a process all the more reified in its transnational transfer. Beginning with the understanding that issues of race, ethnicity, nationality, gender, and class, and other differential modes of identification complicate the production, consumption, and functioning of culture, we wish in this anthology to examine such transpositions and recontextualizations of cultural objects as they move across and between national borders.

Before directly discussing cultural capital within the context of transnational transpositions, it is necessary to acknowledge how problematic the definition of "culture" is. On one hand, it may designate a set of values, beliefs, and practices specific to a particular group; on the other, the production of art and media objects that may variously mediate the representation of values, beliefs, and practices. Within our understanding of culture we include the set of material practices and apparatuses that are involved in the production, enacting, staging, and reproduction of culture. Our task is complicated by focusing specifically on the phenomenon of transnational movements of cultural objects and their recontextualizations and reconfigurations. This may seem an impossibly wide net to cast, bringing together radically different elements whose cultural "charge" may be altogether

[3] "Making Prison Pay," *The Nation*, January 29, 1996, 12.

heterogeneous, but the theoretical loss suffered by not allowing at the outset the possibility of discussing the not-impossible convergence of extremely diverse modes of cultural production and dissemination would seem unwarranted, given the increasingly complex nature of the world today.

We thus ask: How is "culture" recognized, reconfigured, disseminated, appropriated, practiced (i.e., materialized) via the operations of (inter)national and subnational ideologies? How is cultural hegemony refused, diffused, absorbed, reproduced, and reconfigured, given the particularities of its interpolation into multiple contexts and under different pretexts by various agents? How is the materiality of "culture" correlated (or not) with the materiality of the economic? How are these questions complicated by the fact that radically new technologies and modes of production (e.g., faxes; electronic archives; the Internet; global telecommunications networks available through home and portable modems; video, digital tape, and CD copying machinery; computer graphics that can seamlessly alter or invent sounds and "photographic" images) and new skills (e.g., computer hacking, virus production, automatic and random code-breakers) have made the mass (and often "illegal") (re)production and circulation of cultural objects less and less controllable and predictable and their points of origin more and more difficult to discern? Robert Weimann's essay in this volume addresses precisely the need to reevaluate our concepts of value and representation as the spheres of "culture" and "technology" interpenetrate and to conceive of a "new political economy of cultural value" in such scenarios.

The use of the term "cultural capital" in our subtitle is a strategic one: we wish to explicitly evoke Pierre Bourdieu's concept because it provides a crucial mode of understanding the differential functions of "culture" within social space. Nevertheless, the transnational movement of cultural objects today challenges us to think through Bourdieu's concept in very difficult ways. In this section I summarize those aspects of Bourdieu's insights that provide us with a particular point of orientation and then outline a series of complications that arise when we seek to understand the nature of cultural capital in a transnational, postmodern context.

Bourdieu's concept of cultural capital, elaborated in *La Distinction:*

Critique sociale du jugement,[4] is a useful starting point for a meditation on the ideological functions of cultural activity, especially in considering how the definition of cultural space and the positioning of subjects within it evince relationships of power. For Bourdieu, cultural capital denotes a set of accumulated conditions of life (primarily economic and educational) that, once articulated (i.e., "invested"), position the subject in particular relation to others. Basing his conclusions on data derived from interviews with some one thousand French, Bourdieu maps out the positioning of these individuals around culture (paintings, pieces of classical music, popular songs, photographic images, furniture, journals, newspapers, lawn ornaments, "natural" scenery, etc.). His overarching thesis is that the petit-bourgeois notion of culture may be defined by a strident denial of material necessity — art for the petit bourgeoisie exists as a reified symbolic. To acknowledge material necessity is to admit one's residual affinities with the working class; in contradistinction, to opine upon the symbolic is to display one's detachment from "mere" life. The aesthetic perception of objects serves as a pretext for the petit bourgeoisie to announce their right to opinions that identify them squarely within a specific class consensus.

Thus, for Bourdieu, pronouncing culture is an act of articulating positionality. Culture is eminently commodified and conspicuously consumed, viewed for its exchange value. Most useful for our present concerns is Bourdieu's attention to the particularly contestive positioning affected by the recognition, accumulation, and investment of cultural capital: "Hidden behind the statistical relationships between educational capital or social origin and this or that type of knowledge or way of applying it, there are relationships between groups maintaining different, and even antagonistic, relations to culture, depending on the conditions in which they acquired their cultural capital and the markets in which they can derive the most profit from it."[5] The antimetaphysical bent of Bourdieu's critique discloses the ideological foundations of the Kantian ethico-aesthetic and points out the operations of political economies within class "distinctions."

---

[4] Published in 1979 by Les Éditions de Minuit, Paris. In English, *Distinction: A Social Critique of the Judgement of Taste,* trans. Richard Nice (Cambridge, Mass.: Harvard University Press, 1984); all citations are to the English translation.
[5] *Distinction* 12.

The investment of cultural capital is understood as predicated on a particular enactment of Bourdieu's famous concepts — that of a *habitus* within a *field*. The latter designates a particular grid of relations that governs specific areas of social life (economics, culture, education, politics, etc.): individuals do not act freely to achieve their goals, unconstrained by particular regimens. The very imagining of goals and the creation of dispositions must be understood within historically specific formations of fields; each field has its own rules and protocols that open specific social positions for different agents. Yet this is not a static model: the field in turn is modified according to the manner in which those positions are occupied and mobilized. Any field "presents itself as a structure of probabilities — of rewards, gains, profits, or sanctions — but always implies a measure of indeterminacy."[6] The disposition of social agents to variously fill these positions in social space is called a habitus.

The concept of *habitus* is complex. It is purposefully defined vaguely as a system of "durable, transposable dispositions, structured structures predisposed to function as structuring structures, that is, as principles which generate and organize practices and representations that can be objectively adapted to their outcomes without presupposing a conscious aiming at ends or an express mastery of the operations necessary in order to attain them. Objectively 'regulated' and 'regular' without being in any way the product of obedience to rules, they can be collectively orchestrated without being the product of the organizing action of a conductor."[7] Individuals are inclined to act in certain ways given their implicit understanding of, their "feel for," the field. The habitus "expresses first the result of an organizing action, with a meaning close to that of words such as structure; it also designates a way of being, a habitual state (especially of the body) and, in particular, a disposition, a tendency, propensity, or inclination."[8] Hence, declarations on art and modes of consuming culture are seen as outcomes of inclinations, predispositions, habits of thought, all of which

[6] Bourdieu, "Droit et passe-droit: Le champ des pouvoirs territoriaux et la mise en oeuvre des règlements," *Actes de la recherche en sciences sociales* 81/82 (1990) 89; my translation.

[7] Bourdieu, *The Logic of Practice*, trans. Richard Nice (Stanford, Calif.: Stanford University Press, 1990) 53; translation of *Le sens pratique* (Paris: Minuit, 1980).

[8] Bourdieu, *Outline of a Theory of Practice* (Cambridge: Cambridge University Press, 1977) 214.

disclose the way in which the "field" is negotiated as so to situate the speaker in social space.

Both the flexibility of what might otherwise be thought of as a strictly determinative structure (the field) and the ambiguity of a pre-disposed but not mandated agency (habitus) signal Bourdieu's desire to go beyond the usual binary categories of external/internal, con-scious/unconscious, determinism/free agency. The habitus "is in ca-hoots with the fuzzy and the vague. As a generative spontaneity which asserts itself in the improvised confrontation with endlessly renewed situations, it follows a *practical logic*, that of the fuzzy, of the more-or-less, which defines the ordinary relation to the world."[9] As Loïc Wac-quant explains, "The peculiar difficulty of sociology, then, is to pro-duce a precise sense of an imprecise, fuzzy, woolly reality. For this it is better that its concepts be polymorphic, supple, and adaptable, rather than defined, calibrated, and used rigidly."[10]

Recognizing the flexibility of these concepts leads us to examine more closely the nature of agency. On one hand, the individual actor is better understood as a "player" in a game that has preceeded him or her, one that has as its interest the control and management of social space and the traffic therein; on the other hand, the nature of the game at any one moment is eminently relational and subject to the particular disposition of agents within the field. To move more precisely into the notion of cultural capital, we must understand it as (re)instating a particular social position. The consumption of or com-mentary on "culture" is a pretext for the display of a particular mode of knowledge about the world which in turn is an articulation of dif-ferential social power.

It is precisely in this notion of the differential, subject-situating aspect of the deployment and consumption of culture that our an-thology is most interested. Within the circuits of *transnational* trans-positions of cultural objects, however, the predicative powers of those objects may be as uncertain and multiple as the fields and agents involved. In short, transnational movements of cultural objects chal-lenge the notion of a simply produced, disseminated, absorbed, and practiced universal "world culture," which is, after all, often under-

---

[9] Bourdieu, *Choses dites* (Paris: Editions de Minuit, 1987) 96; my translation.
[10] Bourdieu and Loïc J. D. Wacquant, *Invitation to Reflexive Sociology* (Chicago: University of Chicago Press, 1992) 23.

stood simply as an amplified version of a national cultural model. Instead we may focus on uneven flows of culture; multidirectional currents of cultural objects; the relative value of these objects determined by the specificity of each transaction; and, perhaps most important, the indeterminant, syncretic nature of culture as capital even as its investment evinces the desire for a particular positionality. At the bottom of this, clearly, is our uncertainty over the signifier "culture" and our attention to what functions it attends and what functions attend it as it is transposed and objectified by increasingly heterogeneous groups with varying and not necessarily overlapping understandings of what might constitute cultural knowledge and social power.

The habitus we might imagine for social agents has not yet become habituated to postmodern globalized culture that continues to be reshaped as we speak. The field of culture must now be understood to accommodate both dominant and emergent social groups who differently and significantly inflect the consumption and production of an increasingly global and hybrid culture. One focal point of any examination of cultural flows is precisely the moment of habituation and the conditions that allow us to identify it as such; Arjun Appadurai's essay in this volume describes one case of such a reinvention of habitus within global transpositions of culture.

Crucially, the transposition of cultural objects may strongly affect not only the positioning of individuals, but of social groups and collective agencies whose appropriation and reconfiguration of those "foreign" objects signals an attempt to significantly restructure not just the field of culture but contiguous fields of economics and politics. "Culture" is always political, but in what sense(s) can we understand this relationship under the conditions of global movements of cultural objects and their very differing manifestations in sub-, micro-, and transnational spaces? The transposition of culture in our increasingly global age is a transnational *political* phenomenon that tests the notion of unified national cultural hegemony even as it suggests a transnational hegemony taking shape. How can we calibrate the nature and threshold of the double challenge to unified national hegemony from both subnational localities and transnational hegemonies? Or have these challenges been finessed and absorbed by reconstituted national cultures? In this anthology, the basic question behind Bourdieu's notion of cultural capital — how what one *does* with cultural objects predicates other actions and effects — becomes elaborated as a question set within multiple national contexts and performances that complicate and disturb Bourdieu's analysis of cultural capital, which is largely based on a single-nation model.

Bourdieu is certainly aware of the ways in which ideas are reconfigured in different national settings:

> The meaning and function of a foreign work are determined at least as much by the field of destination as by its field of origin. This is so first of all because its meaning and function in the field of origin are often completely ignored. In addition the transfer from one national field to another is made across a series of social operations: an operation of selection (what should one translate? what should one publish? who will translate? who will publish?); an operation of marketing (of a product that has been stripped of its manufacturer's label beforehand, passed through the publishing house, the collection, the translator and author of the preface — who presents the work in appropriating it and annexing it to his or her own vision and, in any case, to a problematic inscription into the field of reception, and who only rarely does the work of reconstructing the original field, mostly because it's much too difficult to do); and to an operation of reading, at last, with readers applying to the work categories of perception and problematics that are produced by a different field of production.[11]

Remarking on the case of circulating texts across national boundaries, Bourdieu notes, "very often . . . it's not what [foreign authors] say that is important, but what one can make them say"; given this necessarily deformative process, "the sense in which symbolic capital circulates is not always the same."[12] Thus Bourdieu's analysis is rigorously context-specific; he argues that the "international" nature of any work is actually to a large extent the product of the eminently *national* context in which it is reconfigured. He explicitly acknowledges the way that cultural objects are appropriated to fulfil different interests.

Extending Bourdieu's critique to try to account for the refiguration of heterogeneous objects in the hands of multiple agents is more difficult; that is, we must ask what happens when one widens the scope of inquiry to accommodate the transpositions of objects in highly differentiated circuits, not only from one publishing house to another, for

[11] Bourdieu, "Les conditions sociales de la circulation internationale des idées," *Romanistische Zeitschrift für Literaturgeschichte* 14: 1-2 (1990) 3-5; my translation.
[12] Ibid.; my translation.

instance, but through nonparallel circuits of production and dissemination and sociopolitical function. The essays of Xiaomei Chen and Mary Layoun both speak to the importation and exportation of political ideology in the guise of the cultural. The production of a "national" character of "international" culture must thus not rest on a reinstantiation of the nation as a simple entity, but must be understood as taking place in insecure, heterogeneous ways that belie the comfortable mastery of the international by the "local" — that is, "national" — contexts into which products from one nation are redeployed.

The notion of competency underlying Bourdieu's concept of cultural capital also becomes highly problematic as one apprehends a number of discontinuous competencies that may be accessed for different ideological purposes by complex and potentially contradictory "habituses," all of which may be revealed at the various moments of a cultural object's transposition into different local, national, and international spaces. Contributions by Bruce and Judith Kapferer, by Anne Knudsen, and by Biodun Jeyifo all focus on the relation of the political to the representation and constitution of the cultural landscape as it is leveraged by the appropriation of specific, varied iconographies and narrative styles. Carlos Rincón demonstrates how the notion of transposition is complicated when one tracks the movement of a cultural object across different cultural sites. Objects may be recontextualized within multiple spheres and circulated variously, outside of particular entitlements and copyrights, between nonhomologous venues, and they may be inflected multiply by recirculations, deformations, fragmentations, and pastiche-ing in various media.

To extend Bourdieu's model in this manner is tremendously daunting for another reason besides its single-nation focus: ironically, Bourdieu's chief project is to uncover a model of understanding that will have "universal validity."[13] In 1989, at the Maison Franco-Japonaise, Bourdieu confidently asserted, "By presenting the model of social science and symbolic space that I have built up for the particular case of France, I shall be speaking to you about Japan (just as, speaking elsewhere, I would still be speaking about Germany or the United States). . . . As a matter of fact, my entire scientific enterprise is based

[13] Indeed, the "universal" is here again revealed to be simply an elaboration of national-style culture. See Bourdieu, "Social Space and Symbolic Space: Introduction to a Japanese Reading of *Distinction*," *Poetics Today* 12: 4 (1991).

on the belief that the deepest logic of the social world can be grasped, providing only that one plunges into the particularity of an empirical reality, historically located and dated. . . . The aim is to try to grasp the invariant, the structure, in each variable observed."[14] Therefore, just as the model engendered in *Distinction* could be used to understand the investments and operations of cultural capital in other countries, one might imagine that one might discover, through carefully amassing and tracking the proper empirical data, the operations of cultural capital as cultural objects are uprooted from their "field of origin" and reconfigured in a "field of destination."

Although Bourdieu's aspirations are toward the universal, he qualifies what exactly he means by "universal": "Social space is constructed in such a way that agents or groups are distributed in it according to their position in the statistical distribution based on the two differential principles which, *in the most advanced societies*, such as the United States, Japan, or France, are undoubtedly the most efficient: economic capital and cultural capital" (my emphasis).[15] He repeats this qualification at the end of the lecture: "I shall undertake in my next lecture to say what the mechanisms are which, in France as in Japan and all other advanced countries, guarantee the reproduction of social space and symbolic space, without ignoring the contradictions and conflicts that can form the basis of their transformation."[16] We might ask what doubt about the actual universal validity of his model cautions Bourdieu into making this qualification.

It would seem that the "nonadvanced" countries of the world may present him with a much more "fuzzy" and "woolly" set of fields. From his perspective, the efficient deployment of cultural and economic capital, confirmed in their clear (if contradictory) articulation in social and symbolic space, is underwritten by a sophisticated and well-established — that is, modern — field of power.[17] Conversely, we might infer that "less-advanced" societies lack precisely such a structure and instead are riddled with incompletely articulated social actions that resist being located within his model. If we remember that,

[14] Ibid., 627f.
[15] Ibid., 631.
[16] Ibid., 638.
[17] For "field of power" see Bourdieu, *The Field of Cultural Production: Essays on Art and Literature*, edited and introduced by Randal Johnson (New York: Columbia University Press, 1993) 38ff.

above all, Bourdieu is interested in understanding the field as a space of struggle and competition between classes, then we can assume that the rules of the game and the modes of articulation in "less advanced" nations make that struggle more complicated. Now, one could say that, by "less advanced" Bourdieu might mean "less bourgeoisified," and that therefore he is perhaps designating societies wherein extremely clear lines of class and caste are solidified, but he does not pursue this line of questioning, and so leaves open a number of suggestive areas of inquiry that problematize his model — for example, the interpenetration of "advanced" and "less advanced" states in new global discursive and economic spheres. The insertion of the products of "advanced" states might actually disrupt the fields of even "traditionally stratified" societies or stabilize in particular ways the unsettled social and symbolic spaces of those societies.

Finally, the crucial issue of adjudication has to be addressed. Bourdieu is careful to outline the particular roles that professionals play in formulating the particular field of culture. Again, his model is inherently nation-based and "top-down," wherein cultural capital is measured according to high cultural standards that have evolved along the trajectory of a national cultural tradition. In fact, mass culture is precisely that negative element against which high culture supposedly is defined. Yet with the transposition of cultural objects across national borders — not necessarily via the modes of transmission Bourdieu comments on in the matter of the translation of scholarly and high literary works, but rather now taking into account the movements of heterogeneous objects into all manners of hybrid spaces that complicate any schematization of high and low culture — we find that this movement runs ahead of the formation of an adjudicating body.

Of course, cultural pundits still proclaim on these phenomena and are granted a certain amount of credibility within their particular circles (academics like ourselves, for example) — Jean-François Lyotard's essay in this volume is an acerbic satire of one particular characterization of cross-cultural globetrotting intellectualism. We have yet to meet the challenge of accounting for phenomena now being produced (even as we write our essays and publish our books) that circulate in spaces that refuse to be contained in our academically prescribed categories. Furthermore, we are uncomfortable with limiting our "social agents" to those who most resemble us. Hans Ulrich Gumbrecht's epilogue names precisely those "without social security

numbers" as one group whose "participation" in culture reparticular-
izes and challenges our theories and conceptualizations. In short, we
have not yet been able to come up with a theoretical model that might
predict the outcome of the transposition of cultural objects across an
increasingly disjunctive world wherein the particular habitus of social
agents is shot through with new information and new objects from
around a globe to which we have yet to be habituated, nor have we
arrived peacefully at a sense of how the differentials of class, race,
gender, ethnicity, sexual orientation, and so forth, might be accommodated in any modeling system.

A critique by Peter Bürger of Bourdieu's analysis of cultural capital has several elements in common with my remarks regarding its
transposability into the terrain of transnational cultural studies.[18] To
begin with, Bürger takes issue with Bourdieu's locating the operation
of cultural capital solely within the dynamic of class conflict. Though
this is an important and viable phenomenon, it is not the only market
of exchange. Indeed, culture may be "invested" in extremely uneven
ways and with unpredicatable results precisely because of the multi-
directionality of that gesture of performance, creation, consumption,
transfer. Bürger's most trenchant criticism, however, is of the position
from which Bourdieu launches his analysis. As useful as it may be to
assume for his particular analytical purposes, this position of one objectively detached from the circuits of cultural capital brings its own
limitations: "The external perspective of the observer which he has
chosen allows him to reveal connections between aesthetic attitudes
and social indices such as class origin, educational training, and social
position; but it does not allow him to pronounce on the intentions
and motivations of those who participate in cultural events, except
as clearly characterized interpretative hypotheses." Bürger concludes,
"The very radicalism of his critique, which unmasks the ruling ideology of art as fetishism, misses its target, because it does not, in turn,
dialectically question its own result again — from the perspective of
the participant."[19] Although Bürger's argument centers on the need
to factor in the perspective of the avant-garde artist, we can broaden

---

[18] Peter Bürger, "The Problem of Aesthetic Value," in Peter Collier and Helga
Geyer-Ryan, eds., *Literary Theory Today* (Ithaca: Cornell University Press, 1990) 23-
34.
[19] Ibid., 24, 33.

that notion to incorporate other agents who produce cultural objects in a variety of ways and in decentered sites. The basic criticism is that Bourdieu's position as observer skews his analysis away from a whole range of cultural activity that exceeds the focus of his particular hypothesis regarding class position.

For our topic, this focus is problematic when one wishes to analyze a terrain of cultural activity made more complex than that which Bourdieu treats — more complex by way of a recognition of how cultural objects are worked upon and reinvented in that movement of transposition, how such refiguration may involve *heterogeneous* agents marked by identities not (only) restricted to class, how the "nation" as a point of consolidation (which allows a particular understanding of "class," for instance) no longer works in any determinative way.[20] While recognizing the emergence of a transnational bourgeoisie and ruling elites, one should not ignore the emergence also of more and more variegated oppositional positions.

It has yet to be shown that this dynamic can be recontained within a rough outline of class conflict (we will return to this topic below), since such groups are imbricated within multiple sites that are not based necessarily on national models. It would be better perhaps to envision different sites of power occupied variously by contingently produced groups and collectives. Bourdieu's assertion of the positioning function of cultural capital allows us to argue the ideological function of culture, but in the case of transnational cultural flows we cannot presume the particular character of that "ideology"; rather, we are drawn to imagine a complex and contradictory set of ideological functions in a late-capitalist, postmodern age. Finally, and most important, we must note that culture may be produced and circulated in ways that ignore or exceed the functional schemes of capital. As Jonathan Friedman points out, "Bourdieu's perspective . . . is rationalistic and economistic, insofar as it reduces all practice to the accumulation of cultural capital, that is, of specific forms of power. As such it fails to account for the essentially a-rational construction of desire."[21] It may be that cultural objects are absorbed within hetereogenous fields and not re-

---

[20] In this regard see Margaret Archer's study *Culture and Agency: The Place of Culture in Social Theory* (Cambridge: Cambridge University Press, 1988) as a social science attempt at linking agency, cultural change, and social realities.

[21] Jonathan Friedman, *Cultural Identity and Global Process* (London: Sage Publications, 1994) 149.

invested, that they are simply consumed or refigured without being placed back into circulation as social icons.

A number of critics from various spheres have commented on the increased complexity of contemporary life, especially as regards the effects of highly accelerated technological and global economic change. For example, in their book, *The End of Organized Capitalism*, Scott Lash and John Urry posit the increased fragmentation of economic and social life, not according to a telos of an advanced capitalist cartel coherently consolidating wider and wider terrains, but according to a progressively disorganized and deterritorialized global economy. Elaborating on Bourdieu's terminology, Lash and Urry assert the emergence and growth of a "destructured and decentered habitus," produced under the specific conditions of disorganized capital: "with the sea change in modern society, in which large organizations, workplaces, and cities are of diminishing significance for each individual, the processes of forming, fixing, and reproducing 'subjects' is increasingly 'cultural,' formed of available 'lifestyles' not at all based on where one lives or whom one knows, that is, on those who are immediately present."[22] While one should note that this observation specifically comments on the emerging service class, Lash and Urry's argument that cultural imagery now forms a basis for subject formation may be particularly adapted to a transnational context: the importation of cultural images reproduces a stock of "lifestyles" that run up against refiguration and recontextualization in different national settings.

Indeed, several scholars of globalization who center on the cultural sphere argue that, unlike the economic and political spheres, which remain bound to local and international relations, the cultural sphere has become delinked from such stable points of operation. Roland Robertson and, following his lead, Malcolm Waters, have reacted against early Wallersteinian world systems theory, which they claim is too functionalistic and deterministic.[23] Instead, they argue that the increased proliferation of symbols and contemporary life's reliance on images and tokens have made the cultural realm *the* most globalized arena, as more and more of our lives' meaning-producing

---

[22] Scott Lash and John Urry, *The End of Organized Capitalism* (Madison: University of Wisconsin Press, 1987) 296, 276.
[23] See Roland Robertson, *Globalization: Social Theory and Global Culture* (London: Sage, 1992), and Malcolm Waters, *Globalization* (London: Routledge, 1995).

activities and transactions take place in that sphere. Hence, Lash and Urry's focus on "lifestyles" is not arbitrary; its selectivity is significant precisely because it asserts that "culture" has become particularly related to the notion of global life in ways that exceed that of the economic and political. Such attenuation of the relations between the economic, the political, and the cultural allows us to entertain a more flexible and subtle sense of the possible formations of transnational culture; yet in seeking to free its analytic framework from what it sees as the rigidity of Wallerstein's model, this attenuation also threatens to overemphasize and reify "culture"; Robertson himself is forced to invent the notion of "metaculture" in order to acknowledge the embeddedness of culture in contexts other than itself.

One attempt to locate transnational cultural activity within a larger political economy is offered by Leslie Sklair, who argues that it is more appropriate to see global culture as imbricated within a general process of capitalist consumer culture's creation and penetration of global markets, with America simply being one of several nations occupying the core: "Contemporary culture industries . . . seek to transform the global audience into consumers of transnational commodities through the propagation of a set of self-serving notions of development, communication, organization, daily life, and change."[24] Yet this attempt at

---

[24] Leslie Sklair, *Sociology of the Global System* (New York: Harvester Wheatsheaf, 1995), 141. Here Sklair is summarizing and endorsing the argument of Armand Mattelart (see Mattelart, *Transnationals and the Third World: The Struggle for Culture*, South Hadley, Mass.: Bergen and Garvey, 1983).

This vision of the propagation and control of "lifestyle" disseminated and maintained by images and symbols found in Sklair, Lash and Urry, Robertson, and others (and in this regard, of course, the work of Jean Baudrillard may be evoked as one possible "end point" of imagining such a society) bears a strong connection to the historical instantiation of what Alain Touraine calls the "programmed society." Touraine argues that in contemporary global society, the issue of class must be read against an entirely new context, that of the "programmed society" in which "domination consists less in organizing work than in managing the production and data-processing apparatus, i.e., ensuring the often monopolistic control of the supply and processing of a certain type of data, hence of a way of organizing social life." Thus, Touraine seems to accommodate an analysis of the control and management of symbols and icons that convey a lifestyle and rhythm of consumption, wherein "culture" is mediated precisely by such data. For Touraine, "the defense against such an apparatus is no longer carried out in the name of political rights or workers' rights but in support of a population's right to choose its kind of life and in support of its political potential, which is often called self-

homogenization runs up against a critique of the possibility of such uniformity of effect and predictability. In his by now famous formulation, Appadurai evokes chaos theory to grapple with an increasingly disjunctive world: "In order for the theory of global cultural interactions predicated on disjunctive flows to have any force greater than that of a mechanical metaphor, it will have to move into something like a human version of the theory that some scientists are calling 'chaos theory.' That is, we will need to ask how these complex, overlapping, fractal shapes constitute not a simple, stable (even if large-scale) system, but to ask what its dynamics are." The particular disjunctures Appadurai notes take place between "five dimensions of global cultural flow": "(a) ethnoscapes; (b) mediascapes; (c) technoscapes; (d) finanscapes; and (e) ideoscapes."[25] As these dimensions split apart and recombine variously, particular formations of what might be called "global culture" are generated contingently and nonpermanently. Our anthology offers a number of case studies: Irmela Schneider's essay outlines the effects of U.S. television programming on Germany; Brad Prager and Michael Richardson's essay traces the manufacturing of leisure spaces and the concomitant production and characterization of "leisure" and "amusement" across national boundaries; Appadurai remarks on the effect of transnational commodification and marketing on the very rhythms of life.

The contingent status of such formations belies the notion that global culture is necessarily homogeneous. As Janet Abu Lughod notes: "We are still very far from [an ideal type of instantaneous, indiscriminate, and complete diffusion of all cultural products, with no need for *intermediate interpretation*]. Rather, what we are experiencing

---

management." He cites the student movements of the 1960s, the feminist movement, and ecological movements as examples of such resistance. As such, "political action is all-pervading: it enters into the health service, into sexuality, into education, and into energy production." Such a vision also extends the political beyond national boundaries and would suggest the possibility of coordinating alternative cultures to that of the capitalist consumer culture remarked upon by Sklair and others. See Alain Touraine, *The Voice and the Eye: An Analysis of Social Movements*, trans. Alan Duff (Cambridge: Cambridge University Press, 1981) 6, 7; translation of *La Voix et le Regard* (Paris: Seuil, 1978). A similar argument for the potential of "postnational" alliances has been made by Appadurai, who implies such alliances might take advantage of the weakening of national confines though they would also have to navigate increasingly disjunctive landscapes.

[25] Appadurai, "Disjuncture and Difference," *Public Culture* 2: 2 (spring 1990) 1-24.

is rapid, incomplete, and highly differentiated flows in global transmission. We have a globalizing but not necessarily homogeneous culture."[26] Homogeneous culture is, in fact, impossible: every instance of receiving any global transmission has to undergo the mediation of a series of receptions and retransmissions grounded in specific material histories. Robertson suggests that "imported themes have been syncretized into unique constellations of ideas with certain elements of autochthony constraining receptivity of some ideas rather than others. The notion of indigenization is relevant because the syncretic bundles are for very 'domestic' purposes."[27] He argues that "the global field increasingly imposes constraints upon, but also differentially empowers, civilizational cultures, national societies, intra- and cross-national movements and organizations, sub-societies, ethnic groups, intra-societal quasi-groups, individualism, and so on."[28]

Ultimately we are faced with a series of paradoxical potentialities with regard to transnational culture that cannot be read according to the old telos of "development" or "modernization." Ulf Hannerz and John Tomlinson, each in their own way, interject needed considerations of the specific unevenness of temporality and spatiality with regard to transnational cultural movement. Hannerz suggests an alternative to the choice between accepting absolutely either the notion of homogenization or that of localized cultural resistance. Rather than assume the saturation of the local by the global, he asserts a notion of gradually unfolding "maturation," as global culture is mediated non-instantaneously by four different "frames": the market; the state; what he calls "form of life" ("the everyday practicalities of production and reproduction, activities going on in work places, domestic settings, neighborhoods, and some variety of other places"); and "movements" reminiscent of Alain Touraine — collective forms of social action such as the peace movement, the women's movement, the environmental movement, and the like.[29] As Hannerz complicates the temporal framing of globalization, Tomlinson persuasively argues that any notion of cultural imperialism infiltrating and warping global culture to its di-

[26] Janet Abu Lughod, "Going Beyond Global Babble," in Anthony D. King, ed., *Culture, Globalization and the World-System* (Binghamton: State University of New York at Binghamton, 1991) 135.

[27] Robertson, 20.

[28] Ibid., 61.

[29] Ulf Hannerz, "Scenarios for Peripheral Cultures," in King, ed., 112-15.

rection must address a series of questions about the firmness of "cultural identity" read as *national* identity.[30]

Returning to our critique of cultural capital in a transnational frame, in this regard one might view the habitus not so much as decentered and detached from the economic and political spheres as multiply centered in relation to various possible economic and political contexts, and the "play" of the game increasingly unpredictable. For instance, how does one gauge the reception of a service-class "lifestyle" in diverse and variegated contexts? Lash and Urry may be too quick to assume the exactitude of the reproduction of such lifestyles, especially in the context of disorganized capital. We must ask how such a lifestyle can cohere in a decentered and temporally disjunctive habitus. These basic arguments provide another way of thinking through the effect of global flows of culture upon discrete localities, an approach reflected in the ways the particular cases in this volume are presented.

To summarize: If the transposition across national boundaries of a cultural object deeply affects its particular function as an object of cultural capital, then what functions might it take on? Once we have taken into account the disjunctive character of globalization that nonetheless is recombinatory — differentiating yet unifying along uneven planes and paradigms — can we achieve anything like the universally valid model Bourdieu claims in *Distinction*, or can we only go by the empirical data of what seems to be an infinitude of isolated cases? How do the differentials of gender, ethnicity, sexual orientation, to name but a few, variously affect the way a "foreign object" is put into play in the field of culture, and what kinds of position-taking are available to heterogeneous social agents? Can we theorize the temporal dimensions of domesticating the foreign, or have such terms as "domestic" and "foreign" lost their semantic tidiness? Even as we are focused on the movement of objects from the core to the periphery, the reception of the products of the "advanced" states within the social space of the "less advanced" states, we must not forget the movements of "peripheral" culture to the center that have always taken place or the recirculation of objects that now bear the traces of their travels and transformations.

Finally, we must recognize that there are multiple ways in which cul-

[30] See John Tomlinson, *Cultural Imperialism* (Baltimore: Johns Hopkins University Press, 1991) esp. 68-101.

tural capital is inflected differently at home. We cannot and should not assume that these issues are neatly sequestered out there, and that locally things move according to a predictable set of rules. Even in "advanced" states, the predication of cultural capital must be read within the context of heterogeneous habituses populated by both "domestic" and transmigrant peoples. For example, Aihwa Ong provides a compelling analysis of how wealthy Chinese capitalists in the American Pacific Rim have tried to acquire the cultural capital proper to those who possess their symbolic capital. Just as Bourdieu asserts in *Distinction* that symbolic capital does not necessarily mean economic power, neither is the reverse true. Ong writes:

> The Westward dispersal of Hong Kong capitalists is connected to the changing conditions of global capitalism and late modernity. Emigrants are engaged in fabricating cultural personae that can operate effectively in the transnational economic arena, while their strategy of cultural accumulation seeks to reproduce their high social status overseas. In California, Chinese investors use wealth, political alliances, and the cultural patronage of "high culture" institutions to transform old racial categories into new ones of higher symbolic value. They soon discover that just as there are limits to flexible accumulation in business, so there are limits to cultural accumulation. Chinese immigrants deploying cultural forms not considered as "belonging" to their ethnic group cannot easily convert such symbolic capital into high social standing in Anglo circles. Their cultural performances as a new faction of the social elite are discredited by a perceived difference in their "money politics," their accent, and the color of their skin.[31]

"Cultural capital" is thus an extremely unstable notion when viewed according to such differential factors. And yet, crucially, social agents continue to "invest" their actions with the understanding that they will produce certain effects. No small part of our task is to trace the disjuncture between this impulse to place culture into a system of value, exchange, and representation, and the actual trajectories of its effect. It may be that we can only name culture retroactively as the sum of such effects; culture is thus recognized as a placeholder of value. In this age of ever-increasing hybridization and uneven recombinations of economic, political, and social systems across and within national

[31] Aihwa Ong, "Limits to Cultural Accumulation: Chinese Capitalists in the American Pacific Rim," *Annals of the New York Academy of Sciences* 645 (1992) 43.

boundaries, the streams of cultural capital may be seen to be extremely "muddy" and variously sedimented. We have yet to theorize a model that might account for the myriad ways cultural objects — now more and more quickly and massively produced and disseminated in increasingly hybrid spaces — might be appropriated and invested with symbolic power by/in populations equally variegated. This anthology presents both theoretical and highly empirical studies as an initial attempt to address precisely such issues regarding contemporary transnational cultural formations and their functions. While acknowledging the need to begin to theorize the impact of flows of cultural objects across diverse spaces, we insist that these phenomena must be recognized as particular, historicized materializations of transnational movements that penetrate specifically constructed localities and that demand particular scrutiny of unruly and as yet undisciplined practices.

Consumption, Duration, and History

ARJUN APPADURAI

Consumption as a topic has always come equipped with an optical illusion. This illusion, especially fostered by the neoclassical economics of the last century or so, is that consumption is the end of the road for goods and services, a terminus for their social life, a conclusion to some sort of material cycle. My main concern in this essay is to show that this view is indeed an illusion, and that in order to get rid of it, we need to resituate consumption in time — time conceived multiply — as history, as periodicity, and as process. From this view follow a series of methodological suggestions and a preliminary proposal about a way to conceptualize what is new about consumerism after the advent of electronic media.

Repetition and Regulation

Like breathing, consumption is a self-effacing habit, which becomes noticeable only when contextually ostentatious. But it is only in ostentation that we often take notice of consumption, and this is the first of the methodological traps we need to avoid, a trap that pertains to many other topics as well. That is, we need to resist the temptation to construct a general theory of consumption around what McKendrick et al. called the "Veblen effect,"[1] namely, the tendency of mobility patterns to be organized around the imitation of social superiors. The fact that consumption may sometimes be conspicuous and imitative should not tempt us to regard it as always being

---

[1] Neil McKendrick, N. J. Brewer and J. H. Plumb, *The Birth of a Consumer Society: The Commercialization of Eighteenth-Century England* (Bloomington: Indiana University Press, 1982). See also, T. Veblen, *The Theory of the Leisure Class* (New York: Macmillan, 1912).

so, not least because various forms of abstinence can be equally conspicuous and socially consequential.[2]

As a general feature of the cultural economy, consumption must and does fall into the mode of repetition, of habituation. In this regard, the observation by Jameson,[3] building on Baudrillard, Freud, Kierkegaard and others, that repetition characterizes the commodity culture of consumer capitalism, can be situated in a wider anthropology of the relationship between consumption and repetition. Even in the most fashion-ridden of contexts, as I shall suggest in the next section of this essay, consumption leans toward habituation through repetition. The principal reason for this is that consumption, in all social contexts, is centered around what Marcel Mauss called the techniques of the body,[4] and the body calls for disciplines that are repetitious, or at least periodic. This is not because the body is everywhere the same biological fact and thus demands the same disciplines. On the contrary, because the body is an intimate arena for the practices of reproduction, it is an ideal site for the inscription of social disciplines, disciplines that can be widely varied. Playing on one of the etymological roots of the word to consume, it is worth noting that eating, unlike say tattooing, calls for habituation, even in the most upscale environments where food has become largely dominated by ideas of bodily beauty and comportment, rather than by ideas of energy and sufficiency.[5]

But even where hedonistic and antinomian consumption practices have taken deep hold, there remains a tendency for those practices of consumption that are closest to the body to acquire uniformity through habituation: food, dress, hairstyling. I stress the force of habituation, since it has frequently been lost sight of, in favor of the forces of imitation or opposition. These latter forces can often be very important, but they always encounter the social inertia of bodily techniques. Thus, even among monks, vegetarians, food faddists, and counter-consumers of every sort, it is extremely difficult to maintain an anarchic consumption regime. The techniques of the body, how-

[2] Arjun Appadurai, *Commodities and the Politics of Value in the Social Life of Things: Commodities in Cultural Perspective* (Cambridge: Cambridge University Press, 1986) 363.
[3] Fredric Jameson, *Reification and Utopia in Mass Culture* in *Signatures of the Visible* (1979; New York and London: Routledge, 1990) 9-34.
[4] Marcel Mauss, "Techniques of the Body," *Economy and Society* 2.1 (1973) 70-85.
[5] Pierre Bourdieu, *Distinction: A Social Critique of the Judgement of Taste* (Cambridge: Harvard University Press, 1984).

ever peculiar, innovative and antisocial, need to become social disciplines,[6] parts of some habitus, free of artifice or external coercion, in order to take on their full power. The core of consumption practices being the body, the habituation that requires bodily disciplines to be successful entails that consumption patterns will always tend to repetition, at least in some regards. This is the inner paradox of hedonism, especially in its anarchic dimensions: even hedonistic consumption requires its bodily disciplines, and these disciplines encourage repetition and discourage inventiveness by their nature.[7] Even an unkempt beard must be maintained.

Naturally, not all consumption need be repetitive or habitual, but any consumption system that strives for freedom from habit is pushed toward an aesthetic of the ephemeral, as I will suggest in the course of this essay. This accounts for some important features of the relation between consumption, fashion, and pleasure, discussed in my conclusion. All consumption practices that endure at all must pay some tribute to bodily inertia, even if this inertia affects very different areas and is anchored in dramatically different ideologies, across time and space. On this inertial base can be built a variety of different periodicities and temporal rhythms, including some driven by Veblen's type of conspicuous consumption.

In any socially regulated set of consumption practices, those that center around the body, and especially around the feeding of the body, take on the function of structuring temporal rhythm, of setting the minimum temporal measure (by analogy to musical activity) on which much more complex, and "chaotic" patterns can be built. Pushing the analogy a step further, the small habits of consumption, typically daily food habits, can perform a percussive role in organizing large-scale consumption patterns, which may be contrived of much more complex orders of repetition and improvisation. The methodological moral here may be put as follows: where imitation seems to dominate, repetition might be lurking.

The inertial logic of repetition is a resource around which societies and their ruling classes build larger regimes of periodicity, typically around some form of seasonality. Our experience of the Christmas

---

[6] T. Asad, "On Ritual and Discipline in Medieval Christian Monasticism," *Economy and Society* 16 (1987) 159203.
[7] Colin Campbell, *The Romantic Ethic and the Spirit of Modern Consumerism* (Oxford: Basil Blackwell, 1987) ch. 4.

gifting frenzy in the United States exemplifies this sort of regime very well. In many societies, important rites of passage have consumption markers, often cohering around obligatory or near-obligatory patterns of giftgiving, typically between predesignated categories of socially linked persons, often kinsmen. But this does not imply a mechanical marriage of van Gennep and Mauss.[8] In fact, the seasonalities which organize consumption are more complicated and less mechanical than is at first apparent.

The acts of consumption that surround routine rites of passage are often less mechanically prescriptive than they might appear. Pierre Bourdieu has shown this very well in his discussion of the gifts between affines in Kabyle marriage alliances in Algeria.[9] What Bourdieu is able to show, as an instance of what he calls the regulated improvisations of the habitus, is that what appear to be a fixed set of prescriptions that govern gift transactions between affines is governed by an extremely complex set of strategic interactions, whose sequence, because improvisatory, is unpredictable, though its general social morphology is known to the actors at the very outset. A crucial source of uncertainty, which can be treated as a strategic resource by the key actors, is the *lapse of time* between various acts of gifting. Malinowski had earlier noted this key role of timing in gift-giving, and so had Mauss, while Sahlins gave it greater typological force.[10] For our purposes, it suggests that the rhythms of accumulation and divestiture that generate particular states of material wealth, in many societies, are products not of mechanical distributions of goods or of predictable patterns of gifting, but of complex calculative sequences, built, like other agonistic forms, on shared understandings of style but considerable latitude in strategy.

This calculative dimension of gift-giving offers a more complex perspective on the relationship between consumption and rites of passage. Acts of gift-exchange, with their attendant implications for consumption and production, are often seen, in the context of rites of passage, as highly conventionalized markers (in Pierceian terms, as icons) of these rites. But it may be more useful to see these con-

---

[8] Arnold van Gennep, *The Rites of Passage* (1908; London: Routledge and Kegan Paul, 1965) and Marcel Mauss, *The Gift* (1923; New York: Norton, 1976).

[9] Pierre Bourdieu, *Outline of a Theory of a Theory of Practice* (Cambridge: Cambridge University Press, 1977).

[10] Bronislaw Malinowski, *Argonauts of the Western Pacific* (1922; New York: E.P. Dutton, 1961) 353; Mauss, *The Gift*; and Marshal Sahlins, *Stone Age Economics* (New York: Aldine, 1972).

sumption strategies as *indexically* related to rites of passage: that is, as creating the meaning of these rites by the way in which they point to their meaning. Let me elaborate. The basic package of rites described by van Gennep, those having to do with birth, initiation, marriage, and death, are usually regarded as cultural regularities with a remarkable degree of universality owing, in van Gennep's argument, to the physiological and cosmological uniformities on which they are built. Using Mauss's ideas about the techniques of the body to turn van Gennep on his head, I suggest that consumption periodicities, mediated by strategies of accumulation and divestiture, often constitute the principal significance of these "natural" events, rather than simply marking them in some loose "symbolic" manner. This is very clear in initiation and marriage, where issues of time and timing are obviously salient, given the degree of play available to key actors in determining when, and who, these events shall affect. With birth and death, the biological clock seems primary, and yet, even here, we know that the ritual marking of these events, which can be lengthy, debated and highly idiosyncratic defines their social salience.[11] What affects social salience is the nature, timing, scale, and social visibility of the material transactions that constitute the ritual process of these rites. The argument would be simpler still in the case of the other rites of passage that van Gennep discussed, rites involving transitions in space, territory, group membership, agriculture and the like. In a word, the socially organized periodicities of consumption, and the calculative strategies that give them agency and amplitude, are constitutive of the social meanings of rites of passage, and not simply symbolic markers of these meanings. Consumption thus, on the larger seasonal scales of seasons, biographies, and group histories discussed by van Gennep and others, regulates the more tight periodicities of temporal rites of passage. In this sense, consumption creates time and does not simply respond to it.

To make this maxim clearer, I return to Christmas. In the United States, as the range of commodities grows, as families find themselves with larger lists of goods and services that might service the desires of family members, and as fashions, particularly for youth, shift mercurially, those who play the crucial "Santa" role find themselves shopping earlier for Christmas. Timing is a delicate problem, since everyone wants to get their shopping done before the Christmas "rush,"

[11] Clifford Geertz, *Ritual and Social Change: A Javanese Example* in *The Interpretation of Cultures* (New York: Basic Books, 1973).

and the ideal thing would be to do your Christmas shopping while you are sweltering in June or July. Absurd as this already seems, it is made doubly difficult by the fact that it is not until September or October that the fashion cycle, especially for such items as children's toys, starts issuing clear signals. So, you have to know how long to wait, before deciding that this year's "favorites" have been established, but not so long that the stores have run out of them. At the other end of the process, all large stores run after-Christmas sales, but frequently, due to low shopper turnout in some parts of the country, there are *pre*-Christmas sales, further distorting the periodicity of prices and sentiments that have to be juggled by American families. The shrewd shopper has always known that the best time to shop for Christmas gifts (especially if you are not worried about goods subject to short fashion cycles) is in the immediate post-Christmas potlatches at the big stores. So Christmas is obviously not a simple seasonal fact. From one point of view, it may be seen as a year-long celebration, with more and less frenzied periods of conscious activity. In this case, it is a lot more like Trobriand yam-gardening than like birth by Cesarean section. The difference lies in the larger social logics of acquisition and divestiture that are coordinated for the particular rite of passage to be successful. The methodological maxim here somewhat complicates the previous one: where repetition in consumption seems to be determined by natural or universal seasonalities of passage, always consider the reverse causal chain, in which consumption seasonalities might determine the style and significance of "natural" passages.

Periodicities and Histories

But the seasonalities of consumption themselves are carved out of more open-ended, more circumstantial, more contingent temporal processes, and it is these that we generally choose to call historical. History, in all societies, irrespective of whether they are hot or cool, literate or not, is by definition the story of the *longue durée*, whether or not we know enough about all the histories we encounter. In regard to consumption the structures of the long run have not been as elaborately studied as regards the world outside the West as they have been for Europe, and the world that Europe encountered after 1500. Yet we know enough about at least some of the histories of the rest of the world, over long spans of time,[12] to know that rather than clear units

[12] Philip Curtin, *Cross-Cultural Trade in World History* (Cambridge: Cambridge University Press, 1984); Marshall Hodgson, *The Venture of Islam: Conscience and History in*

of spatiotemporal process, the world has for a very long time been constituted by overlapping congeries of cultural ecumenes. Central to the cultural economy of distance has been the driving force of merchants, trade and commodities, especially of the luxury variety.[13] Nevertheless, not all structures of the long-run are characterized by the same turns, or contingencies, that in retrospect, take on the appearance of necessity. Literacy did not appear everywhere and neither did bubonic plague or the idea of democratic rights. So patterns in the *longue durée* must be considered, in the first instance, locally, that is, within fairly well-observed and documented spheres of interaction. With regard to consumption, long-term change is not everywhere equally rapid, although it seems increasingly foolish to contrast static with changing societies. The question seems to be the pace and intensity of change, as well as the alacrity with which it is invited.

What we know of Europe allows us to watch a society of sumptuary law slowly changing into a society of fashion. In general, all socially organized forms of consumption seem to revolve around some combination of the following three patterns: interdiction, sumptuary law, and fashion. The first pattern, typical of small-scale, low-tech, ritually oriented societies, organizes consumption through a fairly large list of do's and don'ts, many of them combining cosmology and etiquette in a special way. In these societies, what used to be called taboos in an older anthropology frequently regulate consumption, for certain social categories, for certain temporal contexts, in regard to certain goods.[14] The social life of things in small-scale societies appears to have been driven largely by the force of interdiction. Yet, as we learn more from the archaeological record, small societies in places like Melanesia seem to have long been characterized by long-distance flows, both maritime and landbased, of at least some kinds of goods. Yet, in such societies, interdiction structures of various sorts

World Civilization, 3 vols. (Chicago: University Press of Chicago, 1974); F. Perlin, "Proto-Industrialization and Pre-Colonial South Asia," *Past and Present* 98.30 (1983) 94; Edward Schafer, *Golden Peaches of Samarkand: A Study of T'ang Exotics* (Berkeley: University of California Press, 1963); E. Wolf, *Europe and the People Without History* (Berkeley: University of California Press, 1982).

[13] See Curtin, *Cross-Cultural Trade*; Mary W. Helms, *Ulysses' Sail: An Ethnographic Odyssey of Power, Knowledge, and Geographical Distance* (Princeton: Princeton University Press, 1988); Sidney W. Mintz, *Sweetness and Power* (New York: Viking-Penguin, 1985); and Schafer, *Golden Peaches*.

[14] Mary Douglas and Baron Isherwood, *The World of Goods* (New York: Basic Books, 1981).

appear to have successfully accommodated new commodities into existing structures of exchange and polity, partly because the quantitative explosion associated with the commodity world was yet to appear. Even in such low-tech societies, particular conjunctures of commodity flow and trade can create unpredicted changes in value structures.[15]

It is at this point tempting to pose Campbell's version of the Weberian question regarding the historical conditions for the rise of capitalism, that is, to ask it in a way that highlights the consumption side of things. There seems widespread agreement among historians and sociologists working in Europe and the United States that a major transformation on the demand side appears to have taken place in Europe sometime after the fifteenth century.[16] There is, however, no unanimity on the nature of the conditions that enabled the "consumer revolution," except a broad sense that it was associated with the relationships between traditional aristocracies and ascendant bourgeoisies in the early modern period. But is there a more sharply articulated way to ask the question: When and under what sorts of condition do "consumer revolutions" occur?

I will eventually suggest that the idea of "consumer revolution" is itself in some ways inadequate to the electronic present. Yet it might be of some preliminary value to define "consumer revolution" in a sufficiently narrow way so as to make comparison appealing and in a sufficiently broad way so as to avoid the tautologous question: Why did the history of Europe (or England) happen only in Europe (or England)? I suggest that we define the "consumer revolution" as a cluster of events whose key feature is a *generalized* shift from the reign of sumptuary law to the reign of fashion. This detaches "consumer revolutions" from any particular temporal sequence involving a mobile society, sophisticated marketing on the Josiah Wedgwood model, rising wages, mass merchandising and class conflict. It also detaches consumer revolutions from specific historical sequences and conjunc-

---

[15] Marshal Sahlins, *Historical Metaphors and Mythical Realities: Structure in the Early History of the Sandwich Islands Kingdom* (Ann Arbor: University of Michigan Press, 1981).

[16] Campbell, *The Romantic Ethic*; Chandra Mukerji, *From Graven Images: Patterns of Modern Materialism* (New York: Columbia University Press, 1983); McKendrick et al., *The Birth of a Consumer Society*; Grant D. McCracken, *Culture and Consumption: New Approaches to the Symbolic Character of Consumer Goods and Activities* (Bloomington: Indiana University Press, 1988); and Rosalind H. Williams, *Dream Worlds: Mass Consumption in Late Nineteenth-Century France* (Berkeley: University of California Press, 1982).

tures involving literacy, numeracy, expert knowledge, the book trade and other forms of commoditized information flow, of the sort relevant to England, France, and the United States in the last three centuries. Instead, it opens up the possibility that large-scale changes in consumption may be associated with various sequences and conjunctures of these factors. Thus, in India, department stores are a very late development, coming after advertising had been, for at least forty years, a well-established commercial practice, in contrast with France, where department stores[17] seem to have, in conjunction with national expositions and other phenomena of leisure and spectacle, preceded the modern form of the advertising industry. The relationship of conjuncture and sequence between the English and French consumer revolutions seems itself to be complex and contestible. In Japan after World War II, there is good evidence that mass consumption emerged substantially as a result of television viewing (often of situation comedies from the United States), and that advertising followed, as a postmodernist commentatorial mode upon such consumption, rather than as a primary causal factor.[18] Such differences are, of course, in part a product of the complexities of cultural flow after A.D. 1800, whereby many countries have evolved sophisticated technologies of marketing before becoming massively industrial economies. Thus, if you compare Elizabethan England with India, the right comparison would have to be with India in the late eighteenth century, when the sumptuary reach of the Mughal sovereign was both imitated and contested by all sorts of commercial and political groups in North India.[19] Likewise, the role of class conflicts and sumptuary battles between old and new aristocracies can have very different weightage, if you compare Japan and India, where the dissolution of monarchical ideas and the rise of industrial capitalism have very different internal causal and temporal relationships. Such examples could be multiplied.

The general methodological point is clear: just as we have learned, partly through the proto-industrialization debate, not to prejudge the links between European commercial forms and the rise of capitalist

---

[17] Michael Miller, *The Bon Marché: Bourgeois Culture and the Department Store, 1869-1920* (Princeton: Princeton University Press, 1981); Williams, *Dream Worlds.*

[18] M. Ivy "Media, Knowledge and Consumption in Contemporary Japan: Reflections on the 'Post-Mass' Society," 1987 (unpublished mss.).

[19] Christopher A. Bayly, *The Origins of Swadeshi (Home Industry): Cloth and Indian Society, 1700-1930* in *The Social Life of Things*, ed. Arjun Appadurai (Cambridge University Press, 1986) 285-322.

modes of production and exchange, likewise with consumption, what we need to avoid is the search for preestablished sequences of institutional change, axiomatically defined as constitutive of *the* consumer revolution. What this might encourage is a multiplication of scenarios concerning the appearance of consumer society, in which the rest of the world will not simply be seen as repeating, or imitating, the conjunctural precedents of England or France. Having explored such conjunctural variations, in the links between class, production, marketing, and politics, over long stretches of any particular history, we might be in a better position to construct models of global interaction in the realm of consumption, both before and after the great maritime expansion of Europe in the sixteenth century.

In comparing consumer revolutions in this manner, we can maintain the tension between the *longue durée* of localities, and the variable duration of various world processes, by making a distinction that has proved useful in another context,[20] the distinction between history and genealogy. While each of these words has a host of meanings (depending on your jargon of choice), my own usage is as follows: "history" leads you outward, to link patterns of changes to increasingly larger universes of interaction; "genealogy" leads you inward, toward cultural dispositions and styles that might be stubbornly embedded both in local institutions and in the history of the local habitus. Thus, the "history" of Gandhi's ascetical relationship to the world of goods might lead outward to Ruskin, Thoreau and others in the West who articulated a pastoral, anti-industrial vision. But the genealogy of Gandhi's hostility to goods and to possessive individualism generally probably leads inward, to a long-standing Indic discomfort with "attachment" to sensory experience at large. Furthermore, history and genealogy may, in regard to particular practices or institutions, reinforce each other, to the point where one may disguise the other, or they may contradict one another, as in the following example, also from India. When Indians began to enter the British world of clothing in the nineteenth century, certain desirable items of clothing acquired a history that indigenous elites found appealing, but a genealogy that was more troubling. For Brahman elites, for example, the histo-

[20] Arjun Appadurai, *Global Ethnoscapes: Notes and Queries For a Transnational Anthropology* in *Recapturing Anthropology: Working in the Present*, ed. R.G. Fox (Santa Fe: School of American Research, 1991) 191-210.

ry of hat-wearing linked them to a narrative of their own cosmopolitan, colonial past, but its genealogy was probably less comforting,
for it juxtaposed very different ideas about hair and headgear, also
crucial to the Brahman habitus. In general, in any given social and
temporal location, the study of the *longue durée* with respect to consumption, should involve the simultaneous exploration of the histories and genealogies of particular practices. This double historicizing
is likely to reveal multiple processual flows that underwrite any giv-
en conjuncture, and simultaneously make it possible to compare without sacrificing contrast, in regard to the processual study of consumer
revolutions.

Returning then to the relationship between the small cycles, anchored in the techniques of the body, which constitute the core of all
durable consumption practices, and the more open-ended historical
sequences in which they are embedded, it is important to see that
the tempo of these small-scale periodicities may be embedded in more
than one *longue durée*, with the processes implied by history and genealogy creating multiple temporalities for any given practice.[21] It further follows that in studying the consumption practices of distinct
societies, we must be prepared to encounter a host of different histories and genealogies present at the same "moment." Thus, in France,
the consumption of perfume[22] may, in 1880, be underpinned by one
kind of history of bodily discipline and aesthetics, while the consumption of meat may respond to wholly other histories and genealogies.
The more diverse a society and the more complex the story of its interactions with other societies, the more fragmented the "history" of
its consumption practices is likely to be, even if broad styles, trends,
and patterns are discernable. The move from small to large temporal
consumption rhythms is a move from more to less patterned periodicities. Writing the history of "distinction" in the sense of Bourdieu[23]
will entail openness to such multiplicity. In the following sections, I
confine myself to these societies in which fashion, at least for some
classes, has become the dominant mechanism driving consumption,
and commodification is a critical feature of social life.

[21] Maurice Halbwachs, *The Collective Memory* (1950; New York: Harper & Row, 1980)
106-12.
[22] Alain Corbin, *The Foul and the Fragrant: Odor and the French Social Imagination* (Cambridge: Harvard University Press, 1986).
[23] Bourdieu, *Distinction*.

Fashion and Nostalgia

While much has been said about fashion,[24] it is still not fully under-stood as a feature of the temporal rhythms of industrial and post-industrial societies. While it has been widely noted that fashion is the crucial link between production, merchandising, and consumption in capitalist societies, the relationship of fashion to what has recently been called "patina" by McCracken has not been fully explored.

The problem of patina, which McCracken has recently proposed as a general term to deal with that property of goods in which their age becomes a key index of their high status, disguises a deeper dilemma, the dilemma of distinguishing wear from tear. That is, while in many cases, wear is a sign of the right sort of duration in the social life of things, sheer disrepair or decrepitude is not. Wear, as a property of material objects, is thus itself a very complicated property that requires considerable maintenance: the polishing of old silver, the dusting of old furniture, the patching of old clothes, the varnishing of old surfaces, these are all part of the embodied practice of the upper classes in many societies, or, more exactly, of their servants. We might say, paraphrasing the well-known aphorism, "as for patina, our servants will provide it for us." But poorly maintained patina can become itself a sign either of poor breeding, of outright social counterfeiting[25] or, worse still, of complete penury. In short, patina is a slippery property of material life, ever open to faking as well as to crude handling. The patina of objects takes on its full meaning only in a proper context, both of other objects, of spaces for these assemblies of objects, and of persons who know how to indicate, through their bodily practices, their relationships to these objects: the English country house comes to mind as a good example of this complex set of relationships. When all these conditions are felicitious, then the transposition of temporality, the subtle shift of patina from the object to its owner or neighbor, is successful, and the person (or family, or social group) himself or herself takes on the invisible patina of reproduction well managed, of temporal continuity undisturbed. But patina, the gloss of age, cannot by itself generate the right temporal associations for human beings.

[24] McCracken, *Culture and Consumption*; Daniel Miller, *Material Culture and Mass Consumption* (London: Basil Blackwell, 1987); G. Simmel, "Fashion," *American Journal of Sociology* 62.6 (1904; 1957) 541-58.
[25] E. Goffman, "Symbols of Class Status," *British Journal of Sociology* 2 (December 1951) 294-304.

Here, as in so many other matters involving material life, context is everything. The distinction between an heirloom and junk is not "patina" as such, but the successful semiotic management of the social context. Here, too, there is a delicate temporal rhythm to be managed, particularly where membership in elites is partly constructed through patina. Since all things have a "cultural biography"[26] even those objects that have the most unchallengeable patina have possible histories, some of which include theft, sale or other improper modes of acquisition. As the nouveaux-riches know, the important thing is to regulate the pace at which an ensemble of objects with patina is assembled. If you are too slow, only your descendants will know the pleasures of the right gloss, but if you are too quick, Babbitt's fate awaits you, surrounded as you might be with the right things. Thus the management of temporal rhythms is critical to the exploitation of patina.

Patina, as a key to the material life of aristocracies (and would be aristocrats) feeds a deeper stream in the social life of things, and that is the capability of certain things to evoke nostalgia, a syndrome Proust immortalized. Objects with patina are perpetual reminders of the passage of time as a double-edged sword, which credentials the "right" people, just as it threatens the way they lived. Whenever aristocratic lifestyles are threatened, patina acquires a double meaning, indexing both the special status of its owner and the owner's special relationship to a way of life that is no longer available. The latter is what makes patina a truly scarce resource, for it always indicates the fact that a way of living is now gone forever. Yet, this very fact is a guarantee against the newly arrived, for they can acquire objects with patina, but never the subtly embodied anguish of those who can legitimately bemoan the loss of a way of life. Naturally, good imposters may seek to mimic this nostalgic posture as well, but here both performances and reviews are a more tightly regulated affair. It is harder to pretend to have lost something than it is to actually do so, or to claim to have found it. Here material wear cannot disguise social rupture.

The effort to inculcate nostalgia is a central feature of modern merchandising and is best seen in the graphics and texts of gift-order catalogues in the United States. These catalogues use a variety of rhetorical

[26] I. Kopytoff, *The Cultural Biography of Things: Commoditization as Process* in *The Social Life of Things*, ed. Arjun Appadurai (Cambridge: Cambridge University Press, 1986).

devices, but especially when it comes to clothing, furniture, and design, they play with many kinds of nostalgia: nostalgia for bygone lifestyles, material assemblages, life-stages (such as childhood), landscapes (of the Currier Ives variety), scenes (of the Norman Rockwell small town variety) and so on. Much has been written about these matters, and we now have some excellent work on the relationship of nostalgia and authenticity to collections, toys, and spectacles.[27] But what has not been explored is the fact that such nostalgia, as far as mass merchandising is concerned, does not principally involve the evocation of a sentiment to which consumers who really have lost something can respond. Rather, these forms of mass advertising teach consumers to miss things they have never lost.[28] That is, they create experiences of duration, passage, and loss that rewrite the lived histories of individuals, families, ethnic groups, and classes. In thus creating experiences of losses that never took place, these advertisements create what might be called "imagined nostalgia," nostalgia for things that never were. This imagined nostalgia thus inverts the temporal logic of fantasy (which tutors the subject to imagine what could or might happen) and creates much deeper "wants" than simple envy, imitation, or greed could by themselves invite.

The final twist in the peculiar logic of nostalgia in the politics of mass consumption involves what Fredric Jameson has recently called "nostalgia for the present,"[29] a term he uses to discuss certain recent films that project a future from whose perspective the present is not only historicized but sufficiently misrecognized as to appear already to be something the viewer has lost. Jameson's idea, illuminating in regard to certain strands in popular cinema and literature today, can be extended more widely to the world of mass merchandising. Nostalgia for the present, the stylized presentation of the present as if it has already slipped away, characterizes a very large number of television advertisements, especially those directed at the "youth" market. A whole new video aesthetic has emerged, most notably in the campaigns

[27] C. A. Breckenridge, *The Aesthetics and Politics of Colonial Collecting: India at World Fairs* in *Comparative Studies in Society and History* (Spring 1989) 196-216; Susan Stewart, *On Longing: Narratives of the Miniature, the Gigantic, the Souvenir, the Collection* (Baltimore: The Johns Hopkins University Press, 1984).

[28] For a cryptic precursor to this argument, see Halbwachs (68-71) on "reconstructed remembrances."

[29] Fredric Jameson, "Nostalgia for the Present," *South Atlantic Quarterly* 88.2 (1989) 517-37.

for Pepsi, Levi Jeans, and Ralph Lauren outfits, in which contemporary scenes are lit, choreographed and shot in a way that creates a sort of "back-to-the-future" ethos: spare, surreal, science-fictionish in certain regards, unmistakably evocative of the sixties (or fifties) in other regards. We may wish to label much of this aesthetic as based on a kind of "histoire noire." Bracketing the present in this peculiar way, and thus making it already the object of a historical sensibility, these images put the consumer in an already periodized present, thus even readier prey to the velocity of fashion. Buy now, not because you will otherwise be out of date, but buy now because your period will soon be out of date.

Thus it is that nostalgia and fashion creep up, unknowingly, on one another, not just because nostalgia is a clever instrument of the merchandiser's tool-kit, but because the continuous change of small features (that is at the heart of fashion) now has acquired a recycling dimension, especially in the United States, that is remarkable. Rummaging through history has become a standard technique of advertising, especially of visual and electronic ads, as a way to draw on the genuine nostalgia of age-groups for "pasts" they actually know through other experiences, but also as a way to underline the inherent ephemerality of the present. Catalogues that exploit the colonial experience for merchandising purposes are an excellent example of this technique.[30] This inculcated sentiment, calculated to intensify the tempo of purchasing by toying with the merchandiser's version of "the end of history," is the latest twist in the compact between nostalgia and fantasy in modern merchandising. Rather than expecting the consumer to supply memories while the merchandiser supplies the lubricant of nostalgia, now the viewer need only bring the faculty of nostalgia to an image that will supply the memory of a loss he or she has never suffered. This relationship might be called armchair nostalgia, nostalgia without lived experience or collective historical memory. One methodological issue here is interpretive: when we consider those images to which modern consumers respond, we need to distinguish different textures of temporality from one another. We need to discriminate the force of nostalgia in its primary form from the ersatz nostalgia on which mass merchandising increasingly draws and to attend to how these two might relate in the consumption patterns

[30] P. Smith, *Visiting the Banana Republic* in *Universal Abandon? The Politics of Postmodernism*, ed. A. Ross (Minneapolis: University of Minnesota Press, 1988) 128-48.

of different groups. The other methodological issue is simply a matter of paying attention to the paradoxical regularity with which "patina" and "fashion" in societies of mass consumption, feed and reinforce one other. Mass merchandising techniques construct not only time, as was suggested earlier, but also influence periodization as a mass experience in contemporary societies.

Let us return briefly to the issue of repetition in relation to consumption, touched on in the previous section. How can we connect the problem of repetition to the issue of fantasy, nostalgia and consumption in contemporary consumer societies? Insofar as consumption is increasingly driven by rummaging through imagined histories, repetition is not simply based on the functioning of simulacra *in* time, but also on the force of the simulacra *of* time. That is, consumption not only creates time, through its periodicities, but the workings of ersatz nostalgia create the simulacra of periods which constitute the flow of time, conceived as lost, absent or distant. Thus, the forward-looking habituation to predictable styles, forms and genres, which drives commodity-comsumption forward as a multiplicative and open-ended activity, is powered by an implosive, retrospective construction of time, in which repetition is itself an artifact of ersatz nostalgia and imagined precursory moments.

The Commodification of Time

Consumption not only creates time, but consumer revolutions are also responsible for the commodification of time in a variety of ways. The general lead in this area is, of course, owed to E.P. Thompson, who showed, building on Marx, how the disciplines of the industrial workplace create needs for the regimentation of labor by the prior restructuring of time itself. Extending the transformation of labor into a commodity, labor-time becomes itself an abstract dimension of time experienced as fundamentally productive and industrial. Thompson builds on Marx's discussion of the temporal dimension of labor and identifies the logic that leads to later Taylorean ideas about the body, motion and productivity.[31] Modern ideas of production thus have time as a saleable entity at their heart, evoking Ben Franklin's homily that "time is money."

But we have had fewer fundamental insights into the commodification of time, seen from the consumer's point of view. In early in-

---

[31] E. P. Thompson, "Time, Work-Discipline and Industrial Capitalism," *Past and Present* 38 (1967) 56-97.

dustrial societies, where industrial time sets the rhythm of the work cycle, production defines work, and consumption is rendered residual, along with leisure, which comes to be recognized, logically, as the reward for production time well used. Consumption evolves as the phenomenological marker of time left over from work, produced by work, and justified by work. Leisure activities become the very definition of discretionary consumption[32] and consumption becomes the process that creates the conditions for the renewed labor or entrepreneurial energy required for production. Thus, consumption is seen as the required interval between periods of production.

But once time is commodified, it affects consumption in new ways. First, the degree of time over which one has discretionary control becomes itself an index for ranking and distinguishing various kinds of work, class, and occupation. "Free" time, whether for workers, professionals, or schoolchildren, is seen as quintessentially the time of consumption, and, since discretionary consumption calls both for "free" time (time freed of commodified constraints) and "free" money, at least to some degree, consumption becomes a temporal marker of leisure, of time away from work. Transformed into contemporary forms of leisure, where both space and time mark distance from work, we enter the world of the luxury cruise and the packaged vacation, commodified as "time out of time." But everyone who has taken a vacation within the highly constrained circumstances of an industrial society knows that the commodity clock, of productive time, never ceases to operate. This sometimes leads to the paradox increasingly characteristic of industrial leisure: the harried vacation, packed with so many activities, scenes and choices, whose purpose is to create a hyper-time of leisure, that the vacation indeed becomes a form of work, of frenetic leisure, leisure ever conscious of its forthcoming rendezvous with work-time.

In fact, there is really little escape from the rhythms of industrial production, for wherever leisure is reliably available, and socially acceptable, what is required is not only "free" time, but disposable income, generally money income. To consume, whether in search of subsistence or of leisure, we have to learn to contain money, that most fluid of values. As Mary Douglas has pointed out, money always threatens to slip through the cracks of the structures we build to dam, husband, and restrict its erratic flows.[33] In those industrial societies

---

[32] Chris Rojek, *Capitalism and Leisure Theory* (London: Tavistock, 1987).
[33] Jean Baudrillard, *The Mirror of Production* (St. Louis: Telos Press, 1975).

where consumer debt has become monstrously large, financial institutions have exploited the proclivity of consumers to spend *before* they save, rather than after they do so. From the consumer's point of view, they are not simple dupes of an exploitative system of financial lending. The credit economy is also a way of enhancing buying power in the face of huge salary differentials, an explosive growth in what is buyable, great intensification in the speed with which fashions change, and the like. Debt is income expansion by other means. Of course, from certain other perspectives, paying large amounts of interest to service consumer debt is not healthy. But from whose point of view? The consumer can ratchet up his purchases, financial institutions make a killing, and there is periodic blood-letting, either in the form of major collapses like the recent Savings and Loan catastrophe in the United States or in the form of brutal increases in interest rates that asphyxiate consumer expenditure for a while.

In fact, as the immense popularity of magazines such as *Money* in the United States attests, consumption in complex industrial societies is now a very complex skill, which requires knowledge of a large variety of complex fiscal and economic mysteries, ranging from stock-market volatilities, to housing starts and M-1. In the last decade, a growing proportion of American consumers have had to become literate in the mysteries of macro-economics than ever before, at least to the degree that they are forced to enter the maze of consumer lending. Of course, there is a growing group at the bottom, notably the homeless, who have spent their chips and must now watch, or die, on the sidelines, as their friends and colleagues struggle with the roulette of consumer debt-management. The relevance of these processes to the argument at hand is that in societies like the United States, there is emerging a gigantic, if silent, struggle, between consumers and major lenders, where at issue are rival understandings of the future as a commodity. Where bankers and other lenders are eager to encourage borrowing (their major problem being to minimize bad loans) the consumer has to define an open-ended temporal horizon in which the discounting of the future is an extremely tricky business. Recent debates in the United States over reductions in the Social Security tax reveal that most American consumers are prey to a variety of distorted perceptions about the taxes to which they are subject. A good part of this confusion is rooted in the deformation of the experience of time by the structures through which consumer debt is currently organized. Notable among these is the type of credit line, based on home equity, through which consumers can simply write checks against some specified large sum which defines the bank's sense of their ability to pay. What this involves is taking the small periodicities of the average credit card and turning them into a seductive vista of open-ended purchasing power, which ultimately profits banks and retail businesses while putting increasing strain on household incomes to service these loans.

This feature of the creation of time-discipline on the consumption side of advanced industrial societies is not a simple reflex, or inversion, of the logic of industrial production. The peculiar commodification of the future, which is at the heart of current consumer debt, is intimately tied to the structure of merchandising, fashion, and fantasy that were discussed in the previous section. Late industrial consumption relies on a peculiar tension between fantasy and nostalgia that gives substance (and sustenance) to consumer uncertainty, about commodities, money, and the relationship between work and leisure. It is not simply the case that consumption plays the central role in societies where production once did, as Baudrillard once argued:[34] but that *consumption has become the civilizing work of postindustrial society.*[35] To speak of contemporary industrial societies as "consumer" societies is to create the illusion that they are simply extensions of earlier "consumer revolutions." But consumption today transforms the experience of time in a way that fundamentally distinguishes it from its eighteenth- and nineteenth-century predecessors.

Thus large-scale innovations in lending have had a remarkable cultural effect. They have created an open-ended, rather than cyclic, climate for consumer borrowing: they have thereby linked borrowing to the long, linear sense of a lifetime of potential earnings and the equally open-ended sense of the growth value of assets such as houses, rather than to the short, and inherently restrictive cycles of monthly or annual income. Consumption has thus become not the horizon of earning but its engine for a vast number of consumers in contemporary industrial societies. For the anthropologist, what is striking here (apart from its many implications for savings, productivity, investment, crossgenerational entitlements and the like) is that the small periodicities (typically daily ones) of consumption have now become subtly contextualized in an open-ended, linear sense of the very rhythm

---

[34] Mary Douglas, *Primitive Rationing* in *Themes in Economic Anthropology*, ed. Raymond Firth (London: Tavistock, 1967).
[35] Norbert Elias, *The Civilizing Process*, tr. E. Jephcott (1939; Oxford: Basil Blackwell, 1978) vol. 1.

of consumer life. The equivalent of Thompson's time discipline now reigns not just in the realm of production but also in the realm of consumption. But tied as it is to uneven, complex, and often long periodicities, these temporal disciplines of consumption are more powerful, because less transparent, than the disciplines of production. Anyone who has tried to figure out the exact logic of the finance charge on a monthly Mastercard bill will know about the uncertainty to which I refer.

But it is not simply the case that consumption has now become the driving force of industrial society. The fact is that consumption is now the social practice through which persons are drawn into the work of fantasy.[36] It is the daily practice through which nostalgia and fantasy are drawn together in a world of commodified objects. In the previous section, I argued that a sort of ersatz nostalgia — nostalgia without memory — was increasingly central to mass merchandising and that the interplay of patina and fashion was thus paradoxical. I would now suggest that the commodification of time, on the consumption side, implies more than the simple expansion of wants, of styles, of objects and of choices witnessed in earlier "consumer revolutions." What we have now is something beyond a consumer revolution, something we may call a *revolution of consumption*, in which it has become the principal *work* of late industrial society. By this I do not mean that there have not been important changes in production, in the sites, methods, technologies, and organizations for manufacturing commodities.

However, consumption has now become *a serious form of work*, if by work we mean the disciplined (skilled and semiskilled) production of the means of consumer subsistence. The heart of this work is the social discipline of the imagination, the discipline of learning to link fantasy and nostalgia to the desire for new bundles of commodities. This is not to reduce work to a pale metaphor, mirroring its strong anchorage in production. It is to suggest that learning how to navigate the open-ended temporal flows of consumer credit and purchase, in a landscape where nostalgia has become divorced from memory, involves new forms of labor: the labor of reading ever-shifting fashion messages, the labor of debt-servicing, the labor of learning how best to manage newly complex domestic finances, and the labor

---

[36] Arjun Appadurai, "Disjuncture and Difference in the Global Cultural Economy," *Public Culture* 2.2 (1990) 124.

of acquiring knowledge in the complexities of money management. This labor is not principally targeted to the production of commodities but is directed at producing the conditions of consciousness in which *buying* can occur. Every housewife knows that "housekeeping" is work, as real as any other. We are all housekeepers now, laboring daily to practice the disciplines of purchase, in a landscape whose temporal structures have become radically polyrhythmic. Learning these multiple rhythms (of bodies, products, fashions, interest rates, gifts, and styles) and how to interdigitate them is not just work, it is the hardest sort of work, the work of the imagination. We are back then to Durkheim and Mauss, and the nature of the collective consciousness, but now with a twist. The work of consumption is as fully social as it is symbolic, no less work for involving the discipline of the imagination. But increasingly freed from the techniques of the body, the work of consumption is all the more open-ended, situated in histories and genealogies whose conjuncture has to be examined, alas, case by case. The study of consumption will need to attend to the historical, social, and cultural conditions under which such work unfolds as the central preoccupation of otherwise very different contemporary societies.

Conclusion

From two very different directions, the one drawing on Weber and the other on Elias, Campbell and Rojek suggest that the key to modern forms of consumerism is *pleasure*, not leisure (the crucial alternative for Rojek) or satisfaction (the crucial alternative for Campbell).[37] This turn to pleasure as the organizing principle of modern consumption converges with my own argument in the last two sections of this essay, but it remains now to show how the sort of pleasure I have in mind relates to my arguments about time, work, and the body.

As far as the experience of time is concerned, the pleasure that lies at the center of modern consumption is neither the pleasure of the tension between fantasy and utility (as Campbell suggests) nor the tension between individual desire and collective disciplines (Rojek's proposal), though these latter contrasts are relevant to any larger account of modern consumerism. The pleasure that has been inculcated into the subjects who act as modern consumers is to be found in the tension between nostalgia and fantasy, discussed earlier, where

[37] Campbell, *The Romantic Ethic*; Rojek, *Capitalism and Leisure Theory*.

the present is represented as if it was already past. It is this inculcation of the pleasure of *ephemerality* that is at the heart of the disciplining of the modern consumer. The valorization of ephemerality expresses itself at a variety of social and cultural levels: the short shelf-life of products, lifestyles, the speed of fashion change, the velocity of expenditure, the polyrhythms of credit, acquisition, and gift, the transience of television product images, the aura of periodization that hangs over both products and lifestyles in the imagery of mass media. The much vaunted feature of modern consumption — namely, the search for novelty — is only a symptom of a deeper discipline of consumption in which desire is organized around the aesthetic of ephemerality. Pockets of resistance are everywhere, as aristocrats batten down their sumptuary hatches, as working classes and other disenfranchised groups appropriate and resist mass aesthetics, and as states throughout the world seek immortality by freezing cultural difference. But the dominant force, spreading through the consuming classes of the world, appears to be the ethic, aesthetic, and material practice of the ephemeral.

If this valorization of ephemerality is indeed the key to modern consumption, then the techniques of the body differ in what was earlier contrasted as sumptuary and fashion regimes. In sumptuary regimes, the body is a site for the inscription of a variety of signs and values about identity and difference, as well as about duration (through the rites of passage). In regimes of fashion, the body is the site for the inscription of a generalized desire to consume, in the context of the aesthetic of ephemerality. The techniques of the body appropriate to this modern consumption regime involve what Laura Mulvey has called, in another context, scopophilia (the love of gazing);[38] a variety of techniques (ranging from diets to sex-change operations) for body-change that make the body of the consumer itself potentially ephemeral, manipulable; and a system of body-related fashion practices in which *impersonation* (of other genders, classes, roles and occupations), not indexing, is the key to distinction.[39]

This notion of the manipulation of the body, as well as my general argument about *consumption as work*, raise the question of how the aes-

---

[38] Laura Mulvey, "Visual Pleasure and Narrative Cinema," *Screen* 16.3 (1975) 6-18.
[39] For a discussion of several of these issues on fashion, especially with regard to the female body, see K. Sawchuck, *A Tale of Inscription/Fashion Statements*, in *Body Invaders: Panic Sex in America*, ed. Arthur and Marilouise Kroker (Basingstake: Macmillan Education, 1988) 61-77.

thetic of ephemerality, the pleasure of the gaze (particularly in relation to television advertising) and the manipulability of the body, add up to anything fundamentally new: after all, consumption, particularly at the level of the household, always involved drudgery, visual pleasure is not a modern prerogative, and manipulating the body is as old as gymnastics in Sparta and yogic praxis in ancient India. What is new is the *systematic* and *generalized* linkage of these three factors into a set of practices that involve a radically new relationship between wanting, remembering, being, and buying. The histories and genealogies that criss-cross (in the world of the present) to constitute this new relationship are deeply variable, though they have the valorization of ephemerality at their heart. Consumption creates time, as was suggested earlier, but modern consumption seeks to replace the aesthetics of duration with the aesthetics of ephemerality.

Although the full pursuit of the relation between bodies, consumption, fashion, and temporality in late capitalism is beyond the scope of this essay, one suggestion is worth making by way of conclusion. In her recent essay on the imagery of the immune system in contemporary scientific and popular discourses in the United States, Emily Martin (1992) has drawn on the work of David Harvey and others to show that in the context of the flexibility demanded by contemporary global capitalism, there has been a great deal of compression of time and space, and the body comes to be seen as a chaotic, hyperflexible site, ridden with contradictions and warfare.[40] The argument I have made in this essay is to suggest that this situation can also be looked at from the point of view of the logic of consumption in a highly globalized, unruly, late capitalism. From this point of view, the aesthetic of ephemerality becomes the civilizing counterpart of flexible accumulation and the work of the imagination is to link the ephemerality of goods with the pleasures of the senses. Consumption thus becomes the key link between nostalgia for capitalism and capitalist nostalgia.

[40] Emily Martin, "The End of the Body?" *American Ethnologist* 19.1 (1992) 121-40.

Marie in Japan

JEAN-FRANÇOIS LYOTARD

Any stream of cultural capital?[1] Why that's me! Marie says to herself,
watching the baggage carousel revolve at Narita. A small stream, but
a stream nonetheless. Cultural, that's for sure — they buy me some
culture. Capital as well. I'm not its owner — blessed be he — nor
the director. A small bit of the cultural labor force, which they exploit. But decently, on contract, I insist, and I signed. That is not
a great discovery. Half wage-earner; half artisan. You wished for it.
You cross Europe, the continents, airplanes, faxes, telephones, cou-
rier to the four corners of the world. It's hard, real hard. Agreeable,
but hard. It had been agreeable. Nonetheless, it's also work. One cannot sell the same merchandise all the time. One must invent, read,
imagine. Because without that, they are not content; they say that
you are taking them for fools. Or even declining. You know, Marie,
she has nothing more to say. Fit for the trash can.

Insomuch as things go smoothly, there is a hostess (I see her, that's
her, I'm sure) or an assistant who comes to take you to the airport
in a taxi. A half-hour at the hotel to refresh yourself. Sometimes it's
been a ten-hour nonstop flight, eh? A cocktail and dinner, then the
conference and a drink. Or perhaps a cocktail and the conference,
then the dinner. Everywhere the same, in all the cities of the world.
Sometimes they are apprehensive, sometimes enthusiastic, or a little
wicked. Sometimes, also, a real friend. You are always smiling, Marie,

[1] Passages in italics are in English in the original. Tr. — As part of the problematics
of "streams of cultural capital," one should recognize here the transatlantic mobility
of representations of U.S. "multiculturalism," and the ways such a flow of representation has been received, interpreted, and written into both the popular and political institutions of Europe. One has only to survey the popular journals of Britain,

even if you are sweetly telling sinister stories in your *talk*. I can sell agony, that catches their interest but aimiably. The next day or the day after, one takes leave, one embraces, one is given offprints, books, addresses, one embraces again, so long, we'll see each other again, eh? It's a small world, gestures of the hand, a brief sadness, the suit-cases pass through the security checks. Hi, you're Keiko? Thanks for coming to fetch me. Is Keiko a little stream of cultural capital, she too? Evidently. The white-gloved driver looks at us in the rearview mirror, chatting quite politely, heads propped on immaculate lace headrests. The taxi speeds along like a missile through the highways and interchanges. A stream of capital. We arrive; I am going to have my half-hour. The room is on the 58th floor and everything works.

In the shower Marie remembers that their teacher explained to them that as for capital, it's not only that *time is money*, but *money is time* as well. It's the good stream that arrives the quickest. An excellent stream arrives scarcely having left. On radio and on television they call that real time, or *live* time. But the best feeling is to anticipate the arrival of the stream, its "realization," before it arrives. That's the currency of credit. That's stockpiled time, for dispensing before real time. One gains time, one borrows it. You must buy a *word processor*. It's incredible, the time one gains. But what about writing? You write more quickly, the page formats, notes, corrections, you see?

Poor Marie, you'll never get rich, you love scribbling on your pa-per, too bad. You are a little, sluggish stream. You will be submerged by faster little streams of expeditious culture. Suffice that you'd die before you make yourself ridiculous. She tells herself that thought takes time, there is nothing one can do about it, or in general what they stupidly call creation takes time. That does not resemble streams so much. It's more like pools. One wallows there. That leads nowhere, that's not amusing, not communicative. You remember how he

France, and Germany in the past few years to find a remarkable number of articles on multiculturalism, political correctness, and educational democratic movements in the U.S. The sources for such reports, unfortunately, has largely been uncritical readings of U.S. press articles, rather than direct investigative reporting. For com-ment on this phenomenon, see Hans Ulrich Gumbrecht, "Die Häßlichen und die Dummen? Der amerikanische Multikulturalismus und seine Kritiker" [The ugly and the dumb? American multiculturalism and its critics], in *Merkur* 512 (November 1991) 1074-79, and Naomi Schor, "The Righting of French Studies: Homosociality and the Killing of 'La Pensée 68,'" in *Profession* 92, especially pages 32-33, and Edith Kurzweil, "Multiculturalism Abroad," *Partisan Review* 59.3 (1992).

worked, Don? Oh, not sequestered away, monk-like. But all the same completely somewhere else. His friends come to see him in his country hideaway; he receives them kindly. They tell the tales of artists. One never comes to know whether or not that sticks in his mind. He says next to nothing about his work. And then one day they exhibit a series of fifteen large-scale paintings by him in some gallery, or fifty sketches. Conclusion: true streams are subterranean; they flow slowly beneath the earth, they make sheets of water and springs. One doesn't know where they are going to exit. And their speed is unknown. How would I like to be a subterranean pocket of black water, cold and immobile.

Still ten minutes before Keiko arrives. Marie puts on her makeup. For all there is to gain time, we women are always losers. One always has a face, a body to restore. Men shine with only a bit of rag. Not fair. I am pleased with my talk. They won't understand a word. It's too laconic. And too scripted. As if it were Maurice's. Too "French." Or Irish. That tends toward the minimal. They want good, limpid streams. Explain where it comes from, or where it's going. A little introduction. One places the point in context. Ernst proposed this, Dick objected to that, Ruth explained that the problem is poorly posed — a phallocratic approach. And Ron, that everyone continues to think in Western style although there are others. Oh, the others! They don't have anything else on their lips. Difference, otherness, multiculturalism. It's their hobbyhorse.

My professor, he reminded us of Kant: to think by oneself, to think in accordance with oneself. Today they say that's logocentric, not *politically correct*. Streams must flow in the right direction so that they may converge. Why all this cultural bustling? Colloquia, interviews, seminars? Just to assure oneself that everyone is speaking of the same thing. Of what? Of Otherness. Unanimity on the principle that unanimity, that's something suspect. If you are a woman, and Irish, and somehow a professor in Brazil, and lesbian, and one who writes nonacademic books — then you are a truly fine little stream. You are interesting for the cultural capital. You are a little cultural market on the move. Hurry up. But if you leave them a particle of an analysis a bit tight about the *sense-able*, as Rachael says, and its connection with death, then really, you aren't with it. It's commonplace. How does that express your difference? Where did it go, your otherness? Any old fellow, any honest *Ordinarius* in Bochum, Germany, could do that instead of you. What this cultural capitalism has found is the marketplace of singularities. That each one expresses their own singularity. That he/she speaks of his/her place in the network of sex, ethnicity, language, age, social class, the unconscious. The true universality, they now say, is singularity. Do you think of the pretty Irish lesbian who teaches French at the Universidad de São Paulo and is in the midst of making Kanto-Wittgensteinian analyses? Why, it's appalling. It's, frankly, unintelligent, archaic. What is this philo? It's even scandalous. Well, we'll see if they're like that in Tokyo and Kyoto.

At the appointed minute, Keiko is in the room. Truly very beautiful, no doubt. We have a half-hour before cocktails. Would you like to visit the museum that is in front of the Center where you are going to speak? There is a showing of German drawings and etchings of the fifteenth century. Marie said to herself that it's again a stream of culture, this exposition. A piece of old European cultural capital, very smart, packed off to Japan, that will circulate it here, all to practical ends. Which ends? Well, to show what Europe is — its past, its art — to the Asia that knows nothing of it, evidently. That's good, no? And now Marie, you too, you are a bit of the museum. And Tokyo, too, tomorrow Kyoto with a stop at Nara, three-quarters of an hour thereabouts, all that, it's a museum for you. Not only the promised temples, but the landscapes, the overpopulated suburbs, the town centers, all that to archive catalog. The destination of all streams is the museum. They want singularities to enrich the museum. Which museum? The contemporary cultural world. You remember Lewis? "Cultural capital," that means: all the cultures capitalized in the cultural bank. That is the memory of humanity. It's necessary to saturate each branch. The bulk of the work is done — Lascaux is saved and stocked up, the tombs of the Upper Nile, the Aztec pyramids, and the Maginot line as well, and the tombs of Xi'an, Spinoza, Agatha Christie. Now one must catalog the contemporary. Not only its works, but the modes of life, the ways to cook fish or to excite a woman, the little *patois*, slang expressions, the mid- and long-term fluctuations of the dollar, the posters of 1930.

Marie and Keiko look at the Altdorfers, Cranachs, Dürers. Keiko takes notes. She is making her little archival stream, Marie says to herself, she will succeed. Beautiful and serious. It's as if it were already accomplished. That's today's world. On holidays why do the Caduveo Indians or the Tupi-Kawahib regale themselves on dishes of huge off-white larvae extracted from the trunks of trees? In order to be in an anthropological film or workbook. You see, they say, nothing is nature; all is culture, and each culture is singular. And kinship rules? Do you believe that they spring up *sui generis*? Why no. There are Australian communities where their complexity would make a law clerk lose his head. Isn't that wonderful? Record them before they wear out. And the works of Art brut, you believe that these are crude? They are the most sophisticated drawings one can imagine. Record them. And Saturn, you would believe that it was a ball of gas? Not at all, a space probe has detected a hard core. Redo your cosmological museum.

The next visiting exhibition, said Keiko upon leaving, will be devoted (she speaks a super-correct French) to the costumes, accessories, instruments and decor of Nô theater in the northern part of fifteenth-century Honshû. And the next? The masks and sculptures of Dogon in relation to European Negro art. Say, then, it's rich, your Museum! Keiko smiles to excuse herself: very rich collectors, galleries, *sponsors*. Yes, Marie says to herself, me too, they pay me well. I am part of the museum. No, not yet, we'll see. That's what the game is all about. It's just one try. If there is a second time, well then, perhaps. That's how they want to hear me. Not what I say, but if I keep well, if my junk is worth committing to memory. It is not well targeted, that's for sure. A small sign of anguish from Marie, and a laugh: the poorly targeted is perhaps the best targeted. They expect something from me on minorities, I give them a general analysis of the sensate body: that can appear singular as well. It's necessary for the museum to renew itself all the time. The streams that arrive here demand the right to be preserved and exhibited. They must deserve it. That is to say they must draw high attendance and a lot of reviews must be written. If it was always the same objects, then boredom, the down of audience, a substandard performance, an obverse result.

Marie says to herself, raising her glass with the Center's staff, that basically these *managers* are good only if they never stop innovating. The museums, the cultural institutions, are not only warehouses, they are laboratories. Banks, really. And depositories must work. One takes out pieces, one shows them, one places them back in storage, one compares them, one finds others, analyzes them, restores them, x-rays them. Same thing for manuscripts or musical pieces. If I have luck with my *sense-able*, it will be the same with it. Notoriety, that's it, excitement about a name.

Marie spreads her sheets of paper under the small lamp of the podium and begins, standing before an audience she doesn't see. Only

attending to her text. Someone told her that it was considered vulgar
and bad form to place oneself in the fore. She has confidence in her
text. It must speak all by itself. She makes herself absent. It will find
its tone. Now as for me, meanwhile, I can think of something else;
this is better. This story of the stream of culture and capital, it's really an amusing affair. It's metaphysical. Not only metaphoric. The
metaphysical is made up of realized metaphors. Why, this seems to
interest Keiko on the first row, my *aisthèsis*. Is there a crowd? No time
to look. In any case, I am their Other, that's the advantage of self-
export. There are only a few who are to know if my merchandise is
truly singular. If the room is full, they will say that it was good anyway. If not, the public will have been wrong, and the Center is dis-
credited. A droll metaphysic. Bah, it's simply about capital. Thermal
machines, a hot pole and a cold pole, work. They fabricate differentiation. The entire question is that new energy must always be available. And accommodating. But in order to accommodate them, they
have become very cunning. Their multiculturalism, minorities, singularities, for a hundered years it had no future in the culture industry. Except as a Colonial Exhibition. That required a lot of strategies
of capture and exploitation. Now, finally, it has become profitable.
People are bored, they have had enough of always guzzling up the
same images, the same ideas of cultural *fast food*, they need a bit of
unexpected *live*. A good market opportunity. But they'll need to find
something else in ten years. An amusing metaphysic.

It's not that it must be youthful. It's the dynamic as world system,
which dates at least from Aristotle, but what's peculiar, Marie tells
herself, is that apart from a few crazy megalomaniacs, the theory of
energies interests no one. It interests as a spectacle. It's that, the interest in the dynamic, not force or power, but aesthetic pleasure that
they procure. A human community that contemplates its differences.
A generalized aesthetic. The grand operation of this fin-de-siècle and
perhaps the next ones, too. Eh? Perhaps they'll hear that in my talk.
If so, I'll be saved. They only want one thing and that's that one speak
of them, that one show how they are interesting. Everything must
speak about them. You remember that astronaut who said, "One
understands the earth and mankind a hundred times better seeing
them from space ships and probes"? You recall that a probe encountered Halley's comet after I don't know how many years en route.
She speaks to them about themselves. A humanity as spectator of itself in all its theaters. The repertoire must change. Find new pieces.

Show the old ones something else. All this dynamic in order to arrive *ad panem et circenses*.

The room lights up again, applause. Enough? O.K. Go on to the question and answer game. That's part of the cultural. They have the right to speak, the obligation to intervene, no passivity-animation, interaction. This is the test of a good performance. Marie, this is not the time to show that you don't give a damn about it, that you're fed up. Never exhausted, right? Without that, they won't invite you back. Have I been "Other" enough? At least all this helps to learn that, their dialogue. Respond politely, explain, mark your otherness, don't let yourself be brought back to the well known, defend your difference. Go on, show that the little stream of yours has no equal here. Very animated, eh? All the questions are "very interesting, but all the same I would like to add this..." And not too lengthy, O.K.? There's dinner.

One dines with the *happy few*, in French and in English, or else Keiko translates. The streams in the capital of language, they need translation in order to be operational. Painting, music, that works without transformation. The questions and answers continue over dinner. One swallows the words along with the grub, in bulk. But watch out, my dear, your guests are decision-makers, journalists. Too bad about time zones. Cultural capital doesn't care about drowsiness. Discrepancies between time zones, oh yes, they're important. Since for capitalism everything shuts down in Tokyo and opens up on Wall Street. Your little *talk* is an index to the trend in Paris at this hour. How do you find Tokyo? Is this your first time? Surprising, wonderful, but, you know, I don't have a lot of time. Are you going to stay a while? Alas, I have a seminar tomorrow morning at the University and I take the *shinkansen* for Kyoto. And how about Europe?

Ah, it's hard. It would be a whole lecture, even a one or two- month seminar. You'll suggest it to them? No, the request is theirs, not yours. You know, I'm often traveling, and yet I am only a Parisian poorly educated in the ways of the world. Oh go on! Europe as a marketplace — you know it much better than I. But Europe as culture, that does and does not exist. It's like a family. One is never finished with the great-aunts and the great grand-nephews. Are the Transcaucasians Europeans? And the distribution of the patrimony! For twenty-five centuries not a single border has remained the same in Europe. Jealousies, abductions, rapes, concubinages, marriages of reason, incests, the hegemony of one branch. Everyone adores everyone and detests everyone. And it's not over, you know. Nevertheless, peace has been decided in the family. But all the afterthoughts remain. And culturally, can you imagine? It's a monstrosity. Thirty different languages, without counting linguistic minorities. Every possible version of Judaism, Christianity, Islam, with all the conflicts of living together and being neighbors, of confessionals, of linguistics. That's even without speaking of ethnicities, which don't strictly correspond to the languages. For the multicultural, Europe is unbeatable. There are only strangers in the family. The only real community is interest, that's to say, capital, development. And even on this it's not easy. The invasion of wealthy Europe by miserables produced by fifty years and more of Stalinism. Unequal development, in the middle of Europe. The arrivals from Poland and Hungary packed in Brandenburg, besieged by young, inevitably xenophobic, unemployed, as recounted by Hans-Peter. And meanwhile the German capital sells off the old East German businesses at bargain prices and casts greedy eyes on market opportunities in the Ukraine and Russia. The war goes on, but not with armies, rather, with cash. Then, the culture...

Good, they're no longer listening to me, fortunately. They compare this with their own situation — Japanese capital in Korea, in all Southeast Asia. What will China do, ultimately? I don't understand anything of this, any more than they do of Europe. It's the streams of culture, after all. It arrives no matter where, and is lost in the desert. Words, incomprehensible sentences, music, images, delicious mannerisms, but only from afar, for exoticism. Can one escape from touristic bullshit? Including your own, Marie. But there's not enough time. It's become too weighty for one human life, all that which is there to see, to hear, to understand. The museum is too rich, the laboratory works too quickly. Go on to bed! Have to begin early tomorrow morning. The rituals of gratitude and leave-taking, deferences, the taxi.

At one o'clock in the morning the foyer of the hotel is full of businessmen. They deal in all the languages of the world. One trades culture, between others. What the hell are you doing here, Marie? A little handmade jewel of reflective thought. Is there still some capital interesting in this? Some? Collectors? For how long? We'll soon see. You, perhaps you'll never see, old buddy. Try to smoke less.

Translated by David Palumbo-Liu

Identity in Writing: Four Decades of Corsican Identity Construction, 1890-1936

ANNE KNUDSEN

Corsica has always been different. But Corsicans only began to appreciate this fact around the turn of the century. On several levels, writing played a prominent role in the construction of Corsican identity and the development of a Corsican nationalism. Although economic, political, social, and cultural differences existed between Corsica and the mainland France that governed the island, the problems of being Corsican within the French nation as well as the proposed solutions centered upon questions of *writing properly*, in the literal as well as in the metaphorical sense.[1]

It was through writing that Corsicans realized that they were different. The writings about Corsican identity focused first on the writing of Corsican history, secondly on the proper writing of the Corsican language, thirdly on the writing of texts to incite people to feel Corsican, and, finally, on putting in writing the very content of Corsican identity.

Writing was not introduced in Corsica by the French school system, but these schools were the main vehicle for the spread of literacy among the populace. During this period (as today), the French schools were firmly devoted to a concept of *civilization* strongly opposed to the kind of *culture* defining rural populations and indeed the

[1] This paper presents material and analyses that I will be treating more amply in a forthcoming book, *Identity as Politics: The Dilemmas of Corsican "Culturalism," 1871-1939*. The material was collected during two longer periods of research in Corsica in 1988 and 1989, funded by the Center for Research in the Humanities at the University of Copenhagen. I wish to express my gratitude to this excellent and inspiring center that has now been closed down.

more "Germanic," rural, and popular-based self-definition of nation states north of the ancient *limes*.[2]

It will be my argument in the following pages that the creation of a Corsican regional identity during the French Third Republic cannot be properly understood without taking into consideration the complexity of the actual integration of the Corsican intellectuals into a French value system on the one hand, and the French literary description of Corsican culture as profoundly different on the other hand. The often mutually contradictory ambitions of the regionalist movement — *le corsisme* — can thus be analyzed as the logical outcome of a complex process of cultural integration into a universe defined in writing.

From Dissidence to Otherness

Corsican eighteenth-century history is the history of political dissidence. The uprisings against "feudal" Genova met with widespread approval among European intellectuals, just as the Corsican democratic constitution of 1755 was celebrated by authors such as Rousseau and Voltaire and admired by Robespierre and Saint-Just as well as Lafayette. The democratic Corsican republic — the very first in modern times — was visited and described by James Boswell in 1765,[3] and only ill health prevented Jean-Jacques Rousseau from going to Corsica himself[4] to contemplate this ideal society.

Within the island itself, it is doubtful whether the newly created democracy was understood as anything novel. First of all, Corsica actually had a long tradition of village democracy,[5] and, secondly, it seems from the (not too numerous) contemporary diaries,[6] for instance, that internal competition among would-be leaders loomed at least as large in the local minds as did the fight against the Genoese oligarchy in the senate of La Serenissima Reppublica.

---

[2] The differences between a Vico-inspired view of "the nature of nations" and a Herder-inspired view still divide European countries in a recognizable North (and East) and South.

[3] James Boswell, *An Account of Corsica: The Journal of a Tour to that Island and the Memoirs of Pascal Paoli* (London, 1768)

[4] See Arrighi and Castellin, *Projets de constitution pour la Corse* (Ajaccio: La Marge, 1980).

[5] For a substantiation of this view, see Anne Knudsen, *En ø i Historien, Korsika: Historisk antropologi* 1730-1914 (Copenhagen: Basilisk 1989).

[6] See Père Bettinelli, *Osservazione sur Pasquale Paoli* in *Bulletin de la Société des Sciences Historiques et Naturelles de la Corse* (1881), and Abbé Rostini, *Mémoires d'avant 1773*, in BSSHNC (1881-1882).

Nevertheless, on the eve of the French Revolution, Corsica was firmly placed in European philosophical literature as the political pioneer of republican and democratic enlightenment.

The events in Corsica following the revolution and, in particular the establishment of the First Republic, led to a fundamental revision of this image[7] and eventually to the opinion that Corsica was "un pays oriental" where the inhabitants were "d'une paresse indicible: Agir et réfléchir sont deux peines qu'il, le corse, ne prend jamais qu'à l'extrémité."[8] This image of Corsica, though not always as harshly described as in this pamphlet by the Parisian Feydel, remained predominant in French literature throughout the following century. The deception had several reasons. The special Corsican manner of going about the distribution of power and money was already manifest in 1790. Then in 1793 Corsica defected from revolutionary France to join the British. The final defeat in 1815 of the Corsican-born emperor Napoleon the First only confirmed the image of an incomprehensible and possibly dangerous otherness that incidentally corresponded to the picturesque Corsican landscape. Soon the island became the mere stage set for poetry, novels, theater plays, and operas, the dramatic content of which was enhanced by allusions to the passionate Corsican "génie."

Since Corsican literacy during this period was almost exclusively an ability to read Italian (and Latin), the image of Corsican otherness propagated in French literature had only a very small Corsican audience. As with later "ethnographic objects," Corsicans were mostly strangers to the intellectual milieux articulating their true character. Indeed, the Corsican intellectual history of the early nineteenth century is usually referred to as "The Silent Decades," since virtually no Corsican literature appeared in print. A single "society" for literature, *I Vagabondi*, was created by the author Salvatore Viale in Bastia in 1828 in an effort to protect Corsican literature and to preserve the literary links with Italy, but it never acquired much of a following or members in other parts of the island. When in 1830 Italian university degrees were declared invalid for positions in France (including

---

[7] For details, see Pierrette Jeoffroy-Faggianelli, *L'image de la Corse dans la littérature romantique française* (Paris: Presses Universitaires de France, 1979) and Anne Knudsen, *En banal historie: uropfrelsen. Korsika i 1700tallets samfundsdebat* in *Stofskifte* 9 (Vildhedens Historie, 1983).

[8] "Of an unspeakable laziness. To act and to think are two efforts which he [the Corsican] never takes except in the utmost need." See G. Feydel, *Moeurs et coutumes des Corses. Paris an VII de la République* (1799) 14.

Corsica), all Corsican literature in Italian language was doomed. In French language, by contrast, a steady trickle of nonfictional works continued the defining of "le génie des Corses." Only one of these works — an early example, 1821 — was written by a Corsican, P.P. Pompei,[9] but because it was written in French and published in Paris, its intended audience was obviously not the Corsicans. Numerous French works on Corsica written during the time of the constitutional monarchies are quite levelheaded. And all of them relate to the fact that Corsica was already by then defined as the fatherland of unreason, passion, and vengeance. The authors merely try to nuance this picture by pointing to Corsican qualities. The Corsicans were, we learn, trustworthy, proud, hospitable, well spoken, and honest as far as worldly goods were concerned. They were undeniably murderers, but never thieves.

This early "sociology of Corsica" would, however, become supplanted by a folkloristic ethnography following the general European trend in the mid-century when studies of popular culture, poetry, and customs became fashionable. From the 1850s onward, nonfictional literature focused on the parts of Corsican culture already published as fiction, the *vendetta* and the bandits in particular. Several collections of Corsican *voceri* (death chants) were published within series of folk poetry either of the Mediterranean[10] or French countryside, and travellers from England, Germany, and France interviewed bandits and peasants about *la vendetta e l'onore*. Their findings were published in their own mother tongues. Probably only a fraction of these books were available in Corsica where only a minority would be able to read most of them anyway.

A characteristic of the greater part of the *French* works is that they tacitly pretend their Corsican informants speak French. Only specific Corsican customs are rendered in the original language; *abbraccio*, *vendetta*, *vocero*. Interviews with bandits such as Jean Pedignelli in Gracieux Faures's journalistic work from around 1860 are rendered in French, just as if this outlaw from a distant mountain village were a French-speaker. It is unlikely in the extreme that this was the case — just as it is improbable that the said "Jean" was not in reality called Giovanni or, for everyday use, Giovan'.

---

[9] P.P. Pompei, *Etat actuel de la Corse: caractères et moeurs de ses habitants* (Paris, 1821).
[10] An Italian collection: N. Tommaseo, *Canti popolari corsi, toscani, illirici, greci* (Venice, 1841).

The habit of rendering Corsican names as their French counterpart is systematic in all but Italian works from this period. The printing in *italics* (*sic!*) of the names of spectacular Corsican "customs" with their full, Italian vowels in the middle of the plain French texts tended to underline in writing the more general peculiarity of the Corsican "habits" in the context of a civilized, modern, and comprehensible world.

Thus, the image of Corsica was painted in great and exotic detail for the benefit of audiences abroad, while Corsican everyday life presumably continued largely unaltered. That customs did not change perceptibly can be noted from the fact that new material for the same kind of observations could obviously be collected again and again. The ruling elites of the island became bilingual and literate in French after the prohibition of Italian university degrees, but because of the specific Corsican political structures, these elites were seldom present on the island. They were away in Paris, where they could provide resources for their family, friends, and political allies back in Corsica. Some intellectual members of influential families even engaged in "expeditions" in the Corsican countryside. When for instance Jean Baptiste Frédéric Ortoli (of an ancient family of *notables*) published a collection of Corsican folk tales in 1883, they too were rendered in French with Corsican words in italics and explanations in footnotes. The same tendency could be seen in *Le Bulletin de la Société des Sciences Historiques et Naturelles de la Corse*, which from 1882 published sources to the Corsican history and stated in its first issue that sources in "foreign languages" would be translated into French. The foreign language in question was almost exclusively Italian, even though it was at the time quite well understood all over the island. French had become the language of the educated, just as it was the language of the administrative apparatus — and Corsican was considered either a "foreign" language or a nonlanguage.

Eager Readers

The establishment of the Third Republic's institutions on the island showed that political structures resembled closely those of nearly a century earlier when the First Republic faced Corsican "factionalism." But the Third Republic had a much more efficient administrative system, and the school system of the Second Empire had already provided the peasants with some education. Republican institutions were by now developed to such an extent that every village could become integrated with the larger system, both by way of administrative institutions imposed from above and by way of elected bodies. Concomitantly, the Corsican political press grew rapidly, becoming the battle ground of the innumerable "hommes de politique." Integration was under way, though still mainly through the "broker" activities of political leaders.

But the European agrarian crisis in the late nineteenth century speeded up the integration process immensely. In Corsica, as all over Europe, marginal lands had been brought under the plow during the middle of the century. The English historian Stephen Wilson estimates that by 1870 more land than ever before — or since — had been used for growing wheat in Corsica. The narrow terrasses left on the mountain sides by this short-lived but immense response to demographic growth are still a significant part of the Corsican landscape. But soon the Corsican agrarian economy collapsed — as did other marginal agrarian economies in Europe — under the pressure of cheap American wheat, and the Corsicans had to find other fields for their activities.

The specific Corsican emigration pattern of the late nineteenth century, like the earlier emigration pattern it closely resembled, was linked to the Corsican family structure and the system for landholding prevailing in the island. *L'indivision*, in particular, granted the links between heirs and the house and land of their forebears. This practice of obliging the heirs by will of testament to own the inherited property communally, one single heir being prohibited from buying out the others, bound everybody to his village and property with the links of ownership and economic rights and obligations, even if the property in most cases was far too small to support more than a small minority of its legal owners. Hardly anybody was thus disinherited, properly speaking, though many were forced from the land by economic necessities. The hypothetical inheritance formed a link, binding the families together and thus reinforcing the Corsican family ideology that insisted on an interpretation of families as corporate groups. The Corsican emigrants were to a much lesser degree than the typical European migrating peasants left to their own resources; they still formed a part of the family that had remained in Corsica. This peculiarity had two striking effects. First, that the sons leaving Corsica in search of better living conditions could count on at least some help from their families at home if necessary. Many families went little short of ruin in their efforts to provide sons with education that would ensure better possibilities on the continent. The education of the young had a high priority in the families' economic considerations. Secondly, Corsicans abroad did not entirely lose their sense of origin; they assimilated themselves to the new surroundings more slowly and less completely than many other emigrant groups that had no rights "back home" and who had emigrated as entire families, women, children and all.

In accordance with the Corsican emigration pattern of earlier centuries, Corsican emigration was largely a career emigration. This meant that the population engaged in formal schooling to an exceptional degree compared with other rural areas in France and, in particular, that the mastering of the French language became paramount for pupils and parents alike.

The fundamentally controlled character of the Corsican emigration must also be seen as the reason why the overwhelming majority of Corsican emigrants did not initially go farther than continental France. New World emigrants from Corsica were few, and most of them reached the Americas as employees in French governmental or economic structures. This particular emigration pattern seems to have secured a cultural continuity among emigrated Corsicans. Some of these emigrants would later form a considerable part of the readers of regionalist publications.

The Italianate Corsican language had not only been spoken by Corsicans in the past but was still the everyday language in all rural areas and most urban neighborhoods, even in the administrative center, the coastal town of Ajaccio. Courts of justice still had to employ interpreters, and people adressing themselves to the administration generally had to use intermediaries in order to make themselves understood. The early practice of printing prefectural circulars and all official messages in both languages had been abandoned, and the Corsican language had taken on, to an increasing degree, the aspect of a social infirmity, despite the official affirmations to the contrary:

> C'est ici le cas de relever une erreur dont plusieurs esprits étaient imbus. Ils s'étaient persuadés que l'on voulait anéantir la langue italienne. Ils se trompent.[11]

---

[11] *Journal du département de la Corse, 1818-1983*. "We must correct a misconception here that was shared by many minds. They were convinced that the government would annihilate the Italian language. They are wrong" (*Journal de la Corse. Journal du département de la Corse destiné aux actes administratifs et articles qui s'y rattachent*, Saturday, January 13, 1827: leading article).

By the early 1880s this statement had long since been proven false. The problem was now seen as the almost diametrically opposite, since the mastering of French language was increasingly a question of social competence. Every Corsican ought to learn the national language in order to be able to speak at all in a socially acceptable way. Primary education therefore became a topic of major concern with the Corsican political and social elite. In the autumn of 1882, *Le Petit Corse. Journal Républicain Quotidien* consecrated several front pages to the question of "l'Instruction Publique," bringing in extenso the "Rapport de l'Inspecteur d'Académie, Vice-Recteur de la Corse, sur l'enseignement primaire, adressé à M. le Préfet de la Corse."[12] The report is apparently very thorough and brings out that although in 1881 there were 664 primary schools with 38.436 pupils among them, and although "un grand nombre d'élèves, de garçons surtout, restent sur les bancs de l'école jusqu'à 16 ans et plus,"[13] no school in Corsica met the demands of "l'enseignement primaire supérieure" (September 12). Furthermore, the school buildings are described as follows:

> On ne saurait se faire une idée de l'insuffisance absolue, du délabrement et des mauvaises conditions hygiéniques de nos maisons d'école... La plupart des locaux sont misérables, incommodes, à peine assez spacieux pour le QUART d'élèves qu'ils reçoivent; ils devraient être interdits... sans air, sans lumière, sans cour, nulle part des lieux d'aisance...[14]

But worst of all, in view of the new cultural and linguistic offensive, was the pedagogical weaknesses of the public school personnel. The evaluation of the "Valeur morale et pédagogique" of the teachers takes up two whole days in *Le Petit Corse*. Morally, the teachers are generally deemed sufficient, but

> En ce qui concerne le mérite professionel, je suis forcé de faire des réserves: les écoles véritablement bonnes sont rares; les 3/5 sont médiocres ou mauvaises. (September 14)[15]

---

[12] *Le Petit Corse. Journal Républicain Quotidien*, September 13, 14, and 15, 1882; pp. 1-2.
[13] "A large number of pupils, especially boys, stay in school until 16 years and more."
[14] "One cannot imagine the absolute insuffience and the ruinous state and the bad hygienic conditions in our shool buildings. Most of the rooms are pitiful, unsuitable with hardly have enough space to house one quarter of the pupils they receive; they ought to be prohibited... without air, without light, without a courtyard, and nowhere a toilet."
[15] "With regard to professional merit, I am obliged to make some reservations; really good schools are rare; three fifths are mediocre or bad."

After listing shortcomings as the "ignorance des méthodes ... pas de goût pour la lecture," the report expands on the central insufficience among teachers:

> ...l'usage à peu près exclusif du dialecte du pays avec leurs propres enfants mêmes: voilà ce qui frappe chez le plus grand nombre d'entre eux.[16]

Nevertheless, the Corsican children continued in school "jusqu'à 16 ans et plus"; ten years later the explanation of this extraordinary willingness to learn claimed that "les enfants assis sur les bancs de l'école ne rêvent que des places et képis galonnés"[17] (*Bastia Journal*, December 21, 1894), on the continent or in the French colonies. But by now, this kind of political and cultural integration with France had been spurred on by the agrarian crisis:

> ...l'instituteur ne manque pas de faire à ses élèves le portrait le plus flatteur et le plus riant de la vie champêtre. Mais il a beau s'écrier avec Virgile: "Oh! heureux l'homme des champs, s'il connaissait son bonheur!" les enfants n'en croient rien. C'est qu'ici, comme en toute chose, l'exemple est plus fort que le précepte. La vie du laboureur, l'enfant la connaît pour la vivre, pour y être mêlé. Il connaît le travail acharné et opiniâtre de ses parents qui ne rapporte pas toujours le pain noir de la famille. A la maison, il entend souvent les cris de colère et d'impatience du père qui se plaint de la mévente des récoltes ou des embarras de la famille, et comme conclusion: "Etudie, mon fils, si tu ne veux pas piocher la terre comme tes parents."[18]

Many of the children listened well to their fathers' advice. More and more young Corsicans left their island to work in "képis et positions." But one can only agree with the anonymous teacher in seeking the reasons for this exodous; life in rural Corsica had become very difficult.

[16] "Ignorance of methods... no taste for reading." The almost exclusive use of the dialect of the land, even with their own children; this is what strikes one among the majority of them."

[17] "The children sitting on the school benches dream of nothing but positions and gallonned kepis."

[18] "The teacher conveys to the pupils the most attractive and smiling image of rural life. But well may he exclaim with Vergil 'Oh, happy the man of fields, did only he know his luck!'; the children do not believe him. Here, as in everything, the example is stronger than the admonition. The life of the farm hand is known by the child because he lives it, is part of it. He knows the relentless hard work of his parents which does not always bring even the black bread to the family. At home, he often hears the cries of anger and impatience from his father who complains about

Exotic Spelling

A single populist newspaper, *A Tramuntana*, had in the 1890s taken
for granted that its audience was able to read the paper's variety of
written Corsican. Judging from the observations of the inspector of
the primary school system that "the teachers speak the dialect of the
country, even with their own children," this was an accurate presump-
tion. With the emigration and the increasing number of Corsicans
educated and employed in white collar occupations on the French
mainland, the biligual abilities became more doubtful among Corsican intellectuals. When the very first publication advocating Corsican autonomism appeared in 1914, Corsican language was only to
be found on the cover of the book, *A Cispra, Antologia Annuale*, and
in a poem written by the poet Santu Casanova, who had for decades
been the editor and main writer of *A Tramuntana*. The rest of the publication was written in impeccable French by the editors who were
librarians and lycée professors. *A Cispra* was published on the French
mainland, in Marseille. Unlike *A Tramuntana*, the editors of *A Cispra*
explained its policy concerning the Corsican language. An article (74
ff) entitled "Notre Orthographe" states that

> entre deux formes également usitées nous optons pour celle qui s'éloigne
> le plus de l'italien; nous préférons Côrzica et côrzu (prononciation de
> la province de Vico) à Corsica et corso (formes purement italiennes).
> De même nous préférons pueta à poeta.[19]

In the same vein *I Fundatori* "Prions tous les écrivains corses, sans
distinction de dialectes, d'adopter: Côrzica" (77)[20] because "the sacred language ought to have a Corsican face" (78).

The inspiration to this unusual and, one may add, exotic-looking
way of writing the name of the island came originally from the exclusive poetic society *Cirnea* in Bastia 1905. "Cirnea" was yet another way
of writing "Corsica"; it was a Latinized version of the supposed ancient Greek name for the island Kyrnos. *I Sôcii d'a Cirnea* were interested in finer poetry. Most of the (few) members belonged to the

---

the bad prices of his harvest or the hardships of the family, and who concludes: 'Study,
my son, if you will not toil on the land like your parents.'"

[19] "Between two forms which are equally usable, we will opt for the one which is
furthest away from the Italian; we will prefer Côrzica and côrsu (the pronunciation
of the Vico province) to Corsica and Corso which are pure Italian forms. In the
same way we will prefer pueta to poeta."

[20] "We pray of all Corsican writers, regardless of dialect, to employ Côrzica."

French, Italian, and German *haute bourgeoisie* or nobility and had only visited the island as tourists. *Cirnea* existed for only two years, and was mainly responsible for a few exquisitely illustrated and extremely expensive publications of poems in classical style by the "society's" hero and director, Petru Vattelapesca. And for the introduction of the *accent circonflexe* in the writing of Corsican dialect. *Cirnea* had employed the *circonflexe* in its "Glossario Côrso Cismontano," that is, to designate the Corsican dialect spoken on "this side" of the mountains, in the northern part of the island, as opposed to the Transmuntano — and to Italian, the *Cirnea*'s usual language.

The Z for S in Côrzica, on the other hand, was *A Cispra*'s own invention. According to the founders of *A Cispra*, the use of this hitherto unseen writing of the island's name would signal that "the newborn Corsican literature has as its purpose to liberate itself from the Toscan servitude and live a life of its own" (78).[21] To support this project, the editors "sommes hereux *d'annoncer* que, par les soins de la 'Cispra' une grammaire et un dictionnaire patois verront bientôt le jour" (77).[22]

A Cispra was planned as an annual anthology. But the First World War interrupted this plan. *A Cispra* only appeared once. Its newly invented spelling of Corsica did, however, live on for awhile in various publications.[23] But the grammar did not appear until 1926, and then in the humble form of *A Prima Grammatichella Corsa*.[24] Here, the spelling of Corsican was close to Italian, apart from the systematic use of *u* in word endings, which in Italian would have been spelled with an *o*, and a few other peculiarities such as the use of *gh* for *g* and *ch* for *c* — these last an evident Frenchification. By that time quite a few initiatives had already been taken with the purpose of resurrecting the Corsican language and providing it with a written form. From the date of Mussolini's rise to power in 1922, Corsica had become a matter of intense attention from its two "mothers," Italy and France. Until then the Préfecture in Ajaccio, Corsica, had been understaffed and, it would appear from the sparse documents in the archives, sleepy, if not outright incompetent. But in 1924, a new Préfet

[21] "Son adoption précisera l'orientation de notre littérature nouveau-née: s'affranchir de la servitude toscane et vivre d'une vien bien à elle.

[22] "are happy to announce that by the pains of the *Cispra*, a grammar and a dictionary in the patois will see the light of day very soon."

[23] See, for instance, Petru Rocca, Orsini d'Ampugnani, Matteu Rocca, Michele Coranu, *Catachismu Côrzu* 1 (Ghinaghiu, 1922).

[24] Antone Bonifacio, *A Prima Gramatichella Corsa* (Ajaccio: Stamparia di *A Muvra*, 1926).

was provided with staff, regulation stationery, and a typewriter, and reports to the Ministère de l'Intérieur became regular, meticulously written, and orderly. The program of "liberation from Tuscan servitude" did not convince either of the two interested powers. Both the French and Italian government believed that Corsican aspirations to linguistic independence in reality meant that the island would become Italian.

Emigrant Writers

Two major initiatives propagated the Corsican language at this point. Both were products of emigration from the island. *A Muvra* was a weekly newspaper, founded in Paris in May 1920 by the decorated, invalid — and very bitter — veteran Petru Rocca, originally from the village of Vico. He was in many ways a typical Corsican career emigrant who had at the outbreak of the war already become *lieutenant* in the French infantry under the name of Pierre Rocca. His discovery of his Corsican identity and following conversion to Corsican autonomism can be dated accurately to January 1915 and placed in Bray-sur-Somme, in the most terrible sector of the infernal west front. Here, for the first time in his life, the former Pierre wrote a poem in Corsican, mailed it off to a friend back home, and became Petru. He would remain a central person in Corsican autonomism for the next twenty years. In the beginning, *A Muvra* was written mainly in French, though headlines were generally in Corsican or Italian. There still was no generally accepted Corsican orthographical norm, as indeed there is none to this day.

In 1922, *A Muvra* moved to Ajaccio, and in the summer of 1924 Rocca went on vacation to Italy. Later the same year, he and his brother Matteu bought new printing equipment and extended their activities to comprise an editing company. The *police spéciale* strongly suspected that the Italian fascist ministry of propaganda had financed *A Muvra*'s sudden and unexpected growth, but they were unable to prove anything of the kind. The new *Stamparia di A Muvra* started to turn out a large number of publications in Corsican language, among them the above-mentioned Grammatichella.

At the height of its production, around 1930, *A Muvra* appeared in 2000 copies, less than half of which were bought in Corsica. The rest went to Italy (100 copies), mainland France (500) and to the French colonies. From the reports of the close surveillance by the secret police, it is evident that the newspaper was mailed each week to subscribers in Senegal, Guinea, Cambodia, Madagascar, New

Caledonia, Syria, Saigon, Hanoï, Tunesia, Algeria, Morocco, and Mauretania. Evidently there were Corsicans in all these places, either in the army or in the colonial administrations, eager to read about their native island. *A Muvra* was only the beginning.

From 1923, another influential and long-lived publication adressed itself to the Corsican diaspora: *Annu Corsu. Almanaccu litterariu illustratu. Antologia Regiunalista.* This yearbook was founded in Nice ("Nizza") by the usual (one is tempted to say) lycée professor and a Corsican professor employed at the French university in Rome. The first issue exposes a number of variants in the orthography of Corsican language. The editor Paul Arrighi is designated "prufissore à u Liceu Francese di Roma," while the other editor, Antone Bonifacio (the author of the *Grammatichella* a few years later) is "prufissore à u Liceu di Nizza." The French introduction is preceded by a note written in a straightforward Italian sprinkled with "Corsican" orthographical mannerisms: "...in francese par quelli ch' un capiscenu u côrsu..."[25] "Côrsu" has a *circonflexe*, while no *z*, *un* means *non*, and the *us* are placed at the end of the words. But the rendering of the sound *ch* as *c* ("francese" and "capiscenu") is pure Italian. The introduction of the yearbook calls for contributions with these words:

> nous désirions réserver la toute première place aux oeuvres dialectales, *mais* nous ne négligerons pas celles qui, écrites en français ou italien, intéresseront la Corse.(6)[26]

In spite of the visibly strong influence from regular Italian, *Annu Corsu* felt compelled to specify its distance to Italian political ambitions. Already in the second year, the introduction is addressed to "our Italian friends." And though the tone is not at all hostile to what it labels "la fraternité latine qui devrait être chère à tous les coeurs français et italiens,"[27] the warnings aimed at "certains organes impérialistes"[28] are clear. *Annu Corsu* was Corsican, but politically loyal to France. The subscribers to the yearbook were to be found in the same places as the readers of *A Muvra*, but in *Annu Corsu* they appeared in their capacity of "professional Frenchmen," so to speak. "Corsican Clubs" in Sudan, Casablanca, Saigon, and Cambodia sent in

[25] "In French for the benefit of those who do not understand Corsican."
[26] "we wish to reserve first place for works in Corsican dialect, *but* we will not forget works that are written in French or Italian if they are of interest to Corsica."
[27] "This Latin brotherhood that ought to be dear to all French and Italian hearts."
[28] "Certain imperialist voices."

photographs and reports about their activities, and most of the Corsicans in the pictures were wearing French navy, army, or customs officials' uniforms.

A Muvra and *Annu Corsu* were the two largest Corsican publications during this period. But they were soon joined by others interested in the proper writing of Corsican, such as *La Revue de la Corse*, which, although written entirely in French, dedicated more and more space to linguistic questions, and *Kyrnos, Revue corse et trilingue de haute culture*, which appeared for the first time in 1925 with an issue devoted to the "Formation et développement de la nationalité corse" (Introduction). In the first issue of *Kyrnos*, a certain Martinu Appinzapalu wrote about linguistics. According to repeated reports from the *police spéciale*,[29] M. Appinzapalu was no one other than the ardent priest D. Carlotti, of Italian origin, who was strongly suspected of being a fascist agent for *il irredentismo*. The article (58ff) bears the title: "U Còrsu e i dialetti tuscani, specialmente quelli di a regione Pisa e Lucca." It is clear that Carlotti/Appinzapalu uses a quite new orthography to designate "Corsican"— "Còrsu" with an *accent grave*. The main point of the article is that "l'armatura di a lingua è toscana!... di tipu puramente e magnificamente toscanu."[30] This is demonstrated by sixteen pages of comparison between Corsican and Italian linguistic traits, from "pronunzia identica" and "frase e locuzione" to "aggetivi" and "verbi irregulari" (60-76). In the same issue, the editor P. Graziani tells his readers that "Le public cultivé italien commence à s'intéresser à l'histoire et à la littérature corses"(106).[31] It is evident from the numerous Italian publications on Corsican topics during these years that a certain Italian public — whether "cultivé" or otherwise — was indeed very interested in the island. And from the lavish bindings, paper, and general aspect of the books and periodicals, one might get the impression that the publishers of these works had affluent or influential friends. In the eyes of the French ministry of the interior there was no doubt that the Italian government was directly financing this public relations offensive toward a *terra irredenta* — an interpretation that seems entirely justified.

But the question of the Corsican language persisted, and in Corsica extremely few Corsicans ever stated that their language was sim-

---

[29] In *Les archives départementales de la Corse du Sud, ADS*, fond 280.
[30] "The vocabulary of the language is Tuscan, of a pure and magnificent Tuscanity."
[31] "The educated Italian public is beginning to take an interest in Corsican history and Corsican literature."

ply Italian. Quite the contrary. Corsican intellectuals continued their efforts to define and depict the real Corsican language. In *La Revue de la Corse Ancienne et Moderne* (no. 42, November-December 1926), yet another learned text appears, in French, about the Corsican language, this time written by the late P. Lucciana, alias the poet Vattelapesca. Contrary to earlier writers, Lucciana only recognizes two Corsican dialects. No dialect of the tiny Vico province is to be found here. The distinction between a *lingua transmontana* and a *lingua cismontana*, which already Vattelapesca's Cirnea society propagated, is upheld. In the North, we learn (241 ff.), unstressed *e* in the ending of a Tuscan word is pronounced as an open e, while in the transmountaineous South it is pronounced as an *i*. The dividing mountains themselves are cited as an example: seen from the South, they are *monti*, while seen from the North, they are *monte*. Furthermore, "comme tous les dialectes de l'Italie," these dialects are spoken on three different levels: *le corse vulgaire*, spoken among the plebs of the seaside villages, *le corse courant*, which is the real dialect — "le véritable dialecte," spoken by everyone — and *le corse toscanisant/corsu politu*, which beyond a certain limit ceases to be a Corsican dialect at all and becomes simply Tuscan. Lucciana does not use "exotic" letters in his seven-page description of the Corsican dialects. *Revue de la Corse* finds it necessary (249) to stress that it has absolutely nothing in common with "le corsisme" as it is propagated by *A Muvra*. The objective of *la revue* is to work for "le régionalisme littéraire," and thus the editors are not "corsistes" but adherents of "le cyrnéisme." Though nobility was not apparent within these pages, the position of *Revue de la Corse* was obviously within the royalist right-wing tradition of French regionalism.

Textual Threats

The adherents of political independence in Corsica were probably extremely few throughout the 1920s and 1930s. Even the extremely suspicious *police spéciale* never managed to compile lists of more than forty genuine political suspects for the ministry which insisted again and again on surveillance, lists, and biographies of suspects. Among these forty, only the tiniest handful were pro-Italian apart, of course, from the Italian agents on the island, disguised as archeologists, researchers of dialects, poetry, and the like, and quite a few of them employed by the church as priests. The secret reports on "autonomist and irredentist agitation" often resort to speculations that the Corsican people "devait rapidement passer du régionalisme à l'autonomisme"[32] — and to listing Italian irredentists in Italy. In 1931, the fascist newspaper *Il Telegrafo*, written in Livorno for a Corsican audience, was prohibited, just as several of the Italian books on Corsican topics were no longer admitted. In the same year, only 738 items of this kind were seized in the port of Bonifacio (close to Italian Sardinia), and all of them destined for only 112 persons across the island. Through all the Italian efforts vis-à-vis Corsica it is obvious that it is "extrêmement important pour leurs fins politiques, de démontrer que la Corse n'est qu'un patois italien…"[33] while, as we have seen, the Corsican authors were generally trying to establish that Corsican was a language in its own right. This ambition was not least expressed through orthographic means.

While the Parisian government was deeply alarmed by Corsican pretensions to literary self-determination (which they could only understand as political treason), local authorities were much less worried. Local sentiments were most often described by the agents *en place* as much more complicated. "Le rapporteur signale le caractère anti-irrédentiste de *A Muvra*, journal autonomiste d'Ajaccio,"[34] runs a secret report, and proceeds to examine "ce sophisme," not without success.

Writing the Truth

The Corsican laguage was under attack from all sides. The French and the Italians seemed to agree that the local speech was "nothing but an Italian patois," and, in accordance with views current at the time, the linguistic facts were read as metaphors for cultural, racial, and political tendencies. If Corsicans spoke Italian, they were bound to become Italians. In 1929, the emigrant yearbook *Annu Corsu* opened an *enquête* in order to prove otherwise. After 200 years of foreigners' descriptions of Corsicans, Corsicans themselves were now describing their "esprit" to other Corsicans. However, the overwhelming majority of Corsicans involved in this were in imminent danger of becoming foreigners themselves, as noted by the fact that all the

---

[32] "May quickly go from regionalism to autonomism" (*Report de la Sûreté générale, commissariat spécial d'Ajaccio*, December 5, 1932, in *ADS* fond 280). Henceforth abbreviated *Report*.

[33] "Extremely important for their political ends to demonstrate that Corsican is nothing but an Italian patois" (*Report* 42).

[34] "The agent maintains that *A Muvra*, the autonomist journal of Ajaccio, is of anti-irredentist observation" (*Report* 45).

responses to the enquête were written in French. Most of the answers came from Corsicans abroad where *Annu Corsu* had its main audience.

François Santoni was professor of philosophy at the lycée in Strasbourg. He stated that Corsicans were characterized above all by their disregard for

> pures conventions et le sentiment que le sérieux de la vie réside dans la solidarité des grands corps naturels: race, famille, patrie... L'indifférence aux changements extérieurs... l'antique noblesse de la vie pastorale... les rites funéraires... la vendetta et les lamentations...[35]

This does not differ much from the images of the two preceding centuries; rather, it is straightforward, textbook ethnography. But Santoni has more up his sleeve. He manages to twist the proverbial factionalism of the Corsicans to something positive (49): they are, he states, free of "toute superstition politique," which is why they vote according to "les sérieux intérêts privés et suivant de noble sympathies personelles ou familiales."[36]

The seriousness of the Corsicans is a recurrent theme in all the responses: "le Corse est orgueilleux" but "sous des dehors rudes et brusques se cache son grand coeur." This seriousness distinguishes Corsicans from the surrounding peoples, not least the Italians. "Les Italiens sont plus superficiels que nous."[37] The difference between Corsicans and others runs through all the answers, and most often the Italians and the French are invoked as "les peuples qui ont le plus d'affinités avec le nôtre..." The French are depicted as too explicit, and the Italians as ridiculous compared to "le Corse, réservé et méfiant."[38] Others answer that

> les traits communs de cet "esprit corse" avec l'esprit français et l'esprit italien? Je ne les vois que dans ce fonds humain qui présente de profondes analogies, à des niveaux correspondants de la civilisation au

---

[35] "Pure conventions and the feeling that the serious side of life resides with the solidarity with the great natural bodies: race, family, and fatherland. Indifference regarding external change, the ancient nobility of pastoral life, funeral rites, vendetta and death chants" (*Annu Corsu*, 1929: 47).

[36] "All political superstition... serious private interests and noble personal and family sympathies."

[37] "The Corsican is proud... beneath the hard and harsh surface his great heart is hidden... The Italians are more superficial than we" (Eugène Susini 53-54).

[38] "The peoples who have the most affinity to us... the Corsican, reserved and suspicious" (De Zède [pseudonym], 62).

sein des peuples de même race établis autour du bassin de la Méditerranée.[39]

The efforts to define Corsica as something neither French nor Italian but in between or in the middle constitute the dominant trend in all the answers. This is a rather complex endeavor. French tradition claims that the French mentality has a strong propensity for *the middle line*. This is perceived as something entirely un-Corsican: "L'esprit corse s'écarte volontiers de cette ligne médiane que semble rechercher l'esprit français. Le Français aime le milieu, juste ou injuste..."[40]

Corsica was in an akward position — in the middle between France, which was itself in the middle, and Italy, which coveted the island as "terra frontiera." The suggestions that what Italians, Corsicans and Frenchmen had in common were "profound bases of human civilization" in these circumstances seemed the most useful way of positioning the island. From there the step was not long to statements that Corsican ways of speech were not a dialect spoken by peasants, but something much more venerable, as stated by the famous lawyer César Campinchi:

> Les avocats corses à la barre, nos paysans sur le forum du village, parlent avec fermeté. Peu de charme — en tous cas moins que le continental et surtout que l'italien — mais de la logique, de la clarté, de l'autorité, cette indéfinissable et précieuse qualité de l'orateur. C'est ainsi que parlaient les Latins.[41]

The "Latin" argument was somewhat difficult to uphold, however, because fascist Italy had also appropriated the Roman past. Hence the insistence that "nos moeurs dérivent des moeurs de la plus vieille Italie" or indeed that "nos chants offrent un singulier rapprochement

[39] "Common traits between the Corsican character and the Italian or French character I do not see, except in the human basis which show profound analogies at the levels corresponding to the civilisation among peoples of the same race who have settled around the Mediterranean" (Vincent de Peretti, *Annu Corsu*, 1930: 91).

[40] "The Corsican deviates willingly from this middle line which the French spirit seems to search for. The Frenchman loves the middle, just or unjust..." (Pierre Battistini, professor at the *lycée* in Nice, in *Anne Corsu*, 1929: 9).

[41] "Corsican lawyers at the bar, our peasants in the forum of the village, both speak with firmness. Little charm — at least less than the continental and in particular than the Italian — but logic, clarity, and authority, this undefinable and precious orator's quality. This is how the Latins spoke" (César Campinchi, 16).

avec les mélopées berbères."[42] Here, Corsican identity is thus depicted as something that is not placed among, but beyond present-day
nation states.

The disadvantage of this position was, of course, that times had
changed, and that Corsica would have to change to follow them. The
assertions that Corsica was indeed whàt a century of romantic travelers
had described — an ancient world "inabordable"[43] — were satisfac-
tory in viewing Corsica as something that could not be interpreted
in current political terms. But this was quite unsatisfactory as an argument for the island to be taken seriously as anything but a museum. If its spirit was ancient, it would have to change.

The contents of *Annu Corsu* during the thirteen years of its existence tended to show that Corsicans had indeed changed, and that
the Corsican spirit was increasingly understood as exactly a museum
piece. In *Annu Corsu*, the reports from Corsican Clubs in Madagascar, Morocco, and Indochina were written in French, just as was
everything *factual*. News of promotions, marriages, elections, deaths,
descriptions of rural life, reviews of literature with Corsican subjects
— all of it was in French. Generally, thirty percent of the yearbook
was actually written in Corsican language around 1930, but the only
texts to be found in the 50-70 pages of *Lingua Corsa* were some few
fiction texts — and enormous amounts of poetry.

Thus, the publication demonstrated what many had said, that Corsica was "condamnée à subir la pénétration, la domination de civilisations plus avancées..."[44] Because, "malheureusement, il me paraît
difficile de cultiver la véritable esprit corse dans notre monde continental... Le Corse a toujours l'air un peu "sauvage"...[45]

This contradiction was in fact the main result of thirty years of Corsican identity definition. Corsica was a fact of the heart, but hearts
did not count for much in the modern world. A Corsican in Saigon
expressed it this way:

[42] "Our customs come from the customs of the oldest Italy... Our chants show a
unique closeness to the berber mélopées" (Sébastien Dalzeto, 17).

[43] Pierre Dominique 19.

[44] "Doomed to suffer the penetration, the domination of more advanced civilisations"
(Jean-Baptiste Marcaggi 25).

[45] "Unfortunately, it seems to me difficult to cultivate the true Corsican spirit in our
continental world... The Corsican always seems somewhat 'savage'..." (André Né-
gis 29).

Mais le plus beau joyau de son esprit, est son amour tenace du pays
natal: partout où un Corse se trouve, soit, dans les sables arides de
l'Afrique ou bien encore dans les jungles mortelles de l'Asie, son île est
là, présente sur l'horizon, comme la terre promise vers laquelle on as-
pire chaque jour avec plus de passion.[46]

The land might be promised, but it would never be delivered.

The Language Trap

The chain of events I have presented here is not literary. The Corsican history from 1890 to 1939 was determined by the geopolitical ambitions of European powers, by the integration typical of modern
nation states, by the economic transformations of the European world
during these years, and by the political upheavals and totalitarian ideologies that characterized the period. At first glance, it would even seem
that literature and writing would have very little room within this
history.

Nevertheless, it is remarkable to what degree the Corsican problems were not only *stated* in writing, but did themselves *spring from*
writing. As long as the Corsicans did not read, their involvement with
the world describing them as "savages" was almost nonxistent. Only
when literacy in French had spread all over the island did the question of Corsican language became pertinent. The establishment of
a Corsican written language was not only in principle but also as a
practical fact synonymous with the establishment of a Corsican nationality. This in turn was interpreted by the neighboring powers as
a political statement. Language and political association were identified as one position. The net result of the whole sequence was that
the mere writing of Corsican became impossible for political reasons
— and the Corsican "spirit" doomed to find its expression only in private, unpolitical domains, in poetry. In 1940, Petru Rocca was ar-
rested as a traitor and condemned to fifteen years of hard prison on
the French mainland. Unlike many other "corsistes," he lived long
enough to see the dismal end of the tight-rope walking the Corsicans
had tried for so long.

But it is worth recalling that neither Rocca, nor most of his com-
panions, fled to Italy where Corsican refugees were received with open
arms. *A Muvra* actually criticized Italian political ambitions in increas-

---

[46] "But the most beautiful jewel of his spirit is his love for his native land: everywhere a Corsican finds himself, be it in the arid sands of Africa or in the murderous

ingly vehement tones throughout the 1930s. And *Annu Corsu* stopped appearing in 1936 with a printed statement that the editors would not let the yearbook be appropriated by the fascists as a proof of Corsican Italianism.

In 1932, the *police spéciale* had received a somewhat unusual report on the activities of Petru Rocca (La Sûreté Générale, report no. 3260, December 5). The report comprised an analysis of Rocca's personality and motives and stated that he was in actual fact "tricking both sides." He was, the report claimed, letting his Italian benefactors believe that their funds encouraged Corsicans to become irredentists, and pretending that the Italian cause was much more popular in Corsica than was actually the case. In the meantime, he used the Italian money to bolster a "corsisme" equally inimical to Italy and France.

By the end of the 1930s it seemed that Corsica itself had indeed been trying to "trick both sides" in order to find a true Corsican identity. The entire island was in an impossible political situation between the Italian hammer and the French anvil, just like Rocca who ended up caught in his writings. Not because they were pro-Italian, which they were clearly not, but because they were written in Corsican, a language that looked Italian to the eyes of everyone but the Corsicans themselves.

Nationalism or Identity?

During the last decade, many social anthropologists and historians have turned their attention to nationalism as a globally widespread cultural phenomenon. The Corsican autonomism treated here has clear parallels with its contemporary nationalisms elsewhere. Even though Corsica never again managed to become the independent republic of the mid-eighteenth century, the ambitions of the *corsistes* were clearly national.

Just as Gellner[47] states apropos other nationalisms, Corsican self-identification as a nation was spurred on by economic development, urbanization, work migration, and notably by the ethnic homogenization by the French educational and administrative system. In actual fact, it was the Corsicans abroad who supported the main part of the autonomist publications.

jungles of Asia, his island is there, present in the horizon, like the promised land which he longs for each day more passionately. Raoul Nicolai" (Saigon, 31).

[47] Ernest Gellner, *Nations and Nationalism* (Oxford: Blackwell, 1983), and Ernest Gellner, "Nationalisme en Europe de l'Est," *Le Débat* 63 (1991).

While poverty drove the Corsicans from their island, abroad they were confronted with other nationalisms. This latter aspect — the pre-existence of nationalism elsewhere — was already brought up as a decisive factor in the formation of national identities by Barth.[48] The predominantly national political and cultural discourse of the 1920s and 1930s all over Europe, and the political consequences encountered by, for instance, *La Police Secrète* was, in my opinion, *a sine qua non* in the development of the Corsican national discourse. If *les corsistes* had not been regarded as a national threat by the French (and as a national frontier post by the Italians), probably neither poverty nor urbanization and migration would have radicalized the *autonomistes* into *séparatistes* and *nationalistes*. It is striking that cultural heritage played a much larger part than political questions in the writing of all groups.

Contrary to many other peripheral populations, Corsicans did not feel at all handicapped in politics. After all, they had created a democratic constitution and a modern republic well before the French. As a matter of fact, individual Corsican politicians managed exceptionally well in French politics, notably during the Second Empire and the early Third Republic. The question raised by *le corsisme* was thus largely ideological, a question of an abstract "recognition" of Corsica as something different from mainland France.

The role played by writing, printing, and newspapers in the creation of Corsican national identity should be obvious. But the notion of serial mass populations represented and reproduced in the press invoked by Anderson[49] as part of the background for nationalism seems to have been absent among Corsicans, at home as well as abroad. Even to this day, reading habits among Corsicans do not correspond to Anderson's image of the individual reader. In Corsica, newspapers are predominantly read aloud and discussed by groups in cafés, rather than by individuals. During the period in question here, the newspaper *A Muvra* was mostly delivered to café owners and shopkeepers in the villages, and there is no reason to believe that newspaper reading was then practiced in a different way than it is now. Likewise, the *Annu Corsu* was part of the libraries in the Corsican Clubs in the colonies, though we know nothing about the actual reading situation there.

[48] Frederik Barth, ed., *Ethnic Groups and Boundaries: The Social Organisation of Cultural Difference* (Bergen: Universitetsførlaget, 1969).
[49] Benedict Anderson, *Imagined Communities Reflections on the Origin and Spread of Nationalism* (London: Verso, 1983).

Anonymity and the notion of being "one in a series," however, seems to have been a striking part of the war experience during the First World War. The mass slaughter and the often absurd dispositions of the General Staff seem to have impressed most soldiers with exactly this feeling. The reaction of Petru Rocca cited here can easily be viewed as an alternative identification, and indeed as a way of insisting that violent death cannot and must not be meaningless.

This points to the impact of the specific cultural background on any actual nationalism. Though the "ethnic" Corsican identity cannot in any meaningful way be separated from "national" identity,[50] Corsican nationalism was marked by the specific society that fostered it. The striking change in local attitudes toward bandits that took place during the First World War points in this direction. In Corsican society, violent death had formed part of the structuring of basic social entities.[51] Families had been feuding among themselves, thus establishing a universe composed of families. The murderers were considered *bandits d'honneur* because they suffered for honorable causes. In *la Grande Guerre*, more young Corsican men died in four years than would have been killed during a century of vendetta. This changed the perspective on violent death and on bandits. Where previously only families had been in a position to claim their members' lives, now nations took an even stronger position in this respect.

That Corsican autonomism came to resemble most other nationalisms in Europe during these decades should therefore not only be seen as a result of the similarity among the backgrounds of these nationalisms. The reciprocity among French, Italian, and Corsican national identities played a large part in the process as well. Though for the most part unwillingly, the Corsicans were drawn into a discourse where nationalisms strengthened each other by ignoring all other differences than those understood within the symbolic universe of power play among nations that each represented "a language with an army."[52]

---

[50] As Hobsbawm suggests in Eric Hobsbawm, *Nations and Nationalism since 1780* (Cambridge, England: Cambridge University Press, 1990).

[51] Anne Knudsen, "Die Klarheit des Tötens" in *Paradoxien, Dissonanzen, Zusammenbrüche. Situationen offener Epistemologie*, ed. Hans Ulrich Gumbrecht and K. Ludwig Pfeiffer (Frankfurt a.M.: Suhrkamp, 1991).

[52] This provocative definition of the nation state stems from Uffe Østergaard. See Østergaard, "What is National and Ethnic Identity?" (Aarhus: Center for Cultural Research, 1990).

Monumentalizing Identity: The Discursive Practices of Hegemony in Australia*

BRUCE AND JUDITH KAPFERER

Australians have a phrase, "The Cultural Cringe," or more tersely, "The Cringe."[1] It refers to any presentation of self or identity, to a discursive practice of identity, which in effect devalues or undervalues Australianness. Applied with aggression and contempt it reveals a fundamental inauthenticity in those who assert the knowledge and ways of places beyond Australia's shores as a mark of their own distinction in Australia. It cuts down those would-be "tall poppies"[2] who

* We wish to acknowledge the generous support and fine facilities of the Netherlands Institute for Advanced Study in the Humanities and Social Sciences, where we have been Fellows for the academic year 1991-1992.

[1] Reputed to have been coined by A.A. Phillips ("The Cultural Cringe," *Meanjin* 9.4. [1950]) the phrase postdates the kind of behavior it describes by many decades. Nineteenth-century Australians were even more aware of their colonial status vis-à-vis "the Mother Country" — often wistfully referred to in those days as Home — than those of the twentieth century. In his definitive statement, Phillips himself demonstrates a certain degree of Cringe: "We cannot shelter from invidious comparisons behind the barrier of a separate language; we have no long-established or interestingly different cultural tradition to give security and distinction to its interpreters, and the centrifugal pull of the great cultural metropolises works against us. Above our writers — and other artists — looms the intimidating mass of Anglo-Saxon culture. Such a situation almost inevitably produces the characteristic Australian Cultural Cringe — appearing either as the Cringe Direct, or as the Cringe Inverted..." (Phillips 302)

Phillips, like many Australian intellectuals, before and since, was concerned with a narrow definition of cultural practice as constituted in the works of "high" culture alone. The rise to prominence, both in and outside the academy, of popular or mass cultural practice has affected the posture of the Cringe in subtle ways, some of which we explore below.

[2] The term, widely used and straying far from its original meaning, was invented by the (Labor) Premier of New South Wales in the early 1930s. Jack Lang was dis-

seek to grow a little taller than the rest by dint of adopting the styles, knowledge, and experience of the outer world, "overseas," as Australians are wont to say. The Cringe designates a range of ideas and practices relating to the creation and assertion of a uniquely homegrown Australian national identity, in contradistinction to imported notions of the land and its peoples in a context of competitive nationalism. It demands, in fact, that Australians create, *grow* their own identity and produce their own cultural capital from their native soil and authentic, natural stock.

The emphases in contemporary Australian cultural production, particularly that which is publicly funded and controlled, are thereby firmly placed upon authenticity and (ab)originality. But the Cringe still operates to validate (or to invalidate) "imported" styles of everyday life, manners, tastes and opinions, styles which might otherwise be characterized as imitative or derivative, artificial.

Many such styles are, of course, little more than evidence of conspicuous consumption by the very rich, and many are justified, by them and others, in terms of "standards" and "quality." In their consciousness of overseas trends and fashions, and in their costliness, these imported styles are cosmoplitan class markers in a society that is ideologized as classless. In this, they receive a kind of support from an unexpected and not altogether welcome source, the youth of the urban working and middle classes. In their embrace of foreign material goods and foreign ideas, young people may be seen to be on the same cultural "side" as those who perceive the domestic as valueless. On the other hand, there is nothing of the Cringe in their embrace. They are rather concerned to get what they can from the streams of cultural capital ebbing and flowing along the airwaves and around the shopping malls — accepting, rejecting, or adapting as they see fit and as funds permit. As a social group (and a marketing category) young people are less concerned with "standards of taste" than they are with escape from the boredom of familiar routines to the new and innovative, in conformity to what has become an almost international norm. Their preferences in, for example, television and cinema programs, emanating largely from the United States, are shared throughout the

cussing taxation policy when he stated the necessity to "cut down the tall poppies" — that is, to soak the rich. Today, a tall poppy is anyone whose achievements and rewards are greater than those of others, *and perceived to be undeserved*. The attitude so designated has something in common with attitudes to "curve-raisers" or "goldbrickers" in other egalitarian groups.

industrialized world, as are the argot and dance of black America, learned from music videos, the fashions in fast food and clothing and the popular music of middle America and the urban poor.

But there is also an inverse cringe, what Phillips termed the Strut: "the attitude of the Blatant Blatherskite, the God's-Own-Country and I'm-a-better-man-than-you-are Australian Bore" (299). The Strut, adopted by the much-mythologized (in journals like *Private Eye* in Britain and in films like *Crocodile Dundee* or *Breaker Morant*) Australians Abroad, either as ill-disciplined soldiery or hard-drinking tourists, operates at home to denigrate all things foreign, and most particularly foreign ideas, as intellectual, academic, arty-farty.[3] The manifestations of inverse cringe vary with age, sex, and class, but they have always in common a confidently stated belief that all things Australian are the best, the biggest, sometimes the worst, In The World.

The inverse cringe can nonetheless be seen as a similarly derivative and reactive cultural chauvinism, as much as a self-consciously nationalist statement, or as an egalitarian lack of affectation. It may also be conceived of as a style distinctively of the People, the ordinary working men and women of Australia.

As a result, the styles of international capital in pop music, in print journalism, television and radio programming, film-making, architecture or dress design, for example, tend not to produce the global ecumene of which so much is hoped by writers like Hannerz.[4] Rather, in the hands of local elites, or local youth, their effect is more often than not that of reproducing, as closely as possible, styles that will be instantly recognizable as Cosmopolitan Mainstream, and thereby successful in overseas markets dominated by nations with the greatest purchasing power. Simulacra, empty shells of inauthenticity.

---

[3] It may come as something of a surprise to non-Australians that the terms "intellectual" and "academic" are used pejoratively in Australia — even by intellectuals themselves. They express a widespread anti-intellectualism that has its corollary in the elevation of physicalism, utilitarianism, and materialism to the status of an egalitarian credo of natural common-sense: "the School of Hard Knocks" and "the University of Life." If "Realism," as Lyotard suggests, "always stands somewhere between academicism and kitsch," then popular Australian understandings of realism will always err on the side of kitsch, as evidenced in the antiquarian collections of folk museums around the country. See Jean-François Lyotard, *The Postmodern Condition: A Report on Knowledge* (Manchester: Manchester University Press, 1984) 75.
[4] U. Hannerz, "The World in Creolisation," *Africa* 57.4 (1987) 546-59.

Born as among the younger offspring of the British Empire, in the period 1788-1837, the Australian colonies attained nominal political independence from Britain in 1901, with the achievement of Federation; but the newly created nation is said, by historians, teachers, war correspondents, artists and writers and other mythmakers, to have Come Of Age at Gallipoli, in the calamitous Dardanelles campaign of 1915, fighting and dying for King (George V) and Country (England), defeated and dutiful. It is arguable that the nation today, recognizing Elizabeth II of Great Britain as Queen of Australia, unable to prevent her representative from dismissing an elected government in 1975, and satrap of the United States in military and foreign policy decision making, has still to achieve full political independence from other more powerful states; it is certain that economic independence remains a chimera. In such circumstances, Australia retains, however sullenly or cheerfully, the status of a colony, a junior partner, a subaltern state.

The Cringe is an expression of this status. Forced always to define and express Australianness in terms laid down by others — military might, intellectual eminence, industrial exuberance, financial conquest, artistic excellence, cultural sophistication — Australian definers and propagandists of national identity have been driven to reproduce the outside world in themselves.[5] Like money capital, cultural capital is thereby generated in a world outside and beyond the nation. The owners and controllers of the means of cultural production are always positioned elsewhere, as the Other, with only sporadic interest in the political and social ambitions of their satellites, and none at all in their cultural aspirations.

Meanwhile the client state assiduously reproduces the orders of hegemony characteristic of the dominant polity, and nineteenth century Australians endeavor to become more British than the British themselves. And this not only in the realms of political, artistic, and economic relations, but also in subtler understandings of taste, style and distinction — in speech and demeanor, in dress and manners and cuisine, in a style of life which seeks to transport the accoutrements of British wealth and status and power to a new and largely hostile environment. In the twentieth century, British cultural domi-

---

[5] A not unfamiliar turn of events for the comprador cultural bourgeoisie in a range of subordinate states that find themselves at the mercy of great and powerful nations or trading blocs in a global economic system and a globalizing social-political-cultural order.

nation has been diluted by the insistence of minority ethnic groups on the maintenance of their "own" cultural heritages, and even more by the impact of American mass culture. The late twentieth-century orientation to Asia is still largely manifested in economic terms and continues to present a minefield of contradictions to Australian nationalist mythmakers.

Having to express an identity on terms and conditions promulgated by culturally powerful outsiders, with the inevitable result of those outsiders being supported in the maintenance of their own (superior) identity, constitutes a fundamental attack on those ideals of authenticity that are vital to the creation of a credible and distinctive sense of a national self. The defensiveness that such an attack elicits is a central component of the Cringe, manifested as a kind of wary sycophancy. For it can only assume that Australian realities can never be more than a pale imitation, a simulacrum of a model that is always Outside, constituted in another world. Manifested as chip-on-shoulder braggadocio, the inverse cringe appears as pugnacious whistling in the dark — ineffectual, even pathetic.

Sartre's[6] explorations of authenticity and the tensions between the For Itself and the In Itself have some implications for grasping the complexities and dilemmas of the discourse of the Cringe. Thus the conception of identity through the Other paradoxically involves a negation of that very authentic identity for which individuals search. Conversely, the assertion of an authentic identity, an In Itself, alienates and isolates one in the world, in that flow of global realities in which identity has significance or import. The thrust of so much identity searching in Australia or pressure to realizing a distinctive Australianness is caught in the tensional space between the incorporation of global recognition or the lonely separation of the Australian identified but alone and alienated in a wilderness, globally excluded.

The Cringe and the dilemmas of identity that it expresses are integral to the discourse of monuments within the Australian scene. This monumentalizing discourse, one that is also a discourse of representations on themes of identity, is a process of the realization of symbolic capital,[7] its laying down, and its generation. The monuments

[6] Jean-Paul Sartre, *Being and Nothingness* (London: Methuen, 1969) esp. 306-59.
[7] Pierre Bourdieu, *Outline of a Theory of Practice* (Cambridge: Camridge University Press, 1977) develops this concept from E. Evans-Pritchard, *The Sanussi of Cyrenaica* (Oxford: Oxford University Press, 1949). The latter still gives one of the best examples of its usage. Evans-Pritchard describes how the tombs of marabouts in Cyrenaica,

Figure 1
The Australian War Memorial. Canberra.

we discuss are not fixed representations, although those who relate
to them may regard them in this way. We focus on the monuments'
production in history and also their creation of it. They are fluid signs
always surpassing or going beyond what they may be felt to represent. This generative going beyond is integral to the way they are
brought into discursive relation to each other in the Australian context and their positioning and repositioning in histories that have diverse and often conflicting sources. In vital ways they express traces
of ideological continuity but they are also subversive of the nature
of identity as Australians may diversely conceive of it and, too, of
the histories that are engaged to certain expressions of identity. Both
the Cringe and the inverse cringe are expressions of diverse forms
of nationalist statement and ideology, manifested in a number of sites,
structures and landmarks, built and naturally occurring, which have
achieved the status of national monuments, different modalities of
the discovery of a national self.

We concentrate on four such monuments: The Australian War
Memorial, The Australian Parliament House (both located in Canberra, the national capital), The Stockman's Hall of Fame and Outback Heritage Centre near Longreach in central western Queensland,
and Uluru, the giant red rock that rears out of desert country 470

Figure 2
Australian Houses of Parliament. Canberra.

The parked trucks are in protest at the growing tide of unemployment and the opening of Australian industry to increased foreign competition. Financed by a well-known building contractor it engages national and international symbols. The protest is called the Eureka Blockade after a nineteenth century goldminer's uprising at the town of Ballarat against State regulation. The Eureka uprising is a major Australian symbol of individual autonomy and defiance of state power, along with the bushranger, Ned Kelly, also represented at this protest. The trucks are intended to be representations of the Trojan Horse here indicating a subversive insistence on democratic rights at the center of state power.

kilometres southwest of Alice Springs. These are centrally important in discursive practices of identity in Australia, but they by no means exhaust monuments of significance, especially from the perspective of global outsiders. Readers will find no discussion of Sydney's Opera House or Harbour Bridge here. But we think that the ones we have chosen are vital nonetheless.

All these monuments engage themes of egalitarianism and different orientations to some of the fundamental dilemmas of egalitarianism in the Australian context. One such dilemma is the problematic of individual autonomy and distinct identity within encompassing processes that continually threaten autonomy and the presence of a distinct Australian individual quality in identity. The metaphors of State and Nation express different resolutions. They are most clear in the context of discourses surrounding the Australian War Memorial

Figure 3
Australian Stockman's Hall of Fame.
Longreach, Queensland. Courtesy of ASHF.

and the new Australian Parliament House. But other essentialist themes and metaphors abound and are generated in the context of these edifices. Perhaps the most important surround qualities of The Natural, a natural that is basic in human being and that the Australian monumentalized reveals. The Stockman's Hall of Fame and Uluru intensely elaborate discourses concerning Australian naturalness and its specific character in global processes. They, like the other two monuments, are also mutually subversive, indicating a different positioning in history and bringing forth new paradoxes of the Cringe.

The Cringe/Strut dilemma can be seen as having been resolved in the adoption of The Natural as uniquely definitional of Australianness, no longer in competition with the Cultural pre-eminence of other lands. This solution has entailed the turning of the inverse cringe to productive value in nationalist terms. Nature provides the crucial elements of antiquity, authenticity and physical types (of unique flora and fauna, as well as of human strength and endurance) where the

Islamic holy men who had fled Spain in the eighth century, became the centres of the Sanussi Order. This Order engaged the tombs as symbolic capital in their reorganization of the desert tribes against the Italian colonial invasion of Libya.

manifestations of a material culture derived from a myriad sources fail to do so. It constitutes the Australian *geschlecht*,[8] a cultural *stock* — of knowledge, experience, and habitus exclusively available to Australians in their search for national and cultural distinction.

Throughout their brief recorded history, Australians of diverse political and economic interests and allegiances have sought to capture, fix, and express what it is to be an Australian. The quest for a distinctive cultural identity, formulated in the globalizing processes of colonialism and imperialism, has been framed within the historical experience of transportation, exile or immigration and colonial dependency, a European and specifically British provenance and heritage, the brutal exploitation of the land and its Aboriginal people, the conquest of distance, and participation in foreign wars. Around all these events Australian politicians, scholars and artists have woven enduring mythologies — of the land and "its" peoples (whether they be native born or, telling term, naturalized); of egalitarian social relations expressed as mateship among men and the concept of a "fair go" for underdogs whose misfortune is not of their own making, whipped, like curs, into cowering submission.

In State ideology, the moral discourse of people and sacrifice runs parallel to the monumentalist discourse of State power. But in practice, the discourses of the egalitarian and individualist People run counter to those of the State. The major symbol of this opposition, in Australian public culture, has been the siting of the Australian War Memorial directly opposite Parliament House, at the other end of the American city designer Walter Burley Griffin's "land axis" in Canberra.

The Australian originary myth of Anzac,[9] of the sacrifice of those who laid down their lives for ideals of freedom and equality, has been enshrined in the War Memorial. Its nationalism expressed the dilemma of the Cringe and a wonderful resolution of it. The symbolism of death and suffering in Europe reversed the idea of the creation of the colonial self in the imperial Other. Europe, and most especially the "cradle of civilization" in the Middle East, were made Australian (white and male), egalitarian and secular, by Australian bloodshed and burial in their earth. Australians globalized themselves in war, and in planting the symbolic capital of their Australianness overseas

[8] Jacques Derrida, "Geschlecht II: Heidegger's Hand," *Deconstruction and Philosophy*, ed. J. Sallis (Chicago: Chicago University Press, 1987) 161-96.
[9] Bruce Kapferer, *Legends of People, Myths of State* (Washington: Smithsonian, 1988).

made the other themselves, and themselves the other. Aboriginal people, as we will show, are today engaging in a further negation of the negation. They too have gone global and are magnificently subverting the efforts of non-Aboriginals to strut Aboriginal stuff.

But both the tone and orientation of the War Memorial displays, and the myth itself, have undergone a series of revisions as national geopolitical relations have shifted in the decades since 1945. The welcome afforded to Japanese tourists and investment, the settlement of Vietnamese boatpeople, the rehabilitation of long-denied Vietnam veterans, the recognition of the place of women in the national legend have all combined to reproduce the War Memorial as a sanitized version of its original self. Paradoxically, its appeal as a pilgrimage shrine, steeped in the somber tragedy of bloody sacrifice in alien lands, has been lessened, while the glorification of militarism, so long the target of liberal hostility, has been heightened in the Memorial's transformation as an inoffensive and inauthentic tourist attraction, a museum to be traipsed around like any other.

This transformation tells much of the perceptions of those who control the ideological state apparatuses. The Anzac legend is a tale of human sacrifice and military defeat, from the jaws of which a moral victory is snatched by the valor of the common soldiery.[10] But today, the monumentalist discourse of state power and glory is crossed with the popular discourse of land and labor, of a willingly industrious people toiling to increase personal wealth and gross domestic product (all the while caring for the land as a renewable capital resource, as well as a source of spiritual regeneration) and overwrites the moral discourse (now anyway dismissed as passé) of the War Memorial.

Until 1988, the War Memorial loomed over the old Parliament building in a resonant statement of moral and spiritual hegemony. Now, in a postmodern order of global power and its dissimulation, Parliament House dominates not only the land axis, but also the entire city of Canberra: the State triumphant.

The monumentalist discourse of the State is most fully expressed by Australia's Parliament House, nine years in the building, and opened in May 1988, by Her Majesty Queen Elizabeth II during the Bicentennial celebrations of first European settlement in the penal

[10] See S. al-Khalil, *The Monument* (London: Deutsch, 1991) for the opposite story, wherein an Iraqi defeat is transformed into a glorious victory of the Iraqi State and the Iraqi Leader himself, both of which are monumentalized in Baghdad's Victory Arch.

colony of New South Wales. In tourist guides and brochures, and in a plethora of souvenir publications, the edifice is purported to be

> — [a] grafting of meaning, myths, and symbols into a geometric scheme for the Parliament as a synthesis of the Nation's presence.[11]
> — ... an expression of the Australian democratic spirit... At the very centre of Australian political life [the reflecting pool in the Members' Hall] the political is transcended altogether in a moment that invites an almost mystical communion with nature. It is as if, with its awareness of the consequences of power, the building would have us turn away, as from all human vanities, to contemplate the harmony and the order of the timeless world of nature.[12]

Few buildings in Australia have carried such a consciously heavy meaning load. The American architects, Mitchell/Giurgola and Thorp, expressed a particular concern to downplay what they took to be the inevitable grandiloquence of such a structure, in order to emphasize its popular, democratic meanings:

> Our concept of the building is not as a monumental structure imposed on the landscape, but rather one that is closer in spirit to the Greek monumentalisation of an acropolis... We are aware that in any architectural design of this magnitude there is a sense of grandiosity but it is our intention in the development of the design to resist this connotation of the architectural gesture, and instead to nurture and refine the simple sense of monumentality, in concert with the honest, natural landscape.[13]

Such a formulation stands in stark contrast to that ordered by the Federal Capital Advisory Committee in 1921, for the city and, thus, the buildings of the "old" Provisional Parliament House, which served the federal government from 1927 to 1987. This bureaucratic plan saw the capital city as having "simple, pleasing and unpretentious buildings — mostly single storey — planned nevertheless to afford adequate comfort and reasonable convenience."[14]

While the Federal Capital Advisory Committee was parsimonious in the extreme, with little concern for anything other than cost controls, the architect-planners of the city in 1912 and the Parliament

---

[11] The architects, Mitchell/Giurgola and Thorp, cited in A. Fitzgerald, *Canberra and the New Parliament House* (Dee Why: Lansdowne Press, 1983) 80.

[12] I. Indyk, "The Semiotics of the New Parliament House," *Parliament House Canberra: A Building for a Nation*, ed. H. Beck (Sydney: Collins, 1988) 42, 46.

[13] Fitzgerald 80.

[14] Fitzgerald 83.

House in 1979 (American winners of international design contests in both cases) were intent upon the symbolic expression of national pride and prestige. Nonetheless, all planners have been at pains to ensure the signification of what they have taken to be Australianness, either in terms of "natural" and unaffected simplicity and lack of pretension, as in the case of the bureaucrats and their elected masters like the Minister of Works, or in more contemporary (and globally resonant) terms of democracy, independence, and national identity. All have sought to avoid, for whatever reason, imposing a monumental structure upon a natural, undulating site. In doing so, all have drawn upon two of the most fundamental dichotomies of Australian nationalist discourse: the relation between Nature and Culture, and the relation between Land and People.

At the same time, (and this may have been an aspect of the Australian search for a national identity of which the American architects were unaware) the claim upon roots in the old world, nurtured and appropriated through bloodshed and sacrifice in Mesopotamia and the Dardanelles, and later in Flanders fields, has deep resonance for a people still largely descended from European stock, and still uneasy about their place in Asia and the Pacific. The Hellenic style as symbolic of democracy is a familiar architectural gesture in the United States, as are the Romanesque expressions of power: the eagle of the Great Seal and the dome of the Capitol. But the symbols of the republic and the imperium are alien to a country that remains, albeit with some rancor, a constitutional monarchy, and one whose foundations and originary myths are of the penal colony, the classical warrior-hero and the conquest of nature.[15]

Yet Parliament House presents a discourse of temporal power to the citizens of Australia. The building is huge; far from "nestling" into Capital Hill, in the most favored metaphor of the official guidebooks and other commentators, it in fact squats secretively on the deeply excavated (and later, reconstructed) hillside, its 81-meter high flagmast (the tallest stainless steel structure In The World) totally

---

[15] To Australians, Romanesque domes are just as likely to resonate with the temporal and spiritual power of the Catholic church; the American eagle indeed broods imperiously on a pinnacle high above Canberra, the gift of the American government, while the United States Embassy occupies a prime position opposite Yarralumla, the residence of the Governor General, representative of the monarchy. By contrast, the kangaroo and emu of the Australian coat-of-arms (antipodean versions of the British lion and unicorn) are hardly connotative of power, glory, or widespread dominion.

dominating skyline and landscape, earth and sky. Indeed, the flag-mast, exhaustively "read" by symbolists and semioticians, speaks not of the homely "meeting place of our nation" but rather, of the vaulting power of the State, a power presented as grounded in the earth, in the land itself. But where a natural monument like Uluru is proudly autochthonous, Parliament House can present only symbols of the natural and the originary — green marble pillars claimed to represent a eucalypt forest, basalt and granite not worn by wind and rain, but fashioned by human hands.

Thus the discourse of pride and opulence overwhelms that of popular sovereignty, natural autonomy and national identity. Parliament House, constructed of glass and steel and granite, lavishly furnished with rare Australian timbers and imported marble, is decorated with the commissioned and specially purchased works of the Art Program, making "Parliament a showplace of Australian art and craft and completing the building as an expression of the nation."[16] The choice of art and craft works in the building is evenhanded, devotedly of the People: a gigantic tapestry, for example, woven by the Victorian Tapestry Workshop after a design by the eminent artist Arthur Boyd is matched by a 1902 Tom Roberts painting of the opening of the first Parliament, on permanent loan from the (British) Royal Collection. Parliament House, as patron and custodian, also appropriates the symbolism of Aboriginal art, in a way that other sites that present a conscious discourse on Australianness (the War Memorial, the Stockman's Hall of Fame) do not. The theme of the Forecourt mosaic, for instance, designed by Michael Tjakamarra Nelson, is said to depict "a gathering of large groups of tribes of the kangaroo, wallaby and goanna ancestors, congregated to enact important ceremonial obligations."[17] — a kind of primordial parliament.

The discourse of State power is hereby (mis)presented as a discourse of authentically Australian democracy. Despite so many heavy-handed

[16] Joint House Department (JHD), *Australia's Parliament House: The Meeting Place of our Nation* (Canberra: AGPS, 1989) 22. If it does "express the nation," the expression is not one that is readily intelligible to the majority of the Australian populace, who reside far from the national capital and have never considered the role of collective patron of the arts to be their (or their representatives') own. Recurrent outrage, expressed in Letters to the Editor and in the electronic media, at the cost of subsidies to the Arts, or the purchase of expensive works — most famously Jackson Pollock's *Blue Poles* in the early 1970s — is a feature of Australian artistic debate, characteristic of the anti-intellectualism of a determinedly egalitarian and individualist stance.

[17] JHD, *Australia's Parliament House* 28.

attempts to do so, the building fails to express either the ethical narrative of the War Memorial, or the land-and-people mythology in which understandings of Australian identity have so long been sedimented.

This latter discourse, which also presents and updates a late capitalist moral economy of productivity and efficiency, is monumentalized in the Stockman's Hall of Fame and Outback Heritage Centre at Longreach, built with largely private funds, but handsomely supported by the State, during the financial boom of the 1980s, and opened (again by Her Majesty the Queen) in 1988.

The Hall of Fame (the idea of which was derived from the Cowboy Hall of Fame in Utah) celebrates the lives and works of those generally nameless pioneers who established the pastoral industry and opened up the West to development. Its low-slung complex of buildings appears to be small, with rounded roofs flattened over and dwarfed by the vast expanse of surrounding plains. Despite promotional brochures stressing its centrality, Longreach is remote from the well-trodden tourist track that focuses on the coast and on the desert, and comparatively few travellers undertake the still arduous journey, which the Hall's founders thought would "bring home the vastness of the land and help them understand fully the magnitude of the outback."[18]

At the entrance, those visitors who do penetrate this "Gateway to the Outback" are welcomed by a bronze statue of a stockman in characteristically down-to-earth stance, bearing saddle and bridle and dressed in working clothes. Beyond him and beyond the Hall to the east, stands the tallest structure in the vicinity, a giant "Southern Cross" steel windmill. The juxtaposition of stockman and windmill signs mythic connections between water and fertility, earth and sky, land and people, nature and technology.

The windmill also expresses a pragmatic talent for innovation and adaptation conceived as definitional of all rural workers, cutting across ethnic, gender, and class antagonisms. The fascination with things mechanical and technical that is displayed all around the Hall, achieves its apotheosis in the promise of each individual's ability to discover his or her own genealogy through the personal interrogation of computerized lists. This facility purports to enable all Australians with rural forebears literally to "get their hands on" the Past, and to dis-

---

[18] Australian Stockman's Hall of Fame, *Outback* (Kensington, NSW: Bay Books, 1990) 53.

cover, expropriate and incorporate a unique cultural heritage, finally becoming thereby, in Barthes's phrase, "interior to the sign." The operation of genealogical search has the potential to establish an immediacy of relation between the individual and his or her human past, becoming as one with an unbroken line of unsung heroes that the Hall seeks to commemorate and with which the tourist is enabled to connect.

Such a line reaches back, in the displays of the Hall, to the first settlers of all: the hunting and gathering Aboriginal people. But of these people there are no computerized genealogical records, and very few contemporary Australians can lay claim to actual Aboriginal ancestry, welling up from the bedrock of Nature and the land itself. Laying hold of such a patrimony therefore necessitates the establishment of a direct relation to the Land, unmediated by human others and guaranteeing antiquity, authenticity and natural generation.

The "oldest things"[19] in Australia are the natural features of the land itself: lakes, caves, mountains, riverbends, rocks, gorges, sources of food and water. Venerated by Aboriginal people from time immemorial, they have only recently, in a furore of nationalist affirmation, land-rights struggles, and the vogue for eco-tourism, become crystallized as the core of a *national* heritage. Even thirty years ago, the territory surrounding the great monolith Uluru (then known to white Australians as Ayers Rock, named for a desert explorer) was referred to as The Centre, The Dead Centre, the Dead Heart. Today, according to Australian Airlines[20] it is "the red heart of Australia pulsating with a life all its own" and Uluru and its environs swarm with tourists who are adjured by the writers of travel brochures to respect its sacred character as "the spiritual realm of the Yakunjatjara and Pitjanjatjara tribes that find sanctity in the inviolable permanence and infinite secrets of the moody monolith."[21]

The exploitation and desecration of the ancient homelands and sacred sites of Aboriginal people has been going on for two centuries. In the process, the lands of the desert, in particular, have been reconstituted as *national* heritage, incorporating the very essence of Aboriginality and imposing the civilizsation of the tourist resort — air

---

[19] See R. Handler, "On Having a Culture: Nationalism and the Preservation of Quebec's *Patrimoine,*" *Objects and Others*, G.W. Stocking, Jr. ed. (Madison: University of Wisconsin, 1985) 192-217.
[20] Australian Airlines, *The Centre* (1989-1990) 2.
[21] Australian Airlines, *The Centre* (1989-1991) 5.

conditioning, color television and poolside cocktail bars — upon the time and space of the Dreamtime and its sacred places. The local discourse of non-Aboriginal people thereby appropriates Aboriginal history, and incorporates it as central to the reproduction of white hegemony. But at the same time, Aboriginal people have increasing recourse to global discursive practices (literary, artistic, and political) of racial and ethnic identity that actually subvert the localizing and essentializing discourse of white hegemony and appropriation. Indeed, some Aboriginals are turning the tables, marvellously, on dominant whites and their technologies. Not only are whites being encouraged to go Aboriginal and escape their technological and commodity "dreamings," but the Dreamings of Aborigines have encompassed technology and commodities, and in a way that is globally valued. We have the image of one well-known Aboriginal artist, whose acrylic paintings are highly valued on foreign art markets, driving a car totally covered in acrylic representations of his Dreaming Tracks (the "songlines" about which Bruce Chatwin wrote).[22]

The incessant construction, deconstruction and reconstruction of national identity, perhaps the most egregious global process of the current era — and perhaps the most sinister — is crucially dependent upon the substantializing of history and tradition. And this in the most literal sense, of making solid and concrete, giving material expression to ideals and understandings of what a particular (usually dominant) version of history tells of national "character," of a people's place in time, and in the world. The past is realized in the terms of the present, and of the future.

---

[22] There is a wide discussion in the anthropological literature concerning what is known as the "Dreamtime" or "Dreaming" of Australian Aborigines. Among the better discussions are those by Munn (1971) and Stanner (1959-1961). The Dreaming is fundamental in Aboriginal cosmology and understandings concerning conception and relations to land, territory, and topographical features. The primordial ancestors are potent in the reproduction of Aborigines and are reembodied in the living at the moment of conception. In Munn's explanation, the living environment, as it were, becomes embodied in human beings who also, as they become older and progressively more autonomous and powerful in their social relations themselves become part of the landscape. Contemporary usages of notions of the Dreamtime are extremely diverse but some trace of the kind of orientation to which Munn points could be seen as part of the political rhetoric of the artist who covers his car with Dreaming Tracks. See Nancy Munn, "The Transformation of Subjects into Objects in Walbiri and Pitjantjatjara Myth," *Australian Aboriginal Anthropology*, ed. R. Berndt (Nedlands: University of Western Australia Press, 1970) and W. E. H. Stanner, "On Aboriginal Religion," Oceania Bound Offprint (Sydney, 1959-1961).

The twin processes of political decolonization and economic re-colonisation, characteristic of the later twentieth century, continue to produce cultural crosscurrents that have the potential to enrich or to destroy the lives of millions. In these processes it is *national* pride and self-respect that are turned to the support of augmenting or sustaining a position of power and status in an international politico-economic league table. But such pride and self-respect are rarely grounded in the collectivities of the People, of the national self. Rather, they take their form and substance from the State, and from the priorities of those ruling groups that dominate national political and economic policies and practices to their own advantage. However, such advantage can no longer be secured on a local stage, by being a big fish in a small pond. The rise to power of the so-called multi- or trans-national corporations, still headquartered in specific nation states, is insufficient to confer power or prestige upon the nation itself. Further, the cross ownership of great corporations and their subsidiaries, gives rise to a global bourgeoisie (including several Australians) whose interests are far removed from those of a proletariat whose own matching globalisation (like that of The International Workers of the World in the 1920s and 1930s) is strenuously resisted.

The meanings of the past are fulfilled in the present (and vice versa) in a multitude of ways: history teaching in schools, the collection and publication of letters, memoirs, diaries, ledgers, tombstone inscriptions, the recording of oral history, the discovery, excavation, collation and display of ancient artifacts in museums, Heritage Centres, and galleries, the celebration of past events, the erection (and dismantling) of statues and monuments — all contribute to the building of understandings of the-past-in-our-present. So, too, do "historical" novels, film and television productions, the rehabilitation of previously neglected or suppressed writers and artists, the revival and renovation of past fashions in clothing, interior decoration, landscaping and town-planning, domestic architecture. It is the presencing of history that is so vital to national identity formation; the past is brought into our presence, and our present.

Herein is contained the challenge of globalizing multinational economies: the threat of domination, homogenization and loss of national identity on the one hand, and the promise of ecumenism, creolization and mutual liberation on the other. It is also the challenge of multiculturalism writ large, and as with multiculturalism (often perceived as a softer version of earlier crude attempts to achieve the assimilation of dissident elements into a consensual, harmonious whole), cultural globalization is a doomed enterprise. For two centuries Australia has been in the vortex of global cultural cross-currents and undertows, although it was not until the 1970s that multiculturalism became official State policy. And the search for a uniquely Australian identity provides a stark object lesson in the means by which the symbolic capital of a dominant class owning and controlling the means of not only material production, but also cultural production, becomes constituted as the "mainstream" culture, engulfing and swallowing, expropriating, patronizing or destroying the cultures of backwaters and minor tributaries.

The selection and elevation of local traditions and cultural flows to national — let alone global — hegemony has always been a supremely delicate matter. The process must appeal to most of the people most of the time, subsuming local antipathies and conflicts in a widespread agreement about higher goals and nobler motives. Wars, and the memories of war, are in general good for this; so is religious fervor. Attacks upon language, enslavement or the loss of political freedoms, economic independence or civil rights, whether real or imagined, remembered or currently experienced, are also useful in the mobilisation of nationalist sentiment. What is crucial for the endurance of the nation State and the economic system it supports is always the reiteration of the connection between people and place, territory and citizenry: *dulce et decorum est pro patria mori*.

This is why the sites of national(ist) discourse are in themselves discursive practices. They provide not only a context, but a text. They gather up and decontextualize the residues of the past, recontextualizing, refracting, representing and re-*presencing* them. In their very design and construction, as museums, monuments, tombs, memorials, cenotaphs, and in their presentation as public ceremonial space or landmarks, they assert the significance of their discourse. They are the architecture of national identity.

A Capital Idea: Producers, Consumers, and Re-Producers in "the merchandising of our type of democracy"[1]

MARY N. LAYOUN

> ... all objectified cultural capital, the product of history accumulated in the form of books, articles, documents, instruments, which are the trace or materialization of theories or critiques of these theories, problematics or conceptual systems, present themselves as an autonomous world which, although it is the product of historical action, has its own laws, transcending individual wills, and remains irreducible to what each agent or even the whole population of agents can appropriate...
> (228)

> This crossing point between experience and expression is where the professional producers of discourse come in... The dominant language discredits and destroys the spontaneous political discourse of the dominated. It leaves them only silence or a borrowed language, whose logic departs from that of popular usage but without becoming that of erudite usage... It forces recourse to spokesmen, who are themselves condemned to use the dominant language (which is sufficient to introduce a distance from the mandators and, worse, from their problems and their experience of their problems)... a language which never engages with reality but churns out its canonical formulae and slogans, and which dispossesses the mandators of their experience a second time. (461-62)

Pierre Bourdieu, Distinction[2]

---

[1] From opening remarks by Honorable Mervyn Dymally, Democratic Representative from California, and Chair of the House Committee on Foreign Affairs's Subcommittee on International Affairs, at a meeting of that Subcommittee on "The National Endowment for Democracy and Their Core Grantees" (July 19, 1990).
[2] Pierre Bourdieu, *Distinction* (Cambridge: Harvard University Press, 1984).

While attending carefully to Bourdieu's assessment of the (impossible) speech of the "dominated" — and of the (inevitably compromised) speech in the dominant language of their "spokesmen" and/or of the "agent(s)" of cultural capital in general — it might be useful, in the context of mapping various "streams of cultural capital," to consider a few instances when the "dominated" have in small and momentary ways struggled against "professional producers of discourse" and compromised "spokesmen" in an attempt to articulate their experiences. To say this is not to disagree with the configuration that Bourdieu traces in these passages of *Distinction* (although it is difficult not to flinch a little at formulations like "the spontaneous political discourse of the dominated") or, in fact, throughout that massively impressive work of cultural analysis. His critical charting of and commentary on cultural operations are suggestive and helpful in a number of contexts — including the present one, as I contend with my assigned geographic foci, across which run various "streams of cultural capital." Rather, I wish to set out the historical *tension* that exists between dominant and dominated articulations of cultural discourses; here I outline the appropriation and modification of such a capitalized and overdetermined term as "democracy" in the postwar period, and then attempt to account for its practical reconfiguration by dominant interests. In part to enable comparative reference to such distinctly different areas as Japan and the Middle East, in part to keep "in text" both those areas *and* the United States, and in part to consider from another direction the issue of the production, circulation, consumption, and reproduction of dominant discourses, what follows is an extremely selective and brief consideration of the circulation in recent years of an increasingly privileged and resurgent notion-as-cultural-capital.[3]

It is perhaps rehearsing the obvious to remember that cultural capital, like a dominant language, is an "instrument of domination," which is "predisposed to express or legitimate domination" (Bourdieu 228). And it is no doubt equally clear that "democracy" is a fiercely contested notion — contested not least of all *within* the "dominant language." Such obviously fierce contestation — the commonplace of embattled definition and practice — does not make any less notable the specifics of the struggles over definitions of "democracy" or, conversely, over the refusal of "democracy" as an operative term. For all

---

[3] For a consideration of "streams of cultural capital" with a more literary focus, see my *Travels of a Genre: The Modern Novel and Ideology* (Princeton: Princeton University Press, 1990).

of its vexed rhetorical deployment from multiple directions and its evocation in sometimes bizarrely antithetical situations, the notion of "democracy" has been one of the most frequent (if too often uncritical) citations in dominant and nondominant discourses. Yet, it is useful to recall that "its widespread popularity and appeal are little more than one hundred years old."[4] The term itself, of course, is usually cited as from the classical Greek *demokratia* — the rule or *kratia* of the *demos*. The latter term evolved in ancient Greek from "the land" to "the people of a land" but in practice it probably more often than not designated the (male, free-born, landed) citizen of the city state. But even if we grant authority to this history of the notion, "democracy" was already contested in the classical Greek context — as, for example, even a brief comparison of Aristotle and Herodotus on "democracy" would make clear. Whatever is made of this preferred history, it is in the late nineteenth and twentieth centuries that "democracy" is invoked as a positive attribute, as a virtual orthodoxy of political characterization.[5] With these rehearsals in mind, I would like to turn to the relatively more recent scripting of "democracy" and to a few of the responses to and contestations of those scripts.

The United States entered into the post-World War II contest over "democracy," and on substantially altered political terrain in increasingly direct and dominant fashion, the designated heir of sorts to the waning global hegemons of France and, most especially, Great Britain. The Truman Doctrine (1947) and the Marshall Plan (1948), as textual examples, fairly bristle with the rhetoric of "democracy," "the will of the majority," and the "free world." Unavoidably, "democracy" as "the will of the majority" is constantly menaced by the "will of the minority" and their "terror and oppression." But even prior to the formal dissemination of such constructions of "democracy" in these policy statements, the United States was one of the main protagonists in the (Occupation) drama of constructing "democracy" in post-war Japan. Under the leadership of the "Supreme Commander of the Allied Powers" (SCAP) — General MacArthur, of course — the U.S. set out to "remake" Japan in the image of "democracy."[6] The stated

---

[4] David Held, "Democracy, the Nation-State, and the Global System" in *Political Theory Today*, ed. David Held (Stanford: Stanford University Press, 1991) 197-235.
[5] For a succinct and thoughtful tracing of the emergence of this orthodoxy, see Raymond Williams's discussion in *Keywords* (Oxford: Oxford University Press, 1976) 93-95.
[6] This rather remarkable characterization of the American Occupation as "remaking" Japan is the unabashed title of an ex-Occupation official's memoirs: Theodore

first priority of the Occupation was essentially the demilitarization of Japan but also, if secondarily, its "democratization."[7] The early period of the Occupation of Japan was a time of tremendous turmoil and conflict but also of undeniable opportunity for change. The extent to which the ruling narratives of the 1920s to the mid-1940s in Japan were no longer authoritative was clear to both the Japanese and the Occupation forces in Japan. In the wake of this crisis of legitimation, there was a pitched battle over the role of the Emperor in Japanese political and social life; over the reform of education, labor organization, and business; over the social and political role of women in Japanese society; and over the legal and constitutional system in Japan. There was lively public debate in Japan over the meaning of "democracy" and how it might best be put into practice in Japan.[8] But by the beginning of 1948, official U.S. policy regarding Japan had shifted from demilitarization and democratization to the establishment of Japan as an anti-Communist ally in the "cold war."[9]

> ...with the Greek crisis in March of 1947, the Truman administration embarked upon a policy of active resistance to further Soviet challenges [which]... affected our policy in Asia as well as in Europe... The United States stood in desperate need of a Far Eastern ally strong enough to provide some local assistance in the task of preventing the communization of the entire area. Only Japan, our recently defeated and still mistrusted enemy, possessed the sort of developmental potential that we needed in a local ally. So the embarrassing decision was made... (31)[10]

Cohen, *Remaking Japan: The American Occupation as New Deal* (New York: MacMillan, 1987).

[7] The official version of these original goals is the presidential statement of August 29, 1945: "United States Post-Surrender Policy for Japan."

[8] In "Occupying the National Family: Narratives of 'Production Control' in Occupation Japan," I have looked at some of the critical contradictions and heady openings of the first year or so of the Occupation — most especially, *seisan kanri* or production control in the early postwar labor movement and the simultaneous literary "production control" of Mishima Yukio's *Kamen no kokuhaku* [Confessions of a mask].

[9] A war that was "cold" only from the American and perhaps Soviet points-of-view; in the post-World War II period, it was certainly "hot" in Greece, Guatemala, Korea, Lebanon, etc.

[10] Robert E. Ward, "The Legacy of the Occupation" in The United States and Japan, ed. Herbert Passin (Englewood Cliffs: Prentice-Hall, 1966) 29-56. Parenthetically, the rhetoric of retrospective accounts and memoirs of the Occupation is

Needless to say, the earlier debates over redefining "democracy" and its roles in Japanese society were forcibly concluded by the Occupation authorities, who subsequently enacted even more restrictive bans on public meetings, political parties, and labor organizations and exerted ever more stringent censorship of newspapers, films, radio, and literature. From early 1948, the definition of "democracy" was no longer open to debate or interpretation except as administered by the American Occupation.

If the "Greek crisis" marked a decisive turn in the Occupation's project of Japanese "democratization" and in the role of the United States as "democratizer" (as well as in Japanese responses to that turn), it had equally or even more decisive repercussions in the context of the Greek civil war (1947-1949) itself. The response of the Greek opposition forces during the civil war to the United States attempt to define (and impose) "democracy" world-wide was a refusal of both the definition and the circumscribed arena for practice of "democracy." In an astute if often overlooked maneuver, the Greek opposition insisted that its goal was not "democracy" (*demokratia*) but — rejecting the classical Greek reference of that term and its modern American appropriation — *laokratia*, or popular rule.[11] Not quite an insignificant semantic move, I'd insist. The mobilization of the latter term was a direct refusal of U.S. policy discourse; it was the attempt to link experience to expression without necessary recourse to what Bourdieu calls "professional producers of discourse." The insistence was on *laokratia* as the appropriate expression of already existing practice in the "liberated" areas of Greece (a "mimetic" expression of the present) and

remarkable and in need of a study of its own. *The United States and Japan* originated in a "national meeting" convened October 28-31, 1965, at Columbia University by the American Assembly — a "national, nonpartisan educational institution, incorporated in the State of New York" (Passin 173). In his introduction, Passin calls, with no little urgency, for "anticipating the issues and clarifying our own thinking" on the part of the United States in its relations with Japan, citing the widespread Japanese protests against the 1960 revisions of the Security Treaty between the two countries as an example of what might — but should not be allowed to — happen again at the reconsideration of the Security Treaty in 1970. He concludes by contrasting U.S.-Japanese relations to "political instability, civil disorder and outright warfare" (4) of the rest of the globe. It seems clear enough that, even in 1965, the United States was (still or again) "in desperate need of a Far Eastern ally."

[11] The historian Lefteris Stavrianos reminded me of this fact in the context of a rather different discussion; I would like to express my gratitude to him for that reminder as well as for his kind, open, and relentlessly informed discussion on that occasion.

as the definitive goal for Greek society after "liberation" (a utopic expression for the future). For the duration of the Greek civil war, and still to a certain extent in popular memory, the assertion of *laokratia* over and against *demokratia* was an attempt, not unlike that of early Occupation Japan, though obviously in a distinctly different context, to engage in a debate over definitions and practices that did not simply reduplicate the dominant discourse. Those attempts failed, but their "failure" was more in not achieving their long-term goals. For a short-term moment they did succeed in interjecting alternative definitions (or expressions of their experiences) and practices of "democracy" in the face of the authoritative (U.S.) lexicographer. Still, and only too clearly, generating expressions of experiences is not enough. What the U.S. occupation forces possessed in postwar Japan and what official U.S. policy created in postwar Greece was the power to make their definitions and practices of "democracy" the authoritative ones. It is in that framework that the attempts at social redefinition in early Occupation Japan and in civil war Greece did indeed fail.[12] But almost five decades later, it seems clearer that in these two instances the "dominant discourse" of the authoritative "lexicographer"was not altogether unaffected in the process of interacting with resistance to its authority. Nor was the mobilization of and around notions of "democracy" simply the unmediated reproduction of cultural capital elsewhere. If the collective frame for or preferred trope of all of the essays gathered here is "streams of cultural capital," then these instances are something more like incursions from the bank perhaps, or a confluence of branches and stones in the middle of the stream, that divert and alter its flow.

The even more recent U.S. deployments (discursive and military) of its power to authoritatively define notions of "democracy" and responses to those deployments are perhaps more immediately pertinent. For in the last few years, it has (again) been rather startlingly clear that, in the United States at least, "democracy" is our business. And, if the "cold war" is over, the United States would, it seems, like to claim both the victor's mantle and title as the arbitrator of "democra-

[12] This simultaneous "success" for the moment and "failure" in the longer run is the (trenchant) premise of one of Dimitris Hatzis's short stories of the civil war, the radical 'democratization' of a fiercely cold winter on a northern Greek mountainside, and the virtual irrelevance of what happens on the ground to those in command. The short story is "Anuperaspistoi" [The unprotected] in the collection of the same name (Athens: Kastaniotis, 1979).

cy" in the rest of the world. "The issue," as Secretary of State James Baker recently pointed out in a television interview, "is democracy, freedom, and free markets."[13] That stellar triumvirate glares brightly in much official U.S. policy of late. Especially in the last three or four years — as what was formerly East Germany (GDR) merged with West Germany (FRG), a series of separatist wars began in many of the former states of East Europe, and the former Soviet Union disassembled itself in its own series of wars and confrontations — the U.S. government has solemnly (and rather smugly) intoned the virtues of "democracy" and freedom and pledged its official support for or opposition to foreign governments based on their perceived possession of those virtues. It is, then, surely remarkable that, in the face of popular movements to redefine and implement "democracy" in the People's Republic of China and the more recent and widely televised repression of those movements by the Chinese government — most notably the massacre in Tiananmen Square, the U.S. government did not feel compelled to alter or cancel its designation of the PRC as a "most favored nation" in trade relations.[14] It would seem that the last member of the trio cited by Baker — "free markets" — is the crucial one. But within China, at least ten to fifteen years before Tiananmen, the debate over "democracy" was multivalent, urgent, wide-ranging.[15] And, though it gathered massive and unprecedented support across the country, the democracy movement in the spring of 1989 was not the first instance of student demonstrations and protests against government policies. In her analysis of the 1989 student democracy movement and compelling argument that "state brutality [was] an unnecessary action in its aim of controlling the movement," Josephine Khu describes the student democracy movement as marked

---

[13] The statement was made in the context of Baker's account of U.S. security interests as he argued for the Bush administration's support for increased aid to Russia on "The MacNeil-Lehrer Report," June 18, 1992.

[14] In contrast, the Bush administration continued to deny "most favored nation" status to the (former) Soviet Union until only recently, when it was granted to the state of Russia under Boris Yeltsin.

[15] For an interesting retrospective discussion of some of the intellectual figures in that debate, see Hua Shiping's "All Roads Lead to Democracy" and the three responses to his essay in *Bulletin of Concerned Asian Scholars* 24.1 (1992). Of related interest in the same issue is Richard Lufrano's analysis of the 1989 student movement in the provincial capital of Nanjing, "Nanjing Spring." See also Andrew Nathan, *China's Crisis: Dilemmas of Reform and Prospects for Democracy* (New York: Columbia University Press, 1990).

by problems of rapid growth, disunity between Beijing and non-Beijing students, and — ironically — somewhat limited democratic procedure.[16] The struggle, in this instance, appears to have been equally to link experience to expression rather than exclusively expression to experience. Still, since the spring of 1989 and in spite of both the official pronouncements by the Chinese and U.S. governments that "the incident is behind us" and Chinese government reprisals against supporters of the democracy movements, the debate over the experiences and expressions of "democracy" continues, albeit in a sharply subdued mode.

In the Middle East, in the aftermath of the most recent U.S. led Gulf War against Saddam Hussein and his invasion of Kuwait, and, again, in spite of fierce reprisals against peoples in the region (Kurds and Shiites in Iraq, those demanding democracy in Kuwait and Saudi Arabia, Palestinians in Kuwait and Iraq, foreign nationals engaged in contract labor in the Gulf States), the debate over "democracy" is not yet over there either. In a recent essay, "The Quagmire of Arab Democracy," Hilal Khashan considers post-Gulf war possibilities for and obstacles to democracy in the Arab world — the latter far outnumbering the former in his view.[17] Though Khashan's essay is problematic in a number of ways, it quite aptly points to a renewed concern in the Arab world with definitions and practices of "democracy" subsequent to the Gulf War(s).[18] This concern is, Khashan suggests, the result of "domestic pressures" but also of "an international milieu that is beginning to place a premium on democratic zeal" (20). It is that "international milieu" which does not simply "place a premium on" but rather names, locates, and then values what Khashan calls "democratic zeal" — although I would here limit what Khashan designates a "international milieu" to one increasingly U.S. defined and generated since the end of World War II.[19] It is those dominant de-

---

[16] Josephine M.T. Khu, "Student Organization in the 1989 Chinese Democracy Movement," *Bulletin of Concerned Asian Scholars* 22.3 (1990) 3-12. See also, in the same issue, Mark P. Petracca, "Beyond Tiananmen Square" 13-20.

[17] Hilal Khashan, "The Quagmire of Arab Democracy," *Arab Studies Quarterly* 14.1 (1992) 17-33.

[18] Although that concern with democracy was already present before the Gulf Wars (though given scarcely any attention in the American media), in their aftermath an intense reconsideration of global and regional power hierarchies and of social and political contingencies is taking place.

[19] Although the former West Germany and, more recently, Japan also play significant roles in this regard.

finitions of "democratic zeal" or "democracy" generated by what Khashan calls an "international milieu" that circulate internationally as a kind of "cultural capital." To be unmindful or unaware of that discourse and its definitions, and of those who presume to be their omniscient narrators, is to be at a distinct disadvantage in global "streams of cultural capital" and in global and regional politics. Introducing a more nuanced and diverse discussion of "Democracy in the Arab World" in an issue of that title, the editors of *Middle East Report*[20] pay closer attention to the interaction of international and especially U.S. interests and interventions in the Middle East with local elites and ruling factions than to the "Arab mind" for which "the salient variables [of "participatory democracy"] "have not yet been internalized."[21] The U.S.-led Gulf War and its purported promotion and protection of "democracy" and freedom in Kuwait have made quite clear to the peoples of the Middle East that what is at stake is not quite "democracy" in the region, not even its "internalization" by the "Arab mind." Something like this is what the authors of "The Democracy Agenda in the Arab World" point out in relation to recent events in Iraq.

> At a time when Washington finds it convenient to promote elections from Nicaragua to Kampuchea, and when the Bush administration insists on intruding in every other aspect of Iraqi internal affairs, the absence of a demand for internationally supervised elections there is telling.

They continue in more general reference to the Middle East as a whole:

> Washington's identity of views with its Saudis and other Persian Gulf allies on issues of popular sovereignty makes it abundantly clear that whatever indigenous obstacles confront the champions of democracy in the Middle East, they still have to contend with U.S. fear of what popular rule may mean for its oil interests. (*MER* 47)

In spite of their emphasis on oil as the singular factor in U.S. policy in the Middle East, their identification of U.S. fear of popular rule in the region as an important obstacle to "democracy" is certainly apt. There are, of course, internal restraints on "democracy" as well, and the debates in the Arab world over the term itself (some preferring, for example, the Islamic notion of *shura* or participation-via-

---

[20] "The Democracy Agenda in the Arab World," *Middle East Report* #174, 22.1 (January-February, 1992).
[21] Khashan, "The Quagmire of Arab Democracy" 31.

consultation) and what it might or should mean in practice are diverse and urgent. There are, however, already established instances of the attempt to redefine "democracy" in action — the most notable being that of the Palestinians in their Declaration of Independence and the Palestine National Council Communique issued on the same day, the scrupulous organization and operation of the United National Leadership of the Uprising in the Occupied Territories, and (at its best) the functioning of the PLO as the Palestinian government in exile.

But, finally, the personally most sobering lesson in this summary consideration of "democracy"-as-cultural-capital was not the survey of the contests over "democracy" in contemporary China or the Middle East or Occupation Japan or postwar Greece. Nor was it the attempt to think through the notion of democracy in the context of Bourdieu's shrewd analyses of the workings of cultural capital. Rather, it was the almost mundane "discovery" of the establishment and workings of the U.S. National Endowment for Democracy — which discovery, like many others, was only stumbling on something already there. That discovery made patently apparent the extent to which what I had initially considered a trope of sorts of a hegemonic U.S. narration of the story of "democracy" was not quite so metaphoric — or at least not only as metaphoric — as I thought.[22] What I discovered was a quite literal, "private," nonprofit, incorporated, grant making institution registered in the District of Columbia in November of 1983 with the express goal of "encourag[ing] free and democratic institutions throughout the world through private sector initiatives." The apparently unremarkable link between "free and democratic institutions" and the "private sector" (private business) is more conspicuously loaded when the funding patterns of the National Endowment for Democracy are taken into account. But the links not only to private business but also to official U.S. foreign policy are conspicuous as well. For those "private sector initiatives" are, furthermore, to promote

> the establishment and growth of democratic development in a manner
> consistent both with the broad concerns of U.S. national interests and

---

[22] That access, stumbling though it was, to this collection of "books, articles, documents, instruments" (Bourdieu 228) is of course a comment on my own differential position as an agent of cultural capital.

with the specific requirements of the democratic groups in other countries which are aided by programs funded by the Endowment.[23]

This noble expression is made experience in the noteworthy cultural
efforts of the National Endowment for Democracy. Some of those
efforts at promoting global "democracy" include: funding the translation and publication of George Orwell's *Animal Farm* in the then Soviet Union; support for Violeta Chamorro's newspaper *La Prensa* (more
than $800 thousand between 1984-1989) in Nicaragua; support ($12.5
million between October 1988 and February 1990 alone) for the UNO
coalition in the Nicaraguan elections to the exclusion of any of the
other eight parties challenging Sandinista rule (it being a foregone
conclusion that NED would not support the Sandinista government
itself); funding for the establishment and publication of *The Chinese
Intellectual*, based in Hong Kong; grants to the Cultural Council of
the Afghan Resistance for educational work in areas controlled by
the (U.S. government backed) rebels — that work includes the prepa-
ration, translation, and publication of text books, including Islamic
religious publications and the *Koran* (providing an interesting boost
to the more religious contingent within the Afghan resistance); funding the Exchange Network ($600,000 between 1984-1988) that dis-
tributes (largely neoconservative) articles reflecting the propensities
of the Reagan and Bush administrations to editors around the world
for reprint in their publications; the Libro Libre publishing house
in Costa Rica which, in addition to publishing and distributing
"democratic" (largely, anti-Sandinista) literature, funded and distributed transcripts and recordings of procontra conferences and seminars.[24]
There is perhaps nothing particularly startling in all this; the list of
NED-sponsored activities reads like an overview of official U.S. administration foreign policy of recent years. And, in some bluntly apparent fashion, the establishment and working of the NED is only
an unabashed illustration of an official U.S. attempt to set the terms
and boundaries for a global discourse of "democracy." Those bound-

[23] "National Endowment for Democracy Act," *United States Statutes at Large*, 98th Congress, 1st Session 97 (1983) 1039.
[24] For a detailed critique of the grant award record of the NED and its resistance
to oversight and conflict of interest inquiries, see Beth Sims, *National Endowment for
Democracy (NED): A Foreign Policy Branch Gone Awry* (Albuquerque: The Inter-
Hemispheric Education Resource Center, 1990)

aries are so persuasive that even presumably well-intentioned congressional attempts at investigation into and oversight of NED practices are caught up in the official rhetoric of "democracy" and "freedom" (if not Baker's "free markets" as well). Reading through the U.S. General Accounting Office (GAO) report on the NED — "Promoting Democracy Overseas"[25] — or the records of congressional oversight hearings[26] is to return once more to Bourdieu's commentary cited in opening about "professional producers of discourse" and the (non)"expression of other experience" in the "dominant language."[27]

The return to Bourdieu, however, is on slightly altered terms. For it is not just to the circulation of cultural capital as a heavily, if diversely, orchestrated affair to which I would draw attention in closing. It is also to the role(s) of "each agent or even the whole population of agents" who trade in cultural capital. For that population, what presents itself as an autonomous world with its own laws that we nonetheless know to be "the product of historical action" is not reducible to our appropriation — try as we might to gain mastery. That pertains as well not just to the "art works" and the profit derived from their appropriation (which is more properly Bourdieu's focus in the first of the passages quoted in opening) but also to more broadly construed "social works" — notions of "democracy," for example, and their appropriation. Yet, they are always in excess of the investment in and appropriation of them. That might well be the threat as well as the promise of movements of cultural (and political) capital. Then, the attempt to be the primary story teller of/investment broker in "democracy" on the part of "professional producers of discourse" in the U.S. administration cannot help but collide with counter story-

[25] U.S.G.A.O., "Promoting Democracy Overseas: The National Endowment for Democracy's Management of Grants Overseas: Report to Congressional Requesters" (Washington DC: U.S.G.A.O., 1986).

[26] U.S. Congress, House Committee on Foreign Affairs, Subcommittee on International Operations, *Oversight of the National Endowment for Democracy: Hearings before the Subcommittee on International Operations* (Washington DC: U.S. Government Printing Office, 1986); *The National Endowment for Democracy in 1990* (Washington DC: U.S.G.P.O., 1989); *The National Endowment for Democracy and Their Core Grantees* (Washington DC: U.S.G.P.O., 1990).

[27] Although the testimony presented to the Subcommittee on September 28, 1989 by Dr. Lucius Walker, Jr., Executive Director of the Interreligious Foundation for Community Organization would surely qualify as something of an exception to entanglement in the sticky web of "the dominant language" that characterizes the over-

tellers and stories and, of course, counter power brokers (which is not thereby to identify those counter-agents with the "dominated"). But those collisions are as important for their "failed" attempts as for the damage wrought in the impact. And they might well be marked by traces of (impossible) speech in a(n impossible) counter language. The stories of such collisions and their "failures" — and, of course, who tells them and to what audience — make a substantial difference in the production, consumption, and reproduction of what the Honorable Mervyn Dymally calls "the merchandising of our type of democracy."

This consideration of the circulation of "democracy" as a notion with no little cultural capital is not, however, an argument about what "democracy" is or should be. That argument might be largely superfluous, except for professional discourse production, in any event. Rather, it is, on the one hand, an attempt to point to distinct deployments of "democracy" as an "instrument of domination," as a marker of "legitimate [political] culture." On the other hand, it is to point at specific responses to the deployments of "democracy" by the United States, responses that affect, deflect, and perhaps reflect more than just what was "merchandised" in the first place.

In the conclusion of his chapter on "Culture and Politics," Bourdieu suggests:

> This suspicion of the political "stage,"... is often the source of "apathy" and of a generalized distrust of all forms of speech and spokesmen. And often the only escape from ambivalence or indeterminacy towards language is to fall back on what one can appreciate, the body rather than words, substance rather than form, an honest face rather than a smooth tongue. (464-65)

The workings of the National Endowment for Democracy would surely constitute such a "suspicious political stage."[28] But, in the interaction of culture and politics, and with admittedly highly differential access to the capital therein, there are other definitions and expressions of

whelming bulk of the congressional hearings. Walker's succinct and straightforward statement is the only account in the official records to which I had access of the workings of NED based on a knowledge of some of the countries in which NED is engaged. All other accounts of the work of NED either came from the NED itself or were conducted from offices in the U.S. based on at least second-hand information.
[28] Although, especially in an election year, there would seem to be only too many other such instances.

experience in circulation, other stories being told, perhaps even the potential for a differently figured investment. And if "democracy" is the term of capital privilege, perhaps an antiliteral high-jacking, or kidnapping, or shoplifting of the term is in order? Who knows what the return on that (disorderly and illegal) investment might be.

Determinations of Remembering: Postcolonial Fictional Genealogies of Colonialism in Africa

BIODUN JEYIFO

> It was not a story to pass on
> Toni Morrison, *Beloved*

> I want in particular to trace the development of the messenger class from its inception as actual messengers, clerks, soldiers, policemen, catechists and road foremen in colonialism as seen in *Things Fall Apart* and *Arrow of God*, to their position as the educated "been-tos" in *No Longer at Ease*; to their assumption and exercise of power in *A Man of the People*; to their plunging the nation into intra-class civil war in *Girls at War*.
> Ngugi wa Thiong'o, *Decolonizing the Mind*

> We were together with Paul Ngei in Jail. If you go to Ngei's home he has planted a lot of coffee and other crops. What have you done for yourself? If you go to Kubai's home, he has a big house and a nice shamba. Kaggia, what have you done for yourself? We were together with Kung'u Karumba in jail, now he is running his own buses. What have you done for yourself?
> Jomo Kenyatta[1]

Recent postcolonial critical discourse, especially the intricate analytic construct designated "colonial discourse theory," has applied a neo-Gramscian interest in how hegemony is exercised in any given social formation to colonial rule in Africa and Asia.[2] This is a crucial theo-

---

[1] Quoted in David-Maughan-Brown, *Land, Freedom and Fiction* (London: Zed Press, 1985) 193.
[2] See Benita Parry, "Problems in Current Theories of Colonial Discourse," *Oxford Literary Review* 9.1-2 (1987) 27-58, for a comprehensive review of this analytic con-

retical move, for the dominant memory of colonialism for most post-colonials is the exercise of domination through force, repression and expropriation, together with the rigid separation of the colonizing "subjects" from the "objects" of colonization.[3] But the recent work of some scholars and theorists, especially of the so-called "invented traditions" school,[4] has convincingly showed, if any demonstration or proof of the matter were required, that the political regime of colonialism in Africa and Asia *needed* to exercise hegemony by winning the "hearts and minds" of "native" populations who were not only numerically superior but also racially and culturally "different."[5] The following two quotations show how, under vastly different political and cultural pressures, the hegemonizing project of colonialism in Asia and Africa ultimately involved similar processes of the *naturalization* of colonial rule. First, here is Bernard Cohn on how the British in India, at a critical moment in the consolidation of colonial rule in that subconti-

struct, See also Vijay Mishra and Bob Hodge, "What is Post-Colonialism," *Textual Practice* 5.3 (Winter 1991). For a useful but provocative theoretical reflection on a neo-Gramscian perspective on hegemony, see Stuart Hall, "The Toad in the Garden: Thatcherism Among the Theorists," *Marxism and the Interpretation of Culture*, ed. Cary Nelson and Lawrence Grossberg (University of Illinois Press, 1988). Given the overly textualist post-structuralism of Colonial Discourse Theory, it might be stretching things somewhat to read a "neo-Gramscian" conception of hegemony into its perspectives on colonial domination. Aijaz Ahmad's critique is useful here: "The category of 'Colonial Discourse Analysis,' interdisciplinary in aspirations but usually dominated by teachers of English, has arisen in this space. Apart from the quality of work thus far produced... two tendencies can be remarked in this kind of work quite frequently. One is that the colonial process seems to be analyzed not as a *process* at all but as a discrete *object*, unrelated to the pasts in the plural, both of England and India; and largely unrelated also to the ongoing processes of class formation and gender construction in both the colonizing and the colonized formation." See his "Between Orientalism and Historicism: Anthropological Knowledge of India," *Studies in History* 7.1 (1991 [New Delhi, India) 149-50. It does remain pertinent, however, that Colonial Discourse Theory has been largely responsible for validating in a general way, a *theoretical* interest in hegemony in current scholarship and criticism on colonial and postcolonial cultural production.

[3] See Timothy Mitchell, *Colonizing Egypt* (Cambridge: Cambridge University Press, 1988) for a penetrating Foucaultian analysis of this view of the colonizing project.

[4] Among the more prominent and influential titles of this theoretical orientation are: *The Invention of Tradition*, ed. Eric Hobsbawm and Terence Ranger (Cambridge: Cambridge University Press, 1983); Bennedict Anderson, *Imagined Communities* (London: Verso, 1983); and V.Y. Mudimbe, *The Invention of Africa: Gnosis, Philosophy and the Order of Knowledge* (Bloomington: Indiana University Press, 1988).

[5] Fredric Jameson's cautionary remarks against an approach which, in comparing colonial and postcolonial histories in Africa and Asia, "obliterates profound differ-

nent, began to reconstruct notions of "inside" and "outside" as an index of that surplus of ideology over coercion that hegemony always requires:

> By the middle of the nineteenth century, India's colonial society was marked by a sharp disjunction between a small, alien ruling group, British in culture, and a quarter billion Indians whom the British effectively controlled. The military superiority of these aliens had just been successfully demonstrated in the brutal suppression of a widespread military and civil revolt which had spread through much of Upper India in 1857 and 1858. In the two decades that followed this military action, a theory of authority became codified, based on ideas and assumptions about the proper ordering of groups in Indian society, and their relationship to their British rulers. In conceptual terms, the British, who had started as "outsiders" became "insiders" ...[6]

In many parts of Africa large-scale settler colonialism made this process of the self-constitution of the European colonizers as hegemonic "insiders" a literal fact and the naturalizing ideology of colonial dominance even more necessary and more elaborate. This point is argued forcefully by Terrence Ranger in his important essay, "The Invention of Tradition in Colonial Africa":

> By contrast with India, many parts of Africa became colonies of white settlement. This meant that the settlers had to define themselves as natural and undisputed masters of vast numbers of Africans. They drew upon European invented traditions both to define and to justify their rule, and also to provide models of subservience into which it was sometimes possible to draw Africans... The invented traditions imported from Europe not only provided many Africans models of "modern" behaviour. The invented traditions of African societies — whether invented by the Europeans or by Africans themselves in response — distorted the past but became in themselves realities through which a good deal of colonial encounter was expressed.[7]

ences between a whole range of non-Western countries and situations" are pertinent here. More questionable, however, is Jameson's notion of the "centrality" of "a fundamental opposition between the traditions of the great eastern empires and those of the postcolonial African nation states." In leaving completely untheorized this "fundamental opposition" Jameson raises more problems than his cautionary remarks dispose of. See his "Third-World Literature in the Era of Multinational Capitalism," *Social Text* 16 (Fall 1986) 67.
[6] Bernard S. Cohn, "Representing Authority in Victorian India," Hobsbawn and Ranger, *The Invention of Tradition* 165-209.
[7] *The Invention of Tradition* 211.

In the main, that corpus of postcolonial African fiction that has focused sharply on the founding moment and the early phase of colonialism, which I shall designate "genealogical fictions," has not taken well the fact that this overriding requirement of colonialism in Africa initially had considerable success, even though colonial "hegemony" was persistently challenged throughout the duration of colonial rule.[8] As we shall presently demonstrate, the vast complement of Africans who "embraced" colonialism, who adapted vigorously, sometimes enthusiastically, to the "invented traditions" of the hegemonizing imperative of European colonization, have either not figured prominently, or have been stigmatized in these fictions. By contrast, in the "middle period" of colonialism throughout Africa, there were innumerable popular songs, dances, chapbook romances and even "serious" biographies that not only foregrounded but also celebrated the "success," and the optimistic outlook of these groups and classes of Africans who adapted quite well to the hegemonic imperial discourses, lifestyles and symbols of the colonizers.[9] These groups included African Christian missionaries and catechists, teachers and clerks, "merchant princes," "warrant" or "paramount" chiefs (whose "traditional" legitimacy was often invented by the colonizers), and military NCOs (from whose ranks putschists and coup-makers of the postindependence period, whom Ali Mazrui has described as the "lumpen-militariat," were later to emerge). Above all, the ranks of the African "enthusiasts" of colonial hegemony solidified around a composite social base that included the uprooted, displaced workers, traders, artisans, domestics and the fledgling literati and professionals of the cities and towns built under colonial tutelage who redefined themselves in uneasy, ambiguous, but often disdainful, terms in re-

---

[8] For important titles that document the challenge to colonial hegemony in Africa, see J. Ayo Langley, *Ideologies of Liberation in Black Africa* (London: Rex Collings, 1979), and the three-volume *The African Liberation Reader* (London: Zed Press, 1982).

[9] Among the vast collection of titles on this important subject, the following are particularly useful: Terence Ranger, *Dance and Society in Eastern Africa, 1890-1970: The Beni Ngoma* (Berkeley: University of California Press, 1975); Emmanuel Obiechina, *An African Popular Literature: A Study of Onitsha Market Pamphlets* (Cambridge: Cambridge University Press, 1973); Obaro Ikime, *Merchant Prince of the Niger Delta: The Rise and Fall of Nana Olomu, Last Governor of the Benin River* (New York: Africana Publishing, 1968); and Emmanuel Ayandele, *Holy Johnson, Pioneer of African Nationalism, 1836-1917* (London: Cass, 1970).

lation to the populations mired in the villages and hamlets at the outermost margins of the colonial world.[10]

It is not a case of a simple, expedient distortion of the facts and actualities of the early phase of colonialism that these groups and classes of African "collaborators" have either simply disappeared, or been marginalized in the postcolonial "genealogical fictions" of the colonial epoch. As I shall argue, what we encounter here is an example of the complexly determined cultural process that always attends the reconstruction of the past.[11] In this essay I attempt a mapping of this process as it was expressed in the first dominant trend of postcolonial African fiction, and I try to uncover some of the pressures and motivations that "determined" or produced the process. Concretely, I address the question: if, beyond the technological and military superiority of the colonizers over the colonized, "invented traditions" were so crucial, in a Gramscian sense, to the hegemony exercised by colonialism in Africa, why did it become necessary for a dominant expression of African postcolonial fiction, in its modes of emplotment of the past,[12] to retroactively underplay the impact of these "invented traditions" by peripheralizing and delegitimizing the African colonized "subjects" who embraced them? Additionally, I pose the question: what are the effects and consequences of this revisionist fictional historicization of the colonial past for the postcolonial present?

The following short passage from Chinua Achebe's *Arrow of God*,[13] one of the most important and influential of these "genealogical fictions," serves well to frame our exploration of these issues in the way that it brilliantly encodes many of the "generic" characteristics and ideological features of this school of postcolonial African fiction:

---

[10] Fanon remains one of the foremost theorists of the town and country, urban-rural contradiction of colonial capitalism. See especially the first two chapters of the classic *The Wretched of the Earth* (New York: Grove Press, 1963), for his most penetrating views on the relative privileges of the towns and urban populations under colonialism.

[11] See *Philosophical Analysis and History*, ed. William H. Dray (New York: Harper and Row, 1966).

[12] I have borrowed this term and its heuristic possibilities from Hayden White. See his *Metahistory: The Historical Imagination in Nineteenth-Century Europe* (Baltimore: The Johns Hopkins University Press, 1973).

[13] Chinua Achebe, *Arrow of God* (New York: Doubleday, 1969).

The others conferred anxiously and Akuebue spoke again begging the representatives of "gorment" to believe their story. "What would be the wisdom of deceiving messengers of the white man," he asked. "Where shall we run afterwards. If you go back to Okperi and Ezeulu is not there come back and take not two but all of us."

The corporal thought about it and agreed. "But we cannot come and go for nothing. When a masked spirit visits you you have to appease its footprints with presents. The white man is the masked spirit of today."

"Very true," said Akuebue, "the masked spirit of today is the white man and his *messengers*." (154; my emphasis)

Some of Achebe's celebrated narrative devices are deployed in this short passage that deals with a very minor detail in the plot of the novel, especially devices like irony, condensation and understatement. Two lowly members of the newly created colonial constabulary have descended on the home of the protagonist of the novel, Ezeulu, in order to "arrest" him and forcibly make him a "warrant chief" to mediate between his people and the colonizers in the system of "indirect rule" set up by the British throughout colonial Africa.[14] Ezeulu is the diviner-priest of Ulu, the most important deity in his Umuaro community of several federated villages. But he is no *ruling* chief, since there is no such institution in *this* precolonial republican confederacy. Indeed, some of the most sacred traditions of the community make accession to a ruling "chiefship" by any powerful, wealthy individual or family all but impossible.[15] Significantly, Ezeulu had left very early on the day of this visitation to his home to go and inform the colonial District Officer that he, Ezeulu, as a principled protector of his people's traditions and institutions, will not be the "white man's chief." There is a tremendous moral and spiritual integrity in this refusal, for in the then newly forming power configurations of the regime of

[14] There are useful accounts of this aspect of the British colonial policy of "Indirect Rule" in the two-volume study, *Colonialism in Africa: 1870-1960*, ed. L.H. Gann and Peter Duignan (Cambridge University Press, 1970).

[15] One particularly interesting tradition emphasized by Achebe in the novel is the ritual obligation of any aspirant to a *ruling* chiefship to settle the debts of everyone in the community, woman and man, young and old! However, this in no way reflects a normative absence of precolonial class formation or large, centralized state systems based on exploitation and surplus extraction in Africa. See Samir Amin, *Class and Nation: Historically and in the Current Crisis* (New York: Monthly Review Press, 1980) and John Iliffe, *The African Poor* (Cambridge: Cambridge University Press, 1987).

colonialism, "warrant" or "paramount" chiefs were strategically positioned to accumulate enormous reserves of wealth, influence, and
authority, not only over their own peoples, but sometimes indepen-
dently of and against the very colonial dispensation that "invented"
their institutional legitimacy.[16]

The brief dialogue in this passage from *Arrow of God* plays astutely
and ironically on these dialogical processes of nascent colonialism.
The absence of Ezeulu potentially robs the agents of the "white man"
not only of their quarry, but also of the considerable symbolic exercise of power that the "arrest" of no less a personage than the diviner-
priest of Ulu would have afforded them. But in the delicate and repro-
bate world of creeping colonial (dis)order, all things work for the good
of the African agents and collaborators, including even unexpected
reversals of expectations. And so a "tribute" is extracted from Ezeulu's family. And what is especially telling is that the discourse through
which this symbolic and actual power play is enacted encodes the transactions in the *phantasmatic* order of knowledge that some theorists have
identified as central to the hegemony exercised by the colonizers in
Africa and Asia.[17] Achebe's deflationary, ironic wit is at its most effective here, for in asking to be "appeased" like a "masked spirit," a sacred ritual reserved only for the gods and the ancestors, the corporal
had been careful to speak only in the name of the "white man," while
Akuebue's rejoinder, in tones of unreproachable deference, deliberately *literalizes* the mythicization of the white colonial incursion: "the
masked spirit of our day is the white man and *his messengers.*" Thus
the opportunistic agents extract their "tribute," but at the expense of
a very effective, if understated, rhetorical "unmasking."

This "unmasking," this stripping away of any claims to legitimacy
or dignity by the African groups, classes and individuals who gave
colonial rule its most powerful supports by "collaborating" in the "invented traditions" of colonial hegemony, is a pervasive, dominant topos of postcolonial "genealogical fictions" of the colonial period. Indeed, Achebe's approach in this matter is perhaps more restrained
than that of many other novelists; he is not particularly interested

[16] Terence Ranger, "The Invention of Tradition in Colonial Africa," gives several
historical instances of this phenomenon as a veritable paradox of colonial rule.

[17] For a brilliant theoretical discussion of the phantasmatic aspects of colonial hegemony, see Malick Alloula's *The Colonial Harem* (Minneapolis: University of Minnesota Press, 1986).

in these groups and classes of "collaborators" and therefore he tends to peripheralize them to the margins of his emplotment of the colonial encounter. Novelists like Ngugi wa Thiong'o, Ayi Kwei Armah and Ferdinand Oyono are by contrast much more ferocious in their satirical, mocking depictions of "collaboration" where it involves not merely serving as agents and hirelings of the colonizers but the more fundamental, more constitutive *interpellation* of colonial subjects as enthusiasts and pundits of the ideologies and symbols of colonial domination.[18] In novels like Ngugi's *Weep Not, Child* and *The River Between*, Oyono's *Houseboy* and *The Old Man and the Medal*, and Armah's *Two Thousand Seasons*, considerable narrative energy is devoted to the depiction of African zealots of Christian proselytization, African promoters of the benefits of the schools built by missionaries and secular colonial administrations, and "assimilated" Africans deeply enamoured of the "culture," ceremonialism, and spectacle of imperial glory as opportunists, traitors, fools, or pathetic victims of a grand illusion. And since the authors who have given powerful novelistic inscriptions to this generalized representational profile are some of the most influential of contemporary African writers, the relatively enormous historic success of colonial hegemony in Africa has all but been put under erasure in African postcolonial critical discourse. In the radical rewriting of history in this profile, *only* the outcasts, the pariahs and the malcontents of the precolonial African social formations offered colonial hegemony its social and ideological base among the colonized in the ways in which they enthusiastically embraced the totally unexpected "opportunities" and the realignments of orientations and identities that the colonial order made possible. This point is well illustrated by aspects of *Things Fall Apart*, the most representative and perhaps most influential of this dominant school of postcolonial genealogical fictions of colonial hegemony in Africa. We may recall that Okonkwo's son Nwoye goes over to the nascent community of early converts to christianity and he becomes one of the first pupils of the new mission school. He changes his name and takes the name Isaac, which carries the biblical allusion to the son of Abraham who consolidates a new patrilineage of the "elect of God" (which we may read as the "chosen"

---

[18] I am using *interpellation* in a greatly modified Althusserian sense here. See the concluding section of Pierre Bourdieu's *Outline of a Theory of Practice* (Cambridge: Cambridge University Press, 1977) entitled "Modes of Domination" for an insightful use of this conception of interpellation.

of the new colonial dispensation). But it is not only the case that Nwoye makes this move with a sorrowing heart and a conflicted spirit, the entire episode hovers at the very margins of the plot of the novel and pales into relative insignificance beside the drama of Okonkwo's challenge to the invading colonialism.[19]

It now seems unimaginable in our postcolonial critical discourse that Isaac (a.k.a. Nwoye) could have been the protagonist of *Things Fall Apart*, just as it seems *unimaginable* that his "collaboration" with the colonizers could have been the subject of a "serious," perhaps even celebratory novelistic exploration. But we need to remember that what is unimaginable here is merely the effect of a powerful ideological current powered by the dominant trend of African postcolonial fictions of the colonial past, the fictions of Achebe, Beti, Ngugi, Armah, Oyono and others. For there are novels that indeed imagine the unimaginable and make "collaborators" like Nwoye-Isaac the protagonists, even the heroes, of their narrativization of colonialism in Africa. The point of course is that novels of this kind have not figured prominently in our postcolonial critical discourse as particularly representative *or desirable* fictional recreations of the colonial past. And what is interesting in the way in which this reveals the ideological provenance of what lies within the bounds of the "imaginable" is that while the novels in this category may be said to be in a "minority" school of postcolonial African fiction, some of their authors are in no sense minor. To give examples: Amadou Hampate Ba, Cheikh Hamidou Kane, and Yambo Ouologuem are major contemporary African writers; their respective texts that challenge the dominant revisionary fictional reconstruction of colonial hegemony are major literary works, namely, *The Fortunes of Wangrin*, *Ambiguous Adventure* and *Bound to Violence*. These works depict the structure of colonial hegemony in Africa as complex, often contradictory but mutually beneficial interaction between the colonizers and the African dignitaries, notables and ruling groups of the precolonial social formations, with the "people" represented as mainly passive, manipulated elements. *The Fortunes of Wangrin*, which

---

[19] For the only critical treatment of the biblical Abraham-Isaac motif in *Things Fall Apart*, see Rhonda Cobham, "Making Men and History: Achebe and the Politics of Revisionism," *Approaches to Teaching: 'Things Fall Apart'*, ed. Bernth Lindfors. It is astonishing, however, that in this otherwise perspicacious essay, Cobham exclusively identifies the Isaac motif with Ikemefuna, and she misses the point that Nwoye takes the name Isaac.

is indeed a fictionalization of the life and career of an African middle-level official of the colonial administration of French West Africa, and *Bound to Violence*, are particularly powerful imaginative renderings of a view of colonial hegemony as ultimately dependent on Africans who so thoroughly understood the dynamics of colonialism that they were able to manipulate and outwit the colonizers themselves while serving the basic goals of the colonizing project. This is a tall order and appropriately, Wangrin's exploits in *The Fortunes of Wangrin* and Saif's machinations in *Bound to Violence* are cast in narratives that radically mix genres and liberally employ the same phantasmatic discourse that we have seen Achebe deploy in *Arrow of God* to diminish the self-importance and legitimacy of the African "collaborators" of the colonizers. Here is a typical passage from *The Fortunes of Wangrin*:

> Wangrin, having obtained the highest marks in his final examination, became an instructor, an employment that was reserved for the most deserving pupils. For two years he carried out his duties to the greatest satisfaction of his superiors, especially of the Inspector of Schools. As a reward, he was directed to found and head a school in Diagaramba, capital of Namaci, an area which the French had taken back from the indigenous chiefs in 1893. It was in this handsome and large city that his adventures were to begin. At that time Wangrin had already adopted one of the most significant of his pseudonyms, Gongoloma-Sooke, a legendary deity in Bambara mythology. This god could neither be soaked by rain or dried by the sun. Salt could not salt him, and soap could not clean him. Although he was as soft as a mollusc, no metal, however sharp, could cut through him. The elements did not affect him in the least; he never felt hot or cold. When he slept he closed one eye; because of this, he was feared by night and mistrusted by day. Simultaneously, he married dawn and twilight and had his union blessed by the scorpion Ngoson, one of the oldest patriarchs in the whole world. Before the sun, Gongoloma-Sooke was lunar and before the moon he was solar... Both kindly and indisposed, chaste and libertine, a weird divinity, he used his nostrils to absorb drink and his anus to ingest solid food... He always walked backwards to his destination, and rested with his head on the ground and his feet stuck in the air at right angles with his body. He hurled vulgar abuse at those who had been kind to him but warmly thanked and sang the praises of those who detested him and had caused him the worst kind of trouble. After the first crowing of the rooster at dawn and the last braying of the donkey at dusk, Gongoloma-Sooke climbed the vast mahogany in the sacred forest and shouted for all who wished to hear: "It is true I am Gongoloma-Sooke, a weird divinity, but I also represent the

confluence of all opposites... Come to me and your wishes shall be granted!"[20]

Wangrin assiduously cultivates the favor of the colonizers, applies himself to the mastery of their language and the workings of their pedagogical and bureaucratic apparati; at the same time, he harnesses the ritual values, the sacral significations of an extravagant deity of whom he becomes an avatar. Thus, like the venal constables of *Arrow of God* who, as we have seen, discursively legitimize the cynical opportunism of their collaboration with the colonizers by drawing on the thaumaturgical idiom of ancestral myths and codes, this passage also deploys a mixture of the literal and the metaphoric, of history and mythology. But there is a crucial difference here, and this is the utter lack of the diffidence and restraint that we saw in the constables of *Arrow of God* in the exuberance and imaginative scale of Wangrin's self-mythologization. Through this a basically amoral, pragmatic ethos is affirmed and celebrated, and this prepares us for Wangrin's extraordinary exploits in *The Fortunes of Wangrin* in which our hero both observes and transcends the constraints of colonial domination. *The Fortunes of Wangrin* thus stands as a powerful textual inscription of the "success" of African "collaborators" of colonial hegemony; moreover, it takes its place among other texts like *Ambiguous Adventure* and *Bound to Violence* in which this "success" is given a heroic, if also ironic, representation. But to the extent that our dominant image of colonial domination has not come from texts such as these we may say that they belong to a "minority" tradition of postcolonial genealogical fictions of the colonial past that collectively throw a sort of critical relief on the dominant tradition fostered by Achebe and Ngugi and others. It is useful for our purposes in this essay to apprehend the divergent imaginative and ideological universe inscribed as a composite profile in each of these schools of genealogical fictions.

The fictional genealogies of colonialism represent a major initial expression of postcolonial African fiction. There are important historical and ideological reasons why this category of a revisionary fictional

---

[20] Amadou Hampate Ba, *The Fortunes of Wangrin* (Ibadan: New Horn Press, 1987). This publication date does not reflect either the actual writing of the narrative in the original French of Ba's *L'étrange destin de Wangrin* (Presence Africaine, 1976), or the long process of its transcription and rewriting from the oral accounts of the eponymous hero. These questions are discussed in Abiola Irele's useful introductory essay to *The Fortunes of Wangrin*.

reconstruction of the past emerged in modern African literature in the twilight of colonialism in Africa and dominated novelistic writing of the first two decades of the postindependence period. Before we come to a speculative discourse on this point, it is important to expatiate descriptively on this category of "fictional genealogies" of colonialism. More specifically, I wish not only to draw attention to this "genre" or "school" of contemporary African prose fiction, but also to apprehend it in terms of the basic trends discoverable within it: a "dominant" paradigm for which Chinua Achebe's *Things Fall Apart* is a powerful example; a "minor" paradigm for which Amadou Hampate Ba's *The Fortunes of Wangrin* serves as an exemplar.

If there is a category of postcolonial African fiction that we can designate as fictional genealogies of colonialism, it is to the extent that two distinct but related narrative topoi recur so consistently in individual texts that they come to establish a defining generic identity. There is, firstly, the topos of the founding moment of colonialism as both a central narrative focus and as a moment of epochal significance. Secondly, there is the corresponding topos of *the early phase of colonization as the inauguration of cultural processes and invented traditions hitherto unprecedented in the indigenous precolonial society.*

But if it is the case that these generic features and concerns are inscribed in all texts belonging to this category of modern African fiction, it is equally true that there are important differences in the ways in which they are so inscribed, differences that make it possible for us to perceive a "dominant" as opposed to a "minor" paradigm. What are these differences within the common generic representational and narrative consistencies? For reasons of space I wish to elaborate on the differentiations between these paradigms by constructing a table that shows how each paradigm inscribes the two topoi of the founding moment of colonialism and a nascent "culture of colonialism." (See Table 1).

The generic features and ideological implications sketched here do not apply uniformly and unambiguously to the authors and titles identified. For example, while *Things Fall Apart* is perhaps the most representative of the "dominant" paradigm in its generic features, it is perhaps the least representative in terms of the identified "ideologic implications" of antimodern nativism or revanchist nationalism. The latter would be more appropriately applied to texts like Elechi Amadi's *The Great Ponds*, Armah's *Two Thousand Seasons* and Camara Laye's *The African Child*. This qualification could be extended further:

Table 1

A. *Topos of the founding moment of colonial rule*

Dominant paradigm	*Minor paradigm*
1. Themes	
"Things fall apart": collapse of the precolonial social formation, its institutions, values and practices. Projection of the precolonial society as an organic totality, as communalistic and balanced, if imperfect in many ways.	As "Things fall apart," new coherences and a re-centering of relationships and institutions take place. Emphasis on how the precolonial social formation, being resilient and contradiction-ridden, connects with the invading colonialism in complex ways.
2. Characteristic modes	
Tragedy, elegeiac nostalgia, irony.	Comedy, satire, mock-epic, irony.
3. Protagonists	
Doomed defenders or champions of the precolonial social order. Narrative energy lodged in failed resistance: the "future" does not lie with the protagonist(s). Deep pessimism.	Enthusiastic accomplices or "collaborators" of colonizers. Narrative energy lodged in cynical manipulation of "opportunities" thrown up by colonizers, sometimes in outwitting colonizers: the "future" lies with protagonist(s).
4. Ideological implications of plot and outlook of protagonists	
Revanchist nationalism, utopian communalism, anti-modern pessimism; culturalism, or the autonomization of a domain of customs, beliefs and practices that is self-determining and is abstracted from the material forces and relationships of an invading colonial capitalism.	Anticulturalist, pro-modern, optimistic Westernization or assimilationism.

B. *Topos of the early phase of colonialism*

Dominant paradigm   *Minor paradigm*

1. *Themes*

Incommensurable, ineradicable difference between the culture of the colonizer and the colonized, between their corresponding world-views and ethical systems.

Colonization as process of inventing and improvising "traditions": hybridity, syntheses, "metisage."

2. *Mode of employment*

Immobilization of the colonial dialectic, a dialectic that necessarily and inevitably locks colonizer and colonized in processes beyond calculated or anticipated consequences; corresponding schematization of the colonial dialectic as a binary clash-of-cultures formulaic plot. Peripheralization of characters and forces "collaborating" with the colonizers.

Mobilization of the colonial dialectic: chance, trickery and uncertainty as organizing motifs. Narrativity in fractured, discrepant voices and discourses; absence of schematic, formulaic resolutions of plot conflicts.

3. *Ideologic implications*

Populist, irridentist nationalism; nativism and indigenism as bulwarks of cultural resistance, deepening of antimodern conservatism and idealizations of "origins" and "essences."

"Progressive," self-seeking individualism, often linked with expedient, pragmatic patrimonialism or clientilism. The culture of the colonizer and the colonized synthesized in an emerging "evolue" or "assimile" subjectivity. Consequently an anticulturalist ideological matrix that locates identity in processes determined by class formation, political alliances, material interests and the requirements of social reproduction.

4. *Examples*

Chinua Achebe's *Things Fall Apart, Arrow of God*; Ayi Kwei Armah's *Two Thousand Seasons, The Healers*; Ngugi wa Thiong'o's *The River Between, Weep Not, Child*; Elechi Amadi's *The Great Ponds*; Camara Laye's *The African Child, The Radiance of the King*.

Amadou Hampate Ba's *The Fortunes of Wangrin*; Yambo Ouologuem's *Bound to Violence*; Cheikh Hamidou Kane's *Ambiguous Adventure*; T.M. Aluko's *One Man, One Wife*.

within the established corpus of each author in our selected list, there are great divergences of generic categories, implicit textual ideology, and aesthetic sophistication. An instance: there are vast differences of formalistic, ideological and aesthetic effects and inscriptions between Ngugi's "early" *Weep Not, Child,* and novels of a later period of his writing like *A Grain of Wheat.* And concerning the "minor paradigm," though it has a smaller complement of full-blown texts, its constitutive generic features and ideological tropes pervade many postcolonial African novels, especially those of the Camerounian novelist, Ferdinand Oyono in texts like *Houseboy, The Old Man and the Medal* and *The Road to Europe.*

The corpus of narratives that I have designated "genealogical fictions" and whose generic and ideological features I have mapped in this short, schematic profile does not exhaust the range of postcolonial African prose fiction. For instance, the move away from thematic and representational features of this "school" to explorations of colonialism both in its "stablized" stages and in the resistance movements that paved the way to its decline began almost at the same time, but it became a more discernible, even dominant trend of African postcolonial fiction in the mid-70s.[21] The famous or representative titles here are Achebe's *No Longer at Ease,* Armah's *Why Are We So Blest?,* Ngugi's *A Grain of Wheat,* and Sembenes's *God's Bits of Wood.*

Frantz Fanon, Amilcar Cabral, Jose Carlos Mariategui, and a host of theorists of revolutionary cultural decolonization and social reconstruction of the developing world have reflected extensively on the reappropriation of the past as vital battlegrounds of the ideological discourses of decolonization and the construction of positive, disalienated identities in the formerly colonized nations and societies. Fanon's observation in the following is typical: "The native intellectual who decides to give battle to colonial lies fights on the field of the whole continent. The past is given back its value."[22]

As we have seen in this essay, this process can be very complicated indeed. And what is especially striking in the reconstruction of the past in the dominant paradigm of the "genealogical fictions" that we have examined here is that its overwhelming generalized mood of pessimism, as well as its characteristic tragic and elegeiac modes of

---

[21] For a narrowly positivistic account of the "development" of contemporary African prose fiction, see Eustace Palmer, *The Growth of the African Novel* (London: Heinemann, 1979).
[22] *The Wretched of the Earth* 171.

representation coincided with the twilight of colonial rule and the eve of independence in Africa, coincided indeed with the decades of the euphoria of Afro-Asian solidarity and the world-historical rise of the nonaligned movement.[23] There is thus a profound disjuncture here that involves leading novelists of newly decolonized, "emergent" nations distancing themselves from the optimism and euphoria of the "present" in order to reconstruct the colonial past, in its founding moment and in the early phase of its stabilization, in bitter, melancholic and dystopic terms — failed or doomed resistance and tragic protagonists to whom the "future" did not belong.

I suggest that this disjuncture is explained, at least in *ideological* terms, by the factor of hegemony and the unique forms and modes of resistance that it generates. This issue involves intricate structures of the interpenetration of history and consciousness.[24] For the "future" which, as projected back into the past by these novelists, did not, or could not, belong to their tragic heroes, was already the "present" of departing colonists and the African legatees who were poised to become the postindependence or "neocolonial" ruling groups and classes. These "genealogical fictions" were thus powerful interrogations of the legitimacy and the presumptive hegemony of these nascent African elites and ruling groups and classes.

The first two epigrams to this essay mark distinct but complementary expressions of this complex counter-hegemonic process. In the quote from Toni Morrison's *Beloved* we glimpse the more muted and somewhat more subtle disavowals in texts like Achebe's *Things Fall Apart*, and *Arrow of God*: the colonial precursors of the postcolonial ruling groups and classes are peripheralized in the narrative frames; they are not given even the indirect *mimetic* legitimacy of central, if negative protagonists. The quote from Ngugi logically applies to his own narratives, and to the narratives of writers like Ayi Kwei Armah and Mongo Beti, narratives that inscribe more direct, more savage forms of disavowal. In all of this we can begin to perceive the

---

23 For one important ethnological text of this euphoria, see *New Nations*, ed. Lucy Mair (Chicago: University of Chicago Press, 1963). For a more penetrating account of the historical and theoretical contexts for "Third World" issues in literary and cultural studies, see Aijaz Ahmad, *In Theory: Classes, Nations, Literatures* (London: Verso, 1992).

24 See, Georg Lukács, "Antinomies of Bourgeois Thought," *History and Class Consciousness* (Cambridge: The MIT Press, 1988). See also Franz Fanon, "The Pitfalls of National Consciousness," *The Wretched of the Earth*.

deeper roots of the much debated antagonisms between many of Africa's leading progressive, left-identified writers and the neocolonial regimes of the continent.[25] Such a perception affords us, I believe, a more complex understanding of the somewhat revanchist nationalism of the fictional genealogies of colonialism produced by these writers in their powerful revisionary re-inventions of the past. Such a complex understanding is also useful in engaging the strong discourses of moralism and voluntarism in the counterhegemonic disavowals of these writers, an instance of which we see in the second epigram to this essay from Ngugi.

There remains the tantalizing question why the neocolonial legatees of the colonial system whose presumptive hegemony in the present is so powerfully contested in the revisionary genealogical fictions we have explored in this essay, have not succeeded in generating their own legitimizing genealogical fictions. After all, we do have the possibilities of such legitimating fictions, such vital cultural capital, in novels like *The Fortunes of Wangrin* and *Bound to Violence* and the "minority" tradition of postcolonial fiction to which they belong. But a clue to this problem lies in precisely the characteristic generic modes of representation of this tradition: comedy, satire, irony, the mock-epic. These generic representational modes hint at anxiety, unease and paranoia. Our third epigram to this essay that comes from Jomo Kenyatta's famous attack on Bildad Kaggia, who was perhaps the true conscience of the revolutionary nationalists of Kenyatta's generation, unintendedly captures this collective paranoiac unease of the neocolonial comprador bourgeoisie.[26] For the brutal frankness of Kenyatta's address to Kaggia cannot ignore the elementary fact that the repeated rhetorical question — "what have you done for yourself?" — cannot be posed to every woman and man in neocolonial Kenya, cannot indeed be posed to the majority of workers, peasants, students, the intelligentsia, and the unemployed of Kenya. The rhetoric of repetition and closure in this speech therefore betrays the acute sense of desperation of a class riven by internal splits and lacking the appropriate or effective hegemonizing metanarratives and discourses for the consumption of the subaltern groups and classes of the postcolonial

---

[25] Among the texts by African writers that have documented and explored this antagonism are Ngugi wa Thiong'o's *Writers in Politics* (London: Heinemann, 1981), and Wole Soyinka, *The Man Died* (London: Rex Collings, 1972).

[26] See Bildad Kaggia's autobiography, *Roots of Freedom* (Nairobi: East African Publishing House, 1975).

rentier state. This entails interesting cultural processes, their ideological inscriptions, and the material economic conditions that subtend and complicate them.

The "invented traditions" of colonial hegemony initially provided the African neocolonial ruling groups and classes their means of individual and collective self-fashioning as "assimiles," "evolues" and elites. Beyond this, there has been a strenuous effort on the part of these groups and classes to reinvent themselves in a diversity of discourses and symbolic ensembles, from Senghor's aesthetic theories of Negritude, to Mobutu's indigenist slogans and edicts on "authenticité," to the more progressive variants like Nyerere's "African socialism"[27]. But real, effective hegemony of the type afforded colonialism by its "invented traditions" eludes the African neocolonial bourgeoisie. And herein lies a key to unravelling the problem. For the "invented traditions" of colonialism were forms of "cultural capital" powerfully legitimated by, and inscribed in a superior mode of production, in the material practices and unequal appropriations facilitated by the colonial economy, and ultimately in the then enormous world-scale class ascendancy of the European bourgeoisie as this was consolidated in the imperial state. This historic context justifies stating the obvious: the neocolonial ruling groups and classes of most parts of Africa and the Caribbean, and parts of Asia and Latin America lack, for historic and structural reasons, such legitimating material supports for transforming their, we might say, tireless reinventions of tradition into effective, expendable cultural capital; force and coercion are prevalent, hegemony and civil society very fragile.[28]

---

[27] See Mohammed Babu, *African Socialism or Socialist Africa* (London: Zed Press, 1981).

[28] On the numerous powerful textual explorations of the problems of constructing a *postcolonial* African "civil society," see Chinua Achebe, *A Man of the People* (Garden City: Anchor Books, 1967) and Ousmane Sembene, *The Last of the Empire* (Heinemann, 1981). For a theoretical discussion of this problem in the more general context of the Third World, see also Paul A. Baran, "The Political Economy of Backwardness," *Imperialism and Underdevelopment*, ed. Robert I. Rhodes (Monthly Review Press, 1970).

Wide Worlds in Confined Quarters: American Movies on German Television

IRMELA SCHNEIDER

I

In Douglas Sirk's melodrama *All That Heaven Allows* (1955) children promise their widowed mother that television will bring "life" into the house. Yet the mother leaves the shapeless device in the living room like a foreign body. She does not believe in its life-giving power and leaves her home and the television in order to lead a life in the wilderness with Ron, the gardener. In a conflict between civilization and nature, between society and love, she chooses nature and love. For the movie heroine, television is merely breathless life. Another scenario approximately thirty years later: In an episode of *Dynasty*, Krystle is in the hospital after giving birth to her child. Naturally her room is furnished with a television set, but it is not at all noticeable. It is an integral part of the room's furnishings. In the nightly news that Krystle keeps up with — even this is nothing special, simply an everyday event like eating and drinking — there is a report on a press conference held by her husband Blake. She learns the latest about her husband's business by watching television, but this astonishes neither Krystle nor viewers. Here television provides the heroine of the series with nourishment.

Both of these scenes mark a change in the way people assess television, a medium of communication that has had a substantial influence on the Western world in the second half of the twentieth century. Both examples are from U.S. productions, and most people can easily relate to both of them. Neither the origin nor the genre of these examples is a coincidence. At the same time, both point to one of the central developments in television programs in Germany and nearly world-wide since the beginning of the 1960s: American productions have achieved dominance on the world market and continued to expand their share in subsequent years. According to *Television Business International*, between 1983 and 1988, U.S. export sales to Europe increased from $212 million to $675 million.[1] This economic hegemony however cannot be equated with cultural hegemony or cultural "imperialism."[2] Although the temptation to draw this false conclusion is great, it must be noted that media communication is not determined by what is offered, but rather is dependent on the manner in which the resources available are utilized.

Mass media can be described as social systems differing from other social systems and developing their specific dynamics by means of internal differentiation, interaction with other social systems, and self-reflection. In functionally differentiated societies, the "primary social function" of mass media lies "in everyone's participation in a common reality, or more precisely, in the creation of such an assumption, which then encroaches as an operative fiction and becomes reality."[3] In other words, mass media are agencies of socialization that shape viewers' ideas about reality. Participation in mass media communication, the perception of programs offered by the media leads "to system specific constructions of meaning."[4] Within such a theoretical framework is the question regarding how system specific constructions of meaning can be historiographically constructed (or reconstructed).

Historiographic descriptions are based on a retrospective perspective; from the viewpoint of present experience they depict a time ex-

[1] See R. Negrine and S. Papathanassopoulos, "The Internalization of Television," *European Journal of Communication* 1 (1991) 9-32; see also Andrew R. Horowitz, "The Global Bonanza of American TV," *Media Culture: Television, Radio, Records, Books, Magazines, Newspapers, Movies*, ed. James Monaco (New York: Delta Books, 1978) 115-22.

[2] See Herbert Schiller, "Disney, Dallas and Electronic Data Flows. The Transnationalization of Culture," *Cultural Transfer or Electronic Imperialism?* ed. Christian W. Thomsen (Heidelberg: Winter-Verlag, 1989) 33-44.

[3] [Tr. — All German quotes have been translated into English.] Niklas Luhmann, "Veränderungen im System gesellschaftlicher Kommunikation und die Massenmedien," *Soziologische Aufklärung 3. Soziales System, Gesellschaft, Organisation* (Köln-Opladen: Westdeutscher Verlag, 1981) 309-34, 318.

[4] Siegfried J. Schmidt, "Medien, Kultur: Medienkultur. Ein konstruktivistisches Gesprächsangebot," *Kognition und Gesellschaft. Der Diskurs des Radikalen Konstruktivismus 2*, ed. S. J. Schmidt (Frankfurt a.M.: Suhrkamp-Verlag, 1992) 425-50, 438.

perienced in the past. Such descriptions cannot be an objective stock-taking of what used to be. Historiographic descriptions construct and constitute their subject matter by providing a linear view of history, including certain conceptions about time, which is then divided into groups. The presentation of historical events, the division into phases, the marking off of breaks are results specific to such descriptions which "are used to function as societal self-portraits."[5] Historiographic descriptions seek to order the experience of history; they serve to "discover and confirm societal identity."[6] Based on the knowledge of the present, a time of past experience is presented from the standpoint of identity and difference, continuity and discontinuity compared to the respective experience of the present.

Based on these assumptions, this paper treats part of the history of the media system of television by presenting a historiographic description of American motion pictures shown on television. Two questions are of central significance here:

1. What are the outlines of such a history when the focus is on the role of the producers of the television system, that is, on those responsible for selecting television programs from the arsenal of motion-picture history? When describing the history of American movies on television, it is the history of their broadcast on television that must be followed. This approach differs from methods in the history of filmmaking, in which the attempt is made to delimit phases along the lines of corresponding current film production.

2. Which constructions of meaning can be captured historiographically with reference to the movies on television? Assuming a constructivistic theory, perception must be viewed as an active, goal-oriented process in which perceptive judgments are passed that are based on certain conclusions. Cognition and perception are not separate processes. Cognition can be described as a process, in which hypotheses, based on current information, are posited, assumptions are made about how such information can be combined to form a coherent, consistent unit.

---

[5] Niklas Luhmann, "Das Problem der Epochenbildung und die Evolutionstheorie," *Epochenschwellen und Epochenstrukturen im Diskurs der Literatur- und Sprachhistorie* ed. Hans Ulrich Gumbrecht and Ursula Link-Heer (Frankfurt a.M.: SuhrkampVerlag, 1985) 11-33, 25.

[6] Monika Elsner, Thomas Müller, Peter M. Spangenberg, "Thesen zum Problem der Periodisierung in der Mediengeschichte," *Fernsehen in der Bundesrepublik Deutschland: Perioden - Zäsuren - Epochen*, ed. Helmut Kreuzer and Helmut Schanze (Heidelberg: Winter-Verlag 1991) 38-50, 38.

The active process of forming hypotheses is determined by organized clusters of knowledge. These clusters, which should not be thought of as stored and mentally represented retrievable information, are called *schemes* (or patterns).[7] Such schemes operate in the perception of everyday experience as well as in the perception of art, fiction, television and, of course, movies.

During the perception of movies, schemes become active that have been developed through the socialization provided by the movie theater, the perception of everyday experience, as well as in the daily perception of television. Which patterns of perception become active in the case of American films and to which grouping of patterns they contribute are two questions that have been investigated by Bordwell, who assumes a cognitional-psychological narrative theory.

What follows represents part of a comprehensive research project on American and British influence on German programs on television, and, as regards movies, considers the question of social and individual value preferences that are cognitively processed during reception.

II

Among the programs broadcast on German public television, the number of American movies and series has increased since the beginning of the 1960s in a relatively constant fashion. Today, in the horizontal as well as the vertical context of programs, American and German productions exist side by side, and together they take part in outlining the construction of reality. American productions that make their way into television in Germany are nothing foreign, but on the contrary, they penetrate programs on German television. They form a context for German or European productions in the same fashion as German productions contextualize American series or movies. Television programs as a form of metadiscourse for individual productions, have been transnational for a long time. Within this transnationality there have been shifts of emphasis over the years as well as various forms of public approval. The borders separating cultures have, psychologically at least, become pervious. In the media

---

[7] See Jean Piaget, *Biologie und Erkenntnis. Über die Beziehungen zwischen organischen Regulationen und kognitiven Prozessen* (Frankfurt a.M.: Fischer Verlag, 1983) 241ff (German translation of *Biologie et connaissance* [Paris: Gallimard, 1967]); for a discussion of the notion of pattern (Schema), see David Bordwell, *Narration in the Fiction Film* (London: Methuen, 1985) 31ff.

society the basic dichotomy of national versus international is just as porous as that of real versus not real.[8]

As early as the 1950s, television was advertised as being the "window to the world." The "world" that appears in this window has changed over the course of time in many ways. In the beginning there was only one channel (officially called the "Arbeitsgemeinschaft der öffentlich-rechtlichen Rundfunkanstalten der BRD" [ARD]), adapting to the structure of the BBC, which was organized along the lines of a "public service" institution, i.e., public television. It was financed by fees charged to everyone owning a television set (and, starting in 1954, auditional financing was obtained from the returns of limited advertising) and controlled by a board consisting of so-called socially relevant groups (e. g. political parties, churches, labor unions). The basic idea behind this was the following: Broadcasting was to be protected from commercial dominance as well as state intervention. The warning had been the broadcasting situation from 1933 to 1945: an instrument of state propaganda. In the meantime, however, the dependence on advertising as well as political influence (via political parties) has grown tremendously.

In the first few years, the "world" that television was supposed to be the window to could only be viewed for a few hours each day. Today viewers can tune in around the clock. In the beginning, television was black and white; since 1967 there have been color televisions. In 1963 a second fullfunctioning channel, ZDF (Zweites Deutsches Fernsehen), was added and the broadcast of a third channel, whose reception varied regionally, also began. In addition to the fees charged to finance these public stations were now returns from television commercials, which the public channels were allowed to show on weekdays for a maximum of twenty minutes during prime time viewing hours only (i.e., between 6 p.m. and 8 p.m). Since the mid-1980s satellite and cable channels belonging to private stations have entered the scene, which are financed exclusively by television advertising. These channels not only insert commercials between programs at certain times over the entire broadcasting period but during programs as well. Now, in the early 1990s, households in Germany connected to receive cable television can pick up approximately twenty-five channels. Broadcasting was founded as a national facility; now, toward

[8] See Siegfried J. Schmidt, "Medien, Kultur: Medienkultur. Ein konstruktivistisches Gesprächsangebot," *Kognition und Gesellschaft. Der Diskurs des Radikalen Konstruktivismus 2*, ed. S. J. Schmidt (Frankfurt a.M.: Suhrkamp-Verlag, 1992) 425-50, 431.

the end of the century, television, with all of its unsolved political, legal, and economic problems, has become an enterprise without borders.[9] Now, at the beginning of the 1990s, we are in a situation of radical change, whose consequences can hardly be predicted. Fragmentation of the public, transnationalization, and the globalization of the communications industry as well as distributional systems are all categories characterizing this radical change. The discussion surrounding the consequences of this change leads us to the heart of postmodern discourse. Delocalization, dematerialization, derealization are central concepts with which the consequences should be understood in this context.[10]

The radical change and its consequences mentioned above is not to be the primary focus of this paper. Instead, attention will be drawn to some of the recent historical events that have contributed to this situation. The large number of channels existing in Germany today cannot be viewed as merely a result of the technological advances of cable and satellite. The connection between technological developments and the development of communication media in society must be regarded as an evolutionary process, i.e., "a complex process of the constant differentiation of new and old forms of communication and media, which mutually influence each other and continue to functionally balance each other."[11]

The current programs of private stations, which are decisively dominated by American movies and series, have received the approval of their viewers because the public channels of the 1960s and 1970s created the conditions for such a development. Programs that initially could only gradually establish themselves as segments in the horizontal as well as the vertical programming context, dominate private stations

[9] See Antonio Cassese and Andrew Clapham, eds., *Transfrontier Television in Europe: The Human Rights Dimension* [La télévision transfrontière en Europe dans la perspective des droits de l'homme] (Baden-Baden: Nomos Verlags-Gesellschaft, 1990); John P. Roberts, "The Implication of the Globalization of Television and Its Cultures," *Communications* 3 (1990) 213-23.
[10] See, for example, Gérard Raulet, "Die neue Utopie. Die soziologische und philosophische Bedeutung der neuen Kommunikationstechnologien," *Die Frage nach dem Subjekt*, ed. Manfred Frank, Gérard Raulet, and Willem van Reijen (Frankfurt a.M.: Suhrkamp-Verlag, 1988) 283-316.
[11] Monika Elsner, Thomas Müller, and Peter M. Spangenberg, "Thesen zum Problem der Periodisierung in der Mediengeschichte," *Fernsehen in der Bundesrepublik Deutschland: Perioden - Zäsuren - Epochen*, ed. Helmut Kreuzer and Helmut Schanze (Heidelberg: Winter-Verlag 1991) 38-50, 47.

today. The process of habitualization on the part of German viewers in watching American motion pictures and series on television as well as the "Americanization" of program structures, first in programs shown in the afternoons and then successively in the evenings,[12] are developments of the 1970s and early 1980s. These developments represent part of the conditions under which private television program promoters have been able to increase their market share in Germany. The products are not the reason why they have become so popular. It is rather socialization processes, which have led to the habitual contact with such products. The public channels have, so to speak, tilled the soil in which the private stations have reaped the harvest of economic success.

III

Among programs broadcast on German television, American movies did not gain acceptance until the television medium was about ten years old. In the 1950s motion pictures on TV were shown on a fairly irregular basis. From 1954 to 1959 an average of 49 movies per year were broadcast.

During this period, older German movies enjoyed the highest proportional representation. Beginning in the mid-1950s several movies from European countries traditionally known for their motion pictures, namely, France and Italy, were increasingly broadcast on German television (see Table 1). At this time American movies were more likely to be shown at the motion-picture theater.[13]

The movies broadcast on television in the 1950s took up the entire tradition of the motion picture showings of the 1930s and 1940s. Popular movie stars of the period now left their mark on television: Hans Moser, Zarah Leander, Attila Hörbiger, Hans Albers, Brigitte Horney, Paul Dahlke to name only a few. This was not only a consequence of availability, but was also determined by what was interpreted as being attractive offers for viewers. In the 1950s the acceptability of American movies, especially in relation to German, movies was

[12] See Angela Krewani,"'Amerikanisierung am Nachmittag': Amerikanische Serien in ARD und ZDF. Ein Überblick über quantitative Entwicklungen," *Amerikanische Einstellung. Deutsches Fernsehen und US-amerikanische Produktionen*, ed. Irmela Schneider (Heidelberg: WinterVerlag, 1992) 172-83.

[13] Irmela Schneider, *Film, Fernsehen & Co. Zur Entwicklung des Spielfilms in Kino und Fernsehen. Ein Überblick über Konzepte und Tendenzen* (Heidelberg: WinterVerlag, 1990) 32-48.

Table 1

Movies on ARD and ZDF According to Country of Origin
(Premier Showings and Reruns) Amounts given in percent

Year	*	**	***	USA	GB	A	F	F/I	I	other
1954	78.2	9.1	0.0	5.5	0.0	1.8	0.0	0.0	1.8	3.6
1955	63.3	16.3	0.0	6.1	0.0	4.1	2.0	2.0	4.1	2.0
1956	40.9	27.3	0.0	6.8	2.3	0.0	15.9	4.6	0.0	2.3
1957	50.0	14.8	0.0	0.0	0.0	1.9	14.8	7.4	1.9	9.3
1958	26.1	15.2	6.5	6.5	8.7	4.4	19.6	2.2	6.5	4.4
1959	15.6	20.0	0.0	20.0	8.9	4.4	8.9	2.2	15.6	4.4
1960	6.8	22.0	1.7	11.9	15.3	6.8	8.5	3.4	8.5	15.3
1961	2.9	17.4	1.5	4.4	15.9	7.3	18.8	10.1	8.7	13.0
1962	1.3	10.4	0.0	11.7	16.9	2.6	13.0	7.8	15.6	20.8
1963	3.8	23.4	0.0	20.1	14.4	1.0	11.0	2.9	5.3	18.2
1964	0.0	21.7	0.0	17.7	17.1	1.7	10.3	5.1	4.6	22.3
1965	2.5	17.6	0.0	19.1	21.1	1.5	5.0	4.5	5.0	26.1
1966	3.1	20.7	0.0	15.0	13.2	1.3	9.7	2.6	9.3	25.1
1967	5.5	19.9	0.0	20.6	15.1	4.0	8.5	4.4	2.9	19.1
1968	2.9	18.1	0.4	23.1	11.9	3.2	6.1	3.6	6.9	23.8
1969	4.6	22.0	0.4	31.6	7.8	1.1	5.3	6.0	4.6	16.7
1970	6.6	15.5	0.3	32.6	12.2	3.3	5.3	4.3	3.0	17.1
1971	6.0	13.7	1.2	31.6	11.0	2.4	4.8	6.6	2.7	20.0
1972	5.9	15.2	0.0	41.1	10.0	2.1	4.7	4.1	1.5	15.5
1973	9.5	11.4	1.9	44.5	7.9	3.8	7.9	3.5	1.3	8.5
1974	8.0	16.2	1.2	42.2	10.4	1.2	5.5	4.6	1.2	9.5
1975	9.2	10.7	1.7	43.4	10.1	2.3	4.0	6.4	1.7	10.4
1976	9.0	8.6	2.5	44.4	11.11	3.1	4.3	5.6	1.9	9.6
1977	7.5	10.2	0.6	47.3	6.9	1.2	4.8	6.3	4.5	10.5
1978	3.9	14.0	0.5	47.9	9.2	1.4	5.3	4.4	1.4	12.2
1979	3.7	10.5	0.2	45.0	6.6	0.7	9.5	0.0	2.5	21.1
1980	4.3	10.1	1.8	48.3	8.0	0.9	7.1	0.0	1.4	18.1
1981	4.4	14.1	1.3	41.7	5.4	1.3	8.1	0.0	2.6	21.1
1982	4.2	14.9	2.3	43.8	5.4	1.1	9.0	0.0	3.3	16.1
1983	5.9	14.6	0.7	47.0	7.5	0.9	9.3	0.0	2.2	12.0
1984	6.5	19.1	0.6	39.8	5.2	2.6	10.3	0.0	4.8	11.1
1985	4.0	19.8	0.7	39.2	7.2	1.1	9.8	0.0	5.8	12.4
1986	1.9	17.0	1.3	41.4	9.2	2.1	9.0	0.0	5.2	13.0
1987	3.8	17.0	0.5	41.2	9.6	2.0	9.2	0.0	4.3	12.4
1988	4.3	19.5	1.7	41.4	7.3	1.9	5.7	0.0	5.7	12.6
1989	2.5	17.5	0.6	49.3	7.8	2.0	6.6	0.0	4.3	9.4
1990	3.9	19.6	2.0	44.0	7.6	1.1	7.6	0.0	4.5	9.5

* West Germany (Repeats)
** West Germany (New productions)
*** East Germany

Source: Databank of Project B5 (Special Collaborative Research Department 240 "TV Screen Media," Universität-GH Siegen) through 1985, SPIO: Filmstatistische Taschenbücher 1987-1991.

comparatively low.[14] Newer American movies were especially popular among the adolescent subculture, which formed in protest against the adult world. But the television medium was primarily taken notice of by members of the middle and upper classes.[15] More important still, however, is the fact that television was supposed to become a medium for the entire family. It was supposed to have an integrating and not a polarizing function. At this time, American movies were not yet perceived as being able to fulfill this requirement. Not until the early 1970s did the number of American movies increase, and quite significantly at that. In the second half of the 1970s the broadcast of American movies on German television reached its zenith with in part more than forty percent of all movies shown (see Table 1).

Movies were also broadcast on German public television from the very beginning due to economic reasons, something that was not a favorite topic of discussion on the part of televison officials in the first two decades of operation, because it was thought that television could operate outside of the market mechanism. Nevertheless, movies were comparatively inexpensive and that is what made them attractive for program promoters from the start. The maximum rate for older productions was 1 DM (German Mark) per meter and for newer productions, 1.50 DM.[16] As late as 1964, the average price, 646 DM per minute of broadcasting time, was "the second most inexpensive form of productions' purchased."[17] By 1971, licensing fees to broadcast a movie had reached between 25,000 and 75,000 DM; in exceptional cases fees were as high as 90,000 DM. In the meantime, over 400,000 DM is paid for "movie packets." It can be expected that one day motion pictures will be more expensive than television stations' productions of films made for television. However, it is inconceivable that television will ever be able to do without movies.

A more influential role in the discussion on the meaning of television than that of economic justifications was played by those taking

[14] See Martin Loiperdinger, "Amerikanisierung im Kino? Hollywood und das westdeutsche Publikum der fünfziger Jahre," *TheaterZeitSchrift* 28 (1989) 50-60.

[15] See Hansjörg Bessler, "Entwicklungsphasen in Angebot und Nachfrage nach Fernsehprogrammen," *Rundfunk und Fernsehen* 1 (1978) 12-19, 15.

[16] See Gunther Faupel, *Medien im Wettstreit. Film und Fernsehen* (Münster: Regensburg-Verlag, 1979) 244; Wilhelm Roth, "Kleines Wörterbuch der Filmpolitik und Filmwirtschaft in der Bundesrepublik," *Filmkritik* 9 (1971) 482-94, 487.

[17] Georg Roeber and Gerhard Jacoby, *Handbuch der filmwirtschaftlichen Medienbereiche* (Pullach bei München: Verlag Dokumentation, 1973) 904ff.

the position that it was the specific task of the television medium, in contrast to the cinema, to broadcast live programs. It was believed that there was a fundamental difference between the movie theater and television, and the conclusion was drawn that the products of cinemas, namely, motion pictures, should not be utilized over the long term. Showing movies on television was thus merely a temporary solution.

Television was supposed to become a dependable medium in which "next-door neighbors" could be seen on the screen — and if possible, live. It was studio plays about everyday topics that were thought to be most likely to catch the viewer's eye and not movies, those optically opulent productions depicting great emotion and faraway places. In the beginning days of television, program promoters believed that movies did not have what it takes to familiarize viewers with the new medium.

While the purpose of live programs was still being debated among experts, results from viewer surveys showed that, besides sports broadcasts, movies shown on television were among the "attractions of television programs."[18] Viewers regarded movies on television neither as stopgaps nor as a temporary solution, but could rediscover what they were already familiar with in a new medium. In terms of the products, viewers apparently did not perceive a difference between a trip to the movie theater and watching television, i.e., movies they were possibly already familiar with from the theater they also watched on television. The motion picture as a product is not distinctively linked to the cinema. The theater simply represents a different way of experiencing a movie. It was the movies broadcast on television and not so much the live programs from the studios with which television proved itself to be a "window to the world." "In the living rooms of the 1950s the fusion of a big event and a small room took place."[19] And this "fusion" was especially due to the movies shown on television, for here stars popular around the world could be seen as well as exotic places and magnificient décor and costumes — a big and nice, wide world.

In practice the number of movie showings on television did not increase annually at a continuous rate over the next few years, but an absolute rise can be seen when the period is viewed in sum. From

---

[18] Hans Bausch, ed., *Königsteiner Gespräche. Referate und Diskussionen des Presse-Seminars der ARD in Königstein/Taunus am 27./28. Mai 1975* (Aalen, 1975) 142-43.

[19] C.-D. Rath, "Elektronische Körperschaft," *Tumult* 5 (1983) 36-44, 38.

1960 to 1977 the number of movies shown on ARD and ZDF more than doubled. While the amount of movies out of all programs shown on ARD totalled 4.8% in 1966, it had already reached 7.5% of the programs on ZDF. Over the next few years ARD increased the amount of movies broadcast to 9%. Now, in the early 1990s, the number of movies shown on ARD and ZDF together make up 12% of all programs. On the two most important private television channels, SAT 1 and RTL plus, the amount of movies shown totals 25% and 15% respectively.[20]

After the creation of ZDF (on April 1, 1963) three phases can be posited, which are based on quantitative factors. The first phase is the time period from 1963 to the end of 1977. During this period approximately three movies were shown per week on each channel. The second phase, from 1978 to 1984, marks a period in which an average annual total of approximately 450 movies were shown on the two main channels. By this time the movie had been firmly established as a daily television viewing event. We are now in the third phase, which began in 1985. This phase has been characterized by a further radical increase in the number of movies on both channels. Taken together the number of movies shown on ARD and ZDF in 1988 was over 800. This means that viewers could watch two movies per day on the public service channels. Today, households capable of receiving cable stations have the opportunity to see around 7,000 movies per year. Choosing movies is no longer the responsibility of television stations; the choice can now be made by the viewer. Viewers have always had the opportunity to decide whether or not they want to watch a movie on television. Now, they not only have this decision to make, but must also decide from the abundance of movies offered which movie they want to watch and which one they do not want to watch.

The enormous upswing that movies are currently experiencing — not only the movies broadcast on television but also those available on the video market — has also had an effect on the aesthetics of movies as well as on the selectional strategy with which television stations can operate. A movie's topicality is shriveling up timewise. The challenge to innovate is constantly increasing, and this challenge is being met by a variety of methods: technological innovations in the

---

[20] See Christa-Maria Ridder, "Das europäische Dilemma oder: Woher kommen die Programme der Zukunft?" *Medium* 4 (1991) 58-62, 58.

form of special effects, innovations in narrative discourse by mixing genres. Another innovative development is the constantly increasing speed of frame sequences. Today, increasing a stimulus means increasing the tempo. Movies cannot be easily brought into a chronological line and ordered according to narrative sequences. Time sequences are now reduced to a sum of individual moments, resembling the aesthetics of television commercials.

Regarding the selectional strategies available to television stations, the accelerating pace at which movies are broadcast has meant constantly shrinking options. In view of private stations and the video market, a competitive market situation has been created, in which public stations have become one buyer among several. The demand for movies is currently higher than motion picture production. Thus, compared to the 1960s, the reverse situation is now the case: In the 1960s there was a wide variety of movies, and aside from motion-picture theaters, the stations ARD, ZDF and the regional channels were the only distributors. Neither the goods nor the money were scarce. At this time, the fact that movies on television operate according to the code of the haves vs. the have-nots, i.e., form a part of the economic system,[21] could be concealed, whereas today this fact is readily apparent: Goods and money are scarce, not only in terms of the limitations of goods and results, but also with reference to the fact that "the satisfaction of future needs is treated as a current problem."[22] For movies on television, it has become a problem in the early 1990s to decide how needs are to be created, which can then also be satisfied.

This situation did not come about because of private television channels, but rather because movies on television became a daily attraction on the two public channels. This, however, resulted from the fact that, starting in the mid-1970s, long before private channels were in existence, both channels looked at the problem of viewer approval as a scarcity. To win the approval of as many viewers as possible became a problem at a time when nearly every household in Germany had a television set and the number of television viewers decreased. This is when the struggle began between the two public channels to win over as many viewers as possible. At the same time it became

---

[21] Niklas Luhmann, "Wirtschaft als soziales System," *Soziologische Aufklärung* (Küln-Opladen: Westdeutscher Verlag, 1970) 204-31.

[22] Siegfried J. Schmidt, "Werbewirtschaft als soziales System," *Arbeitshefte Bildschirmmedien, Universität Siegen* 27 (1991) 5.

apparent that there were to be new distribution techniques in Germany over the next few years to promulgate movies. Program promoters had to realize that viewer approval would become even scarcer in the future, since the number of programs and not the number of viewers would continue to increase. Another reason why approval decreased was that the primary social function of both channels was the same, namely, to allow viewers to take part in the "operative fiction" of a common reality. Both of these reasons for the downswing in viewer approval led to the battle for viewer ratings. And this battle is characterized by a constant expansion in the number of movies among television programs. Among the wealth of options television stations could choose from, experience showed that movies were among the attractions having a good chance of winning public approval. It should thus come as no surprise that the available broadcasting time for movies continued to be increased at a time when figures for viewer approval were falling.

When the question is raised as to how the broadcasting time available for movies in successive years was filled, and which strategies were employed to select movies, one must assume a differentiated structure of phases in the recent history of movies on television.

When ZDF (the second public channel) began broadcasting programs on April 1, 1963, station managers were able to look back on the developments of ARD, which had already been in operation for ten years. As far as the movie is concerned, ZDF disregarded program selectional policy practiced in the 1950s, when the movie served the purpose of a temporary solution and laid down from the very beginning: "The movie is not to be a stopgap, not 'chewing gum in one's eye'; it is one of the options available to inform and to educate viewers."[23] Strategies employed for the selection of movies were the same as those for all programs: the movie was to offer something new, it should be current and should also give viewers the opportunity to learn a little about the history of film-making. The requirement for a movie to be current could be justified by showing motion pictures on television that could not be seen at the theater, i.e., television premiers. What exactly was meant by "learning about the history of film-making" and how this was relevant for those participating in this form of media communication, remained vague. Movies shown on television were

[23] Klaus Brüne, "Möglichkeiten des Spielfilmprogramms," *ZDF-Jahrbuch* (1967) 42-43, 43.

supposed to be "better than the motion-picture theater." Television was explicitly dissociated from the movie theater: "Karl May and James Bond were for moviegoers. Most of the time, thriving success for television stations comes from films taken from the experimental scene."[24] In adopting this policy, ZDF aligned itself with the generation of film-makers characterizing a radical change in the German movie. This radical change was initiated by means of a declaration of young German film-makers such as Alexander Kluge, Edgar Reitz and Peter Schamoni in 1962 ("Oberhausener Manifest" [Manifest of Oberhausen]). However, not only did movies of the older generation dominate among daily program attractions, but West European and American productions as well. The intent to represent cinematic art meant in practice that international movie debuts, primarily of West European and American movies, were broadcast. This intent came about at a time when the number of moviegoers fell drastically and the reputation of the cinema, even within film criticism, increasingly declined. In the most important movie magazine of the day, "Filmkritik" [Film Criticism] Wilfried Berghahn wrote in 1963: "We will have to accept the fact that in the future the première of many an important motion picture will not be at the movie theater, but rather on television."[25] Movie critics writing for movie periodicals as well as daily and weekly newspapers attentively accompanied, indeed systematically treated, movies broadcast on German television, just as they had done earlier in the case of movies shown at the theater. For almost a decade movie criticism primarily focused on movies on television.

From the mid-1960s to the mid-1970s movies on German television were selected not exclusively, although to a large extent by experts, by motion-picture historians and critics. At this time, the question concerning a movie's appeal for a large viewing audience was secondary. TV guides such as "Hör Zu" [Watch and Listen] registered this kind of policy as early as the mid-1960s with reserve: "ARD, so it seems, does not have the feel for movies which the public likes. The list of movie titles now purchased would indeed do every cinematic-art theater honor. It is just that by no means do all viewers prefer the cinematic-art theater."[26] Television thus allowed itself

---

[24] *Spielfilme im ZDF* (1965-1966) 3.

[25] Wilfried Berghahn, "Im Fernsehen," *Filmkritik* 2 (1963) 49-50, 49.

[26] Quoted in *Spielfilme im Deutschen Fernsehen* (1967-1968) 95.

to refrain from being a mass medium at certain times. During this phase, a significant change occurred in the acceptance of the classic Hollywood motion picture.

IV

With a few exceptions, American movies shown at the theater in the 1950s were met with only minor approval by the public. Box-office successes were enjoyed by the main German sentimental movies idealized in regional settings. American movies did not belong to the sophisticated film culture even within the movie-critical public. Instead they were all judged collectively as products stemming from the detested Hollywood motion picture industry. Not only were American movies, but also jazz and rock-and-roll music, the favorites of the adolescent subculture. Here James Dean and Elvis Presley became idols whose behavior was imitated in protest against the older generation. In the 1960s a historical change in mentality occurred, which proceeded in several steps and at different levels.

In the 1960s and early 1970s the reputation of American motion pictures improved among television viewers as well as cinéastes. The American movie advanced to the status of a role model function at a time when the European movie found itself in an aesthetic crisis. Above all, theoreticians of motion pictures written and directed by the same artists discovered that Hollywood directors had developed their own cinematic signature, and that one could not make defamatory remarks about Hollywood motion pictures across the board by saying that they were nothing more than products designed to meet industrial interests: "The art cinema accustomed critics to looking for personal expression in films, and no one doubted that it could be found in the works of Antonioni, Bergman, et al. Auteur critics went further and applied art-cinema schemata to classical Hollywood films... Ironically, the 'rereading' of Hollywood, which has been so central for film theory in recent years, has it roots in the schemata of European 'artistic' film-making."[27] This interest was initially prevalent in France and England and then made its way to young German filmmakers. Motion picture and television directors like Rainer Werner Fassbinder, Rudolf Thome, Roland Klick or Klaus Lemke soon discovered with enthusiasm precisely those directors "who had proven

---

[27] David Bordwell, *Narration in the Fiction Film* (London: Methuen, 1985) 232.

themselves to be responsible film-makers even in the dreamland factory of Hollywood."[28] Quotes from films by John Ford, Howard
Hawks, or Alfred Hitchcock are so much a determining factor in
numerous movies by these directors that they "can also serve as evidence today for the all-powerful influence of the industrial landscape
of American culture as a whole."[29] This influence exerted by American film culture in the 1960s and 1970s is expressed in the aesthetics
of their films as well as in the subjects they treat: they take up the
topos of America as the land of limitless opportunity and give it a
special twist. The most popular (and most successful) film in this context is Werner Herzog's *Stroszek* (1976).

Cinéastes thus isolated a few Hollywood directors so they could
adapt to them their own idealistic concepts about filmmaking. They
were liberated from the aura of having produced mere commercial
products. Television probably did not cause this change, but it contributed to it insofar as in this transitory phase a large number of Hollywood movies were shown on television. Against the background of
the recent history of American motion pictures, the development of
German movies as well as films made for television can best be understood via the distribution of Hollywood films on television.

By no means did Hollywood films on German television initially
enjoy great success. When ZDF showed the first western classic *Rio
Grande* (1950) by John Ford in 1963 as part of its evening programs,
the public did not express enthusiasm but more likely became irritat-
ed.[30] American movies became an important component of the movies shown on television at a time when the battle for viewer approval
had not become a problem. They were chosen because they were available and because experts regarded them as being significant in the
history of film-making. As late as 1968 ARD justified the broadcast
of Howard Hawk's *Red River* as follows: "Even a public that on its
own accord probably would not tune in to a western on Saturday night
should be confronted with an excellent example of this genre and possibly learn to like it. On the other hand it should be made clear that
westerns and gangster movies are not necessarily a vice among television programs, but rather an integral part of our overall concep-

---

[28] Hans Günther Pflaum and Hans Helmut Prinzler, *Film in der Bundesrepublik Deutschland. Der neue deutsche Film. Herkunft/Gegenwärtige Situation. Ein Handbuch* (München-
Wien: Hanser-Verlag, 1979) 22.
[29] Pflaum/Prinzler, *Film in der Bundesrepublik Deutschland* 23.
[30] See *Spielfilme im Deutschen Fernsehen* (1968-1969) 4.

tion, which aims to take great care in the selection and broadcast of films."[31]

In broadcasting movies, television popularized the historically important, and to a lesser extent, the more unimportant films of the 1930s, the 1940s and above all the 1950s in such a way as to greatly exceed the options available to movie theaters. The number of movies from the fifties was especially high. In part over half of all television viewers tuned in to these films in the late 1960s and the early 1970s. In terms of popularity among viewers, the movie reached its zenith during these years.

Ideas about film entertainment have been developed along the lines of Hollywood movies. This demand placed on films has also affected attitudes toward European productions and German films in particular. Attributes of Hollywood movies have become common knowledge and a yardstick for other films. It is along the lines of Hollywood's narrative movie that conventions for watching a film have developed. At this time the American narrative movie became the film prototype of pictures shown on television.

Television thus played a decisive role in the changes that occurred in the course of the 1960s. These changes extended parts of the adolescent subculture of the 1950s to include all generations, gradually gaining acceptance by German culture as a whole. At the same time, reactions to products of the American entertainment industry — not only its films, but for instance its music as well — were initially installed in the traditional idealistic concept of culture and in turn modified. The debate over triviality and appreciation of the masses, which was vehemently revived in the late 1960s, is to be seen against the background of these changes. It increasingly became a problem to label a production as trivial, as it could no longer be disputed that American movies increasingly influenced the media's realm of experience, nor that these films were shifting the conception of reality and changing expressive values. Movies broadcast on television accelerated this process, in the course of which the dominant code of conduct became more flexible, more plural and more differentiated. This "informalization" of the behavioral standard[32] is documented in statements such as the following: "Intellectuals have become accustomed not to judge the 'dreamland factory' (i.e., Hollywood) and

[31] *Spielfilme im Deutschen Fernsehen* (1968-1969) 7.
[32] Norbert Elias: *Studien über die Deutschen* (Frankfurt a.M.: Suhrkamp Verlag, 1989) 41ff.

the patterns of certain film genres solely in a condescending manner, but rather to recognize their legitimacy over and above all ideas of 'cultural goods' and even tend to discover their (pop) pleasure in them. In cultural criticism (even among sociological critics) entertainment and pleasure are no longer concepts having negative connotations."[33] In the cultural change indicated by such words, the traditional dichotomy of art vs. commerce, of the idealistic vs. the materialistic concept of culture has weakened. Normative confines have been relaxed.

Television has contributed to the fact that ideas about the world that are encoded by watching American films have now become common knowledge. Scenarios from westerns and adventure movies represent an essential part of the connotations of freedom and independence, of nature and civilization, of good and evil. Scenarios from crime movies leave their mark on associations regarding criminals, crimes and crime fighting as well as perpetrators and victims. Mental pictures of landscape, cities, streets and houses are influenced by the topography of films. Long before skylines developed in German cities television viewers were well familiar with such panoramas from American movies. The meaning of concepts such as love, intimacy, fidelity and unfaithfulness, freedom and constraint, became inseparable from experiences offered by television. The conflict between blacks and whites is a topic that is always discussed based on knowledge gained by watching television.

Such phenomenological observations can be supplemented by some considerations concerning which forms of narrative codification in these films have now become part of the social conscious.[34] Here attention is to be focused on the asymmetry between production and reception, between global tendencies and specific ethnographic developments.[35]

[33] *Spielfilme im Deutschen Fernsehen* (1968-1969) 4.
[34] See Bordwell (156-204), who, assuming narrative theories of cognitional psychology, has investigated narrative codification exemplified in Hollywood films. In order to be able to make profound statements about which forms of narrative codification are part of the social conscious, one could of course not only concentrate on movies, but should also include a comprehensive treatment of genre types in the investigation of narrative forms on television.
[35] For a discussion of ethnographic criticism, which cannot be treated here in detail, see, for instance, George E. Marcus and Michael M. J. Fischer: *Anthropology as Cultural Critique* (Chicago-London: University of California Press, 1986); Janice Radway: "Reception Study: Ethnography and the Problems of Dispersed Audiences and Nomadic Subjects," *Cultural Studies* 2.3 (1988) 359-76; Ien Ang: "Culture and Communication: Towards an Ethnographic Critique of Media Communication in

In the time period between the 1950s and the 1970s a change occurred in the general values observed by German society that can be described as a change "from values of duty and acceptability (which are falling overall) to values of self-development (which are rising overall)."[36] Klages summarizes the events of this change in values over the last few decades with three successive phases:

> Phase 1 (to the early/mid-1960s): Predominance of values which, compared to others, are clearly distinctive of duty and acceptability; exhibiting partial growth;
>
> Phase 2 (mid-1960s to the mid-1970s): Phase of clear decline in values of duty and acceptability accompanied by a simultaneous increase in values of self-development;
>
> Phase 3 (mid-1970s to today): Stagnation in the movement of changes in values accompanied by a comparatively high instability ('fluctuation') of values observed by people (or at least by a large number of people). (20)

Value orientations refer to standards to which human behavior aligns itself. They become effective when nonphysical conditions or social, political, or economic constraints determine behavior:

> Whenever people desire something or consider something to be 'important', whenever they follow role models or give their opinion on something as a person and pass judgment, 'values' play a decisive role. Those holding particular values needn't necessarily be consciously aware of them, as values can be embedded in social habits and 'norms' and in culturally determined forms of 'natural behavior'. They can also find expression in 'ideals' and in differentiated systems of societal ethics. (10)

Values function to guide behavior. Not all behavior, however, is guided by values. There are various "topicalization levels of value orientations" (12). In this connection it is helpful to distinguish between values and needs. Values have the character of internal plans, whereas needs or aspirations become effective in concrete behavioral situations. They are typically forms of behavior coupled with desires, goals, and intentions, in which considerations of the attainable and realizable play a role. Values are, according to Klages, "simply what is present 'inside of people' as a potential for evaluating, showing preference

the Transnational Media System," *European Journal of Communication* 5.2-3 (1990) 239-60. The following statements are hypotheses and not the results from empirical studies.
[36] Helmut Klages, *Wertorientierungen im Wandel* (Frankfurt a.M.-New York: Campus-Verlag, 1984) 17. Henceforth page numbers indicated within parentheses in the text.

and motivation, while 'needs' represent 'topicalized' values to be found at the level of behavior" (12). The division into two large groups of values which Klages assumes is a construct not so neatly present in social life and of which individuals in their everyday routine are not aware. Such typological descriptions in sociology have been commonly practiced and regarded as a generally accepted methodological approach since Max Weber.[37]

Thus, when investigating value preferences that are topicalized (i.e., become relevant) during the reception of movies, the relationship between the topicalized values ascribed to actors and their possible, hypothetical reference to viewers' value orientations can be taken into consideration.

The change in general values occurred during the phase in which television was becoming a mass medium. It is of course not being argued here that television or even movies broadcast on television alone brought about this change. Nonetheless, a relationship can be seen between the values encoded via American movies on the one hand, which formed an important part of programs aired on television, and the change in general values on the other. American films did not cause this change in values, but they certainly contributed to it, because the plots of these movies simply do not operate with the values of duty and acceptability, which are firmly established in German society. American films, as products of American society and its system of values, are not influenced by the typically German idea of authority, always including references to the authority of the state. They operate more commonly with the values of self-realization and self-development. The fact that American movies are more likely to operate with these values does not mean that emancipation in the political sense is the subject dealt with, nor does it mean that authorities or loyalty or discipline do not play a role. But one is not loyal, disciplined or humble toward a state authority, but toward a social group or community. The loyalty or discipline shown toward this group is not the same thing as the fulfillment of duty in the German sense. Rather, it always serves the purpose of self-development insofar as it brings happiness. Happiness in these films is not a social category, but has an individual or interpersonal reference: Happiness of the individual, between lovers, in the family. This happiness is not a variable of social significance, but primarily a psychological category.

---

[37] This methodical approach can also be found in the study by Milton Rokeach, *The Nature of Human Values* (New York, London: Collier Macmillan Publishers, 1973).

Attributing values to American movies on television in the manner discussed here means generalizing and making sweeping statements. This kind of value association can nonetheless be demonstrated in each of the genres of American film dominant on German television, namely westerns, crime films, comedies, melodramas and adventure movies (see Table 2).

The western hero is true to his own principles and not to any authority. The western scenario is dominated by the idea that the individual and lone hero will do justice for himself as part of his duty toward society. In movies by John Ford or Howard Hawks the western scenario is typically characterized by the idea that the individual and often lone hero sees to it that justice is done for himself and also as an obligation toward society. John Wayne became the archetypical western hero in movies like *Fort Apache* (1948), *The Man Who Shot Liberty Valence* (1962), *Rio Bravo* (1959) or *Hatari* (1961), in which he portrays the role of a rough and independent person, but never mean or cruel. The bad guy is the person who has no principles whatsoever and not the person insubordinate toward some authority. Since the film noir, the crime film is not distinguished by the fact that the criminal is depicted as the adversary of law and order. It is rather crime and laws which are made the issue here. Examples of this are movies like *The Big Sleep* (1946) by Howard Hawks, *The Street with No Name* (1948) by William Keighley, *The Dark Mirror* (1946) by Robert Siodmak or *Key Largo* (1949) by John Huston.

The characters of Alfred Hitchcock, the director whose films have been shown the most often on German television, do not experience a conflict with society, but rather an internal conflict. The psychological exploration of one's own past and one's own feelings is one of the methods of resolving the conflict. Conflicts occur in comedies such as *Hands across the Table* (1939) or *Midnight* (1939) by Mitchell Leisen and melodramas like *Casablanca* (1942, directed by Michael Curtiz) by means of interpersonal intrigues, misunderstandings or failings. The adventure film is meant for those who are interested in adventures that broaden the horizon of individual experience. A final fact can be mentioned which seems to demonstrate the orientation of American movies to values of self-development and self-realization: The majority of films consists of a double plot, one of which is centered around a love story, most of the time having a happy ending. Happiness in love, however, is a very seldom outcome of a film oriented to the values of duty and acceptability. These more often lead to failure in love.

In the 1960s and early 1970s, when these American genres became increasingly more dominant on German television, not only in a quantitative sense, but also as an attraction appealing to viewers, the change in general values mentioned above took place, embedded in a number of other factors. The fact that television made its contribution to this change in the role of a socialization agency cannot be disputed. Which role American films played cannot be explained by the pattern of cause and effect. The only aim here is to make reference to the fact that these movies are among the indicators of the change.

The reasons why American movies enjoyed comparatively little popularity when they were shown at movie theaters in the 1950s, but then achieved great success in the late 1960s and early 1970s, seem to lie within the bounds discussed above. American motion pictures of the 1950s became attractive items in the 1960s and 1970s because they corresponded more to the changes in the ideas about reality, which occurred at that time in comparison to the restorative orientations of the 1950s.

V

From the mid 1960s to the mid 1970s, American movies were initially shown on television because they were felt to represent the best in film-making history. The following period was a phase of familiarization, during which films became increasingly attractive for viewers. This time period is linked to two conditions that were not present in subsequent decades: (1) Movies could be selected from a wide variety of available films and acquired at prices that were affordable. Neither movies nor money were scarce. (2) The number of viewers and the amount of television consumption continuously increased during this time. Achieving viewer approval was not yet a problem.

In the early 1970s the question as to which movies could become "hits" played an increasingly important role. The success of movies on television was no longer measured according to the nature of the films themselves, but rather the number of viewers they could reach. The question regarding how such films would be judged by film experts became a secondary issue. These movies were considered to be a guarantee for public approval that offered viewers "exciting entertainment." "Not only is Hollywood the most productive film capital of the world. It is simultaneously the most reliable guarantee for the quality of entertainment, that the public unequivocally expects."[38]

[38] *Der Spielfilm im ZDF* 2 (1975) 2.

Viewer demands were interpreted not in a plural manner, as was the case in the first two decades of television, but rather in a uniform way, oriented to the narrative films of Hollywood. The American movie genres represented on German television were primarily crime films, westerns, comedies, melodramas and adventure movies. From the beginning of broadcasting in 1954 up through 1985, these genres together make up 61% of all American movies shown on ARD and 70% of those on ZDF (see Table 2).

Table 2

Film Genres of U. S. Movies Broadcast on ARD and ZDF: 1954-1985
(Amounts given in percent)

Adventure	10.1	Horror film	1.0
Animal film	1.3	Literary classic	0.8
Animated film	0.2	Melodrama	12.1
Biography	2.5	Musical	3.9
Catastrophe film	0.9	Political film	0.1
Children's film	1.4	Psychological film	1.7
Comedy	16.2	Satirical film	0.5
Crime film	9.9	Science fiction	1.6
Current events	1.3	Short film	0.0
Documentary	1.0	Slapstick	3.3
Domestic drama	2.0	Spy film	0.5
Experimental film	0.1	Thriller	6.8
Fantasy film	1.3	War film	1.0
Historical film	1.6	Western	16.7
		Other	0.1

Source: Databank of Project Section B5 (Special Collaborative Research Department 240 "TV Screen Media," Universität-GH Siegen).

Edgar Wallace and Karl May movies were no longer for moviegoers but for television viewers, who could watch these movies on ZDF in 1973 during prime time viewing hours. In the 1970s both of these groups of movies were among the most successful television programs in the eyes of the viewers. According to a survey conducted at this time, it was determined that viewers "expect all of the things from this kind of program that they expect from a good movie theater, above all entertainment, excitement, variety, international stars, in short, that great viewing pleasure that makes the motion picture theater so unmistakable."[39]

In the early 1970s it was already becoming apparent that the demand for movies for television programs was greater than the available potential of films that were affordable and could be broadcast.

[39] *Der Spielfilm im ZDF* 2 (1976) 2.

Especially the American market was now putting together more colossal productions, "that in the foreseeable future will no longer be available to television, because they are likely to achieve long-running commercial success."[40] These monumental productions have enjoyed great success in German movie theaters. The number of B-pictures has decreased. The war for film licensing rights has intensified due to the competition of private television stations and the ever expanding video market. Acquisition rights have been purchased for amounts that go far beyond what stations can afford to pay.[41] One way out of this situation in which stations found themselves was to repeat the broadcast of movies they already had the rights for. As far as American films are concerned, besides the growing number of reruns, two tendencies can be observed since the mid-1970s, which can both clearly be seen in the context of movie scarcity: First, program planners continue to dig around in the archives, but have increasingly had to make do with the "second choice," because the first choice is no longer sufficient to meet demand. Second, planners increasingly attempted to procure newer movies. All of these efforts could not prevent the American movie on German television from gradually losing popularity in the course of the 1980s. They were no longer a guarantee for high viewer ratings, but achieved average, relatively stable ratings instead.

As a reaction to higher market competition for film rights brought about by the private stations, a hectic purchasing policy developed in the early 1980s. In 1984, ARD acquired the rights for 1,350 films from a total stock of approximately 3,000 movies from the American film company Metro-Goldwyn-Mayer/United Artists for $80 million. Almost at the same time ZDF purchased a package of 1,264 films for 258 million German Marks which, among others, contained the rights for the popular film classic *Gone with the Wind.*

These package purchases made by ARD and ZDF led to the first large-scale public debate on the number of American productions on German television. The discussion was dominated by polemic formulations such as "Americanism until the year 2013"[42] and the public television stations were blamed for being on "a commercial course that could hardly be reconciled with international treaties."[43] A new debate began regarding quotas, as those that have long been prac-

---

[40] *Spielfilme im Deutschen Fernsehen* (1979) 8.

[41] See *ARD-Jahrbuch* (1982) 103.

[42] Vera Gaserow, "Amerikanismus bis ins Jahr 2013," *Die Tageszeitung/taz*: December 12, 1983.

[43] Werner Grassmann, "Das zweite Kino-Sterben," *Die Zeit*: November 22, 1985.

ticed in France.[44] The discussion focused on two issues: (1) Both film-makers and film critics assumed that movies on television would reduce the number of moviegoers. In the first half of 1985 movie theaters experienced losses of up to 40%, which was attributed to television. (2) Politicians for cultural issues of various political parties as well as producers assumed that money used to purchase licenses for American motion pictures would continue to deplete the budgets for German productions. They demanded that the national film culture be protected. Both arguments overlook the fact that over the past thirty years of television history viewers have formed certain habits that cannot be changed by mere legislation. Empirical analyses of motives for going to the movie theater show that television without movies will by no means increase the number of moviegoers. In a world community created by modern communication media, the demand for a national film culture seems to be a *petitio principii*, even for many producers. As the producer Günter Rohrbach commented in 1988: "Hollywood has made the American way of life a kind of world standard. In comparison, films from other countries of the world have a provincial effect, admittedly with a little luck more specific and more real."[45] This "luck," however, is very seldom and more seldom still is the public for these lucky films, because the world standard of movies is tied to the world views of producers and their audiences. And these world views are apparently less influenced by national and specific elements than by notions of delocalization, dematerialization and derealization. The choice between the American way of life and the specific assumes the option of a cultural identity, which is contemplated independent of cultural frames that are formed by the media of the world community.

American motion pictures on German television are part of the recent history of the postmodern discourse, and they contribute to the postmodern situation when the television viewer, during an evening in front of the television set, can flip through half a century of the film history of the Western world. The movie does not offer a look out into the wide world, but rather a world which has become so within the confines of one's small quarters.

Translated by Ron Kresta

---

[44] See Andreas J. Wiesand, "Dämme gegen eine Flut von Billig-Programmen?" *Media Perspektiven* 3 (1985) 191-213.
[45] Günther Rohrbach, "Würgen und Streicheln. Film und Fernsehen: Partner oder Konkurrenten," *Rundfunk und Fernsehen* 59-60 (1988) 5-10.

Occidentalist Theater in Post-Mao China: Shakespeare, Ibsen, and Brecht as Counter-Others

XIAOMEI CHEN

The current debate on postcolonial and postmodern conditions has produced a number of exciting scholarly inquiries, among them Jyotsna Singh's insightful historical recount of the cultural imperialism manifested in the production of Shakespeare in India. Singh demonstrates how the English Bard "kept alive the myth of English cultural refinement and superiority — a myth that was crucial to the rulers' political interests in colonial India."[1] This study is an especially valuable contribution to the current debate because of the way it illustrates how the construction of English literature and the exporting of the English language consolidated the political and ideological hegemony of the colonial Empire in Third-World countries. Singh's study has ramifications beyond India, however. It certainly encourages following her model in producing reception histories of other non-Western cultures that shared some of the historical conditions that marked colonial India. Among these is twentieth-century China, where the introduction of English and other Western literary and philosophical traditions have fundamentally shaped the theory and practice of literature since the beginning of the May Fourth movement (1919).[2]

A recent study of modern Chinese literature along these lines can be found in Rey Chow's *Woman and Chinese Modernity: The Politics of*

---

[1] Jyotsna Singh, "Different Shakespeares: The Bard in Colonial/Postcolonial India," *Theater Journal* 41.4 (1989) 445-58.

[2] On May 4, 1919, citizens and students of Beijing protested in the streets against the Versailles treaty that granted Japan the right to station police and to establish

155

Reading between West and East. Exploring China's contact with the West during the May Fourth period, Rey chow observes: "the espousal of the Western as the 'new' and the 'modern,' and thus the 'civilized' (*wenming*), meant the beginning of a long process of cultural imperialism that was to last beyond China's subsequent retrieval of her leased territories and official concessions."[3] In the area of feminist discourse in a non-Western context, I have argued elsewhere that the image of Western education originally deployed in May Fourth fiction and drama as a strategy against the traditional culture at home turned out to be politicized in the international arena as yet another way in which Western fathers subjugated and colonialized Third-World women. Thus Bing Xin, the much celebrated "first woman writer" in modern Chinese literature, presented herself as a "privileged" and "superior" woman who sees her sisters' problems in male terms — and especially in Western male terms — thus creating her own vision of what I call "Chinese Western-cultural-imperialism."[4]

Arguing against cultural imperialism is, however, to explore only one side of the coin, albeit an important one. It can indeed become problematic when considered in the broader context of cultural and ideological specifics within a totalitarian society. In this essay, I will demonstrate that on the contemporary Chinese stage the production and reception of Shakespearean and other Western dramas — the literary and dramatic representations of an Occidental "Other" — can help, and perhaps even inspire, the Chinese "Self" to express the politically forbidden and ideologically impossible within the limitations of their indigenous cultural conditions. Thus, the representation of a Western "Other" imposed from within — which can easily be characterized as an act of "cultural imperialism" — can also be understood

military garrisons in Jinan and Qingdao in spite of the fact that China was among the winning countries after the war. The movement embraced an important period of unparalleled intellectual exploration and debates among Chinese intellectuals on the future of China, especially on the values of new forms in language, education, and cultural forms. For a comprehensive survey of the movement, see Chow Tse-tsung, *The May 4th Movement: Intellectual Revolution in Modern China* (Cambridge, Mass.: Harvard University Press, 1960).

[3] Rey Chow, *Woman and Chinese Modernity: The Politics of Reading between West and East* (Minnesota: University of Minnesota Press, 1991) 35.

[4] Xiaomei Chen, "Fathers and Daughters in Early Modern Chinese Drama: On the Problematics of Feminist Discourse in Cross-Cultural Perspective," in *Understanding Women: The Challenge of Cross-Cultural Perspectives*, ed. Marilyn Robinson Waldman, Artemis Leontis, and Müge Galin, Special Issue of *Papers in Comparative Studies* 7 (1991-92) 205-22.

as a powerful antiofficial discourse that has been persistently employed by the Chinese intelligentsia to achieve a political liberation against the ideological oppression within a totalitarian society.[5]

Seen in this light, post-Mao Chinese theater presents us with a compelling example of "Occidentalism," by which I mean a Chinese representation of the Occident as "its deepest and most recurring images of the Other."[6] Such "Occidentalism" may be considered as a counter-discourse, a counter-memory, and a counter-"Other" to Edward Said's "Orientalism." These terms, of course, evoke Michel Foucault's notion of "discourse," employed also by Said in his definition of "Orientalism," as "a Western style for dominating, restructuring, and having authority over the Orient."[7] Yet a critical difference between Said and Foucault's conceptions, as noted by Uta Liebmann Schaub, resides in the fact that "whereas Foucault allows for the emergence of counter-discourses beneath the official discourse of power, Said ignores Western discourses about the Orient that oppose Western expansionism and subvert, rather than support, Western domination."[8] The same can be argued from yet another angle: Said does not explore the possibility of any antiofficial discourse that employs "Occidentalism" to combat the official cultural hegemony at home within a non-Western culture. In such a case, the Western "Other" becomes a metaphor for a political liberation against indigenous forms of ideological oppression.

Here we see two different power structures interacting with each other: on the one hand, a "global" Western cultural imperialism may employ "Orientalism" for its political and economic gain of power, as Said has made abundantly clear; on the other hand, a local ideological and literary "Occidentalism" can, in turn, be employed as an antistructural device to challenge an indigenous totalitarian regime within a non-Western society. What was once conceived of as the global, central discourse of "Occidentalism" can, for the most part, be used or "misused" as a locally "marginal" or "peripheral" language against the centrality of the dominant power in an indigenous culture. The evocation of the West, as a counterpart of the indigenous Chinese

---

[5] For a more elaborated analysis of Occidentalism and its politically liberating function in post-Mao China, see my article, "Occidentalism as Counterdiscourse: *He Shang* in Post-Mao China," *Critical Inquiry* 18.4 (1992) 686-712.

[6] Edward Said, *Orientalism* (New York: Vintage, 1979) 1.

[7] Said 3.

[8] Uta Liebmann Schaub, "Foucault's Oriental Subtext," *PMLA* 104.3 (1989) 306-15.

culture, has more than once set in motion a kind of "dialogic imagination," which in turn becomes a dynamic and dialectical force in the making of modern Chinese history — both literary and political. One problem, therefore, with the ongoing debates on Orientalism — and by extension, on certain aspects of Third-World and anticolonial discourses — is that it is possible to interpret Said's *Orientalism* as working under the assumption that any kind of cultural appropriation is necessarily negative, being either an act of imperialistic colonialization when performed by the "superior" culture, or of self-colonialization when conducted by the "inferior" culture in the context of global domination. These certainly are assumptions that are traceable in Said's work and, hence, very much in the air in the current debate on Third-World discourse. I hope to illustrate in this essay, however, that ideas of ideological concepts are never intrinsically negative in themselves. The Chinese appropriation of the image of the West, then put into critical use against the domestic hegemony of the ruling ideology, can be viewed, at least when seen from certain perspectives, as commendable and even desirable.

Before going into the cultural and historical specifics of the post-Mao theater, several points must be clarified. I have argued elsewhere that Chinese Occidentalism, characterized as it is by a paradoxical and problematic relationship with the Western Orientalism, might be regarded as consisting of two quite different appropriations of the same discourse for strikingly different political ends. In what I term "official Occidentalism," the Chinese government uses the essentialization of the West as a means for supporting a nationalism that effects the internal suppression of its own people, as exemplified in Mao Zedong's theory of "three worlds." Although self-proclaimed as an anti-imperialist discourse against the two superpowers, the United States and what used to be the Soviet Union, Mao's global theory of world revolution was part and parcel of his radical ideology to promote the Chinese Cultural Revolution. Alongside this official Occidentalism, we can readily find examples of what we might term "antiofficial Occidentalism," the purveyors of which are usually the Chinese intellectuals whose knowledge and literacy are maneuvered into its own practice of power against the powerful status quo. In my article "Occidentalism as Counterdiscourse: *He Shang* in Post-Mao China," I focused on the controversial television series *He Shang* as a quintessential example of antiofficial Occidentalism.[9] In this essay, I will

[9] Chen 693-704.

elaborate a third kind of Chinese Occidentalism, in which the anti-official Occidentalism against the Maoist autocracy in early post-Mao China significantly overlapped with the official Occidentalism of the current regime, which, for reasons of its own, briefly tolerated, and even encouraged, the intellectuals' anti-Maoist sentiments that could easily be manipulated into legitimizing the political legacy of the post-Mao regime itself.

In this instance, we see an interesting transaction of what Pierre Bourdieu terms "cultural capital" in which the knowledge, qualification, and recognition associated with the image of the West became political capital for the predominant ruling ideology of the post-Mao regime.[10] The "cultural capital" of things Western had accumulated but remained untapped since the repression of the West in the Maoist era. Indeed, its value had increased by virtue of its association with all things repressed by a tyrannical regime. Thus, its considerable assets were ready to be tapped for a variety of different ends in the post-Maoist era. The attractiveness of the West in early post-Mao China is best demonstrated in the popular productions of Shakespearean plays; indeed, any Western play — no matter who wrote it — could have had a large following in this specific moment in time since the very act of performing Western play on stage was itself a form of political discourse directed against the previous regime. By liberating the previously repressed Western discourse, the post-Mao regime was able to draw upon its cultural prestige and present itself as a liberator. In this particular circumstance, the Chinese intellectuals found a temporarily overlapping space between the official ideology and the antiofficial discourse, a space in which Chinese dramatists could wear Western costumes and speak in the voice of the "other," while spontaneously expressing their grievances against the political power, which the post-Mao regime has just inherited from its predecessor. It is thus important to bear in mind that when the Chinese intellectuals were promoting the West in their theater productions, their seeming celebrations of the current political regime were

---

[10] See Pierre Bourdieu, *An Outline of a Theory of Practice*, tr. Richard Nice (Cambridge: Cambridge University Press, 1977), *Distinction: A Social Critique of the Judgment of Taste*, tr. Richard Nice (Cambridge: Harvard University Press, 1984), *Homo Academicus*, tr. Peter Collier (Cambridge: Polity Press, 1988), *The Logic of Practice*, tr. Richard Nice (Cambridge: Polity Press, 1990), *Language and Symbolic Power*, ed. John B. Thompson, tr. Gino Raymond and Matthew Adamson (Cambridge: Polity Press, 1991).

on many occasions used as a cover-up for criticizing the communist system in general, a system that produced a Maoist regime as well as a Dengist one, and one which was soon, in 1983, to turn its back against the West and the intellectuals who had openly advocated its values and system.

In early post-Mao China, for instance, an otherwise "alien" production of Shakespeare's *Macbeth* [Makebaisi] was popular precisely because the Renaissance text was appropriated by the Chinese audiences as immediately relating to their traumatic experiences during the Cultural Revolution. The Chinese intelligentsia in the early 1980s felt an urgent need to revive the Shakespearean canon after the political upheaval of the Cultural Revolution, an event which, to most Chinese, was an approximation of chaos, brutality, conspiracy, and repression. The political atmosphere after Mao Zedong's death in 1976 and his widow Jiang Qing's later arrest endowed the play with a particular significance that only the Chinese who had survived the Cultural Revolution could fully appreciate. For many Chinese audiences, Macbeth's tragedy reminded them of Mao's sad history of how a national hero, who had fought courageously for the founding of his country, was declared a traitor and finally driven to death — both spiritually and physically — by his power-hungry wife.

During a discussion of the Central Drama College production of *Macbeth* that premiered in 1980 in Beijing, many critics focused on the significant theme of the play and its immediate relevance to the social and political concerns of contemporary China. They all agreed that the play was about "how the greed for absolute and supreme power finally turned a hero into a traitor." Owing to the strict censorship of the Chinese government, which at that time was still reluctant to openly admit Mao's mistakes, there were, naturally, no direct connections spelled out between Mao's errors during the Cultural Revolution and the thematic concerns of the play. The similarities between the drama of Mao and Macbeth, however, were clear to almost any Chinese who had seen and somehow "understood" the play. Indeed, the allusions to Chinese political life were more than transparent to many. Zhao Xun, the Deputy Chairman of the national Association of Chinese Dramatists observed that "*Macbeth* is the fifth Shakespearean play produced on the Chinese stage after the smashing of the Gang of Four. This play of conspiracy has always been performed at critical moments in the history of our nation."[11] In the same letter and

---

[11] Furong Wu, "Macbeth and Chinese Stage" [Makemaisi he zhongguo wutai]," *Foreign Drama* [Waiguo xiju] 2 (1981) 90-92.

spirit, the program notes of *Macbeth* viewed the play as a vivid depiction of the moral decline in Macbeth and Lady Macbeth, and as a play that explored the theme of how "desire for power and ambition are the roots of evils," which "will eventually be punished by the people." Thus, the performance of this tragedy has its "realist significance" especially today, it was claimed.[12]

No theatergoers in 1980 China could have missed the implied message. Indeed, for the majority of the members of Chinese audiences that watched the Shakespearean world of intrigue and conspiracy in *Macbeth*, it was no doubt difficult to forget their terrifying experiences during the Cultural Revolution, a national catastrophe in which Mao and his followers persecuted numerous Party officials, state leaders, and old "comrades-in-arms." Contrary to their own wishes, however, both of them — Macbeth the character and Mao the historical figure — had only brought ruin and disgrace on themselves. Such a reading of *Macbeth* was perhaps the only way that the remote English play could become meaningful to its Chinese audiences in the year 1980.

In contrast to the Chinese audiences' likely reception, the producers and directors of *Macbeth* claimed that they sought to produce *Macbeth* according to the "authorial intention" of the playwright in order to explore the artistic style of Shakespearean drama. After the downfall of the Gang of Four, it was argued, they tried to produce as many "authentic" foreign plays as possible since they were strictly forbidden to do so during the Cultural Revolution. Even during this "purely artistic" experience, however, Xu Xiaozhong and Li Zibo, the directors of this production of *Macbeth*, had to admit the fact that the play "bears a significance which reaches beyond its own historicity" for "reflecting the nature and law of a specific historical period."[13] Such a remark suggests a recognition on their part of the fact that, for most of their audience, *Macbeth* could not but be a commentary on the Cultural Revolution, and its lasting psychological effects. Seen from this perspective, this post-Cultural-Revolutionary Chinese production of *Macbeth* is at least twice removed from the "original intentions" of either its early seventeenth-century English playwright or of its twentieth-century Chinese producers. Yet it would be difficult, and foolish, to

---

[12] Quoted from "Directors' Words" in the program notes of *Macbeth* produced by the Central Drama College, directed by Xu Xiaozhong and Li Zibo, Beijing, 1980.
[13] Xiaozhong Xu and Li Zibo, "The Tragedy of the Horse-man: On *Macbeth* and Its Production" [Marende beiju: tan beiju Makebaisi jiqi yanchu], *People's Drama* [Renmin xiju] 2 (1982) 40-44.

fault this historical and cultural "misunderstanding," or to criticize this example of a Chinese Occidentalism. Under these circumstances, who could possibly prefer an "authentic" *Macbeth* in Beijing? And who could define what would constitute "authenticity" and "correctness" in these circumstances? Short of converting twentieth-century Chinese into seventeenth-century Elizabethans, what kind of "authenticity" might have been possible? Indeed, it is here in the production of the English Bard's renaissance play that we see a re-enactment of the twentieth-century Chinese everyday reality of intrigue and conspiracy. Both by acting the roles of the Occidentalist Other and by watching the Occidentalist Other being enacted on stage, the Chinese people experienced a catharsis during which the memory of the past was cleansed and a reconciliation with the present was at least temporarily granted possible during the limited time and space of theatrical experience. Here, the Occidentalist theater played an important role in the Chinese recovery from the tragedy of an immediate cultural past.

This enactment of the Occidental Other on the Chinese stage as a means of political liberation can also be found in other Shakespearean productions in post-Mao China. The 1982 production of *King Lear* [Li'erwang] by the Director Training Class of Shanghai Drama School was applauded by the distinguished Shakespearean scholar Fang Ping as a "significant event" because the play above all else reminded the Chinese people of "the moral decline of the Cultural-Revolutionary days when human beings' souls were so polluted that they even maltreated their aged parents" — just like the two oldest daughters who abuse their own father King Lear.[14] Another "realistic significance" of the play, Fang continues, is that it teaches us a lesson about the tense and complex political struggle in which we must learn how to differentiate friends from enemies, or how to differentiate the flattering, hypocritical Goneril and Regan from the honest and filial Cordelia. Furthermore, Fang claims, the play bridges the historical and cultural distance between an Occidental past and a Chinese present through a vivid characterization of King Lear as "the highest rule of a monarchy," who creates a chaotic world in which "the loyal are punished and the treacherous are rewarded."[15] This is, of course, another allusion to Mao's irrational behavior in his old age and its trag-

---

[14] Ping Fang, "Welcome You, King Lear [Huanying ni, Lie'wang]," *Shanghai Drama* [Shanghai xiju] 5 (1982) 19-21.
[15] Fang 20.

ic consequences in the life and conduct of the individual during and after the Cultural Revolution.

In contrast to these negative traits of human beings, the play was also viewed as a eulogy of the "pure love" and the "beautiful souls" of Goneril and Edgar. It is here that we found perhaps one of the most unexpected readings of *King Lear*: "although our concept of love is different from that of the Renaissance humanist in the Occident," Fang claimed, "we nevertheless need the same kind of beautiful soul, which is full of warmth and noble love, not just for our relatives and families, but also for our comrades, our motherland, and our dear party in the construction of our glorious socialist society. We should live as a poet, who loves everything that is beautiful."[16] This is, of course, a typical expression of early post-Cultural-Revolutionary political jargon that always demanded an affirmation of a bright future for the Party and its "triumphant" socialist course, even after a necessary exposure of the bad Party renegades, such as the Gang of Four, who "temporarily" usurped the Party's leadership during the Cultural Revolution. Yet it clearly testifies to the multifaceted appeal of a popular Shakespeare, who was appropriated as something "Chinese," and who for this very reason — and this reason alone — came to play his own dramatic role at this moment of cross-cultural literary history in early post-Mao China.

Likewise, the 1981 China Youth Theater production of *The Merchant of Venice* [Weinisi shangren] also foregrounded the theme of "eulogizing *zhen-shan-mei*, or "the true, the good, and the beautiful" as a counter-discourse against "the fake, the evil, and the ugly" Cultural-Revolutionary life and politics.[17] "After so many years of turning the good into the evil," Director Zhang Qihong recalled with emotion, "how urgently do we need to promote justice and friendship in our life."[18] Such a promotion of a better life was not surprisingly achieved through Chinese dramatists' annexation of the Occidental play. In

[16] Fang 21.

[17] According to Chen Dingsha, *The Merchant of Venice* was first produced in China in 1913 by New People's Theater [Xinminshe]. During several different productions mounted around that time, the play's titles varied from *A Pound of Flesh* [Yibangrou], *A Pound of Flesh as Loan Payment* [Jiezhai gerou], to *Meat Money* [Roujuan] and *Woman Lawyer* [Nülüshi]. See Chen Dingsha, "Shakespearean Productions in Early Modern Chinese Stage," *Drama Journal* [Xijubao] 12 (1983) 57.

[18] Qihong Zhang, "A Few Words about My Experience and Experimentation in Directing *The Merchant of Venice* [Zai shijian he tansuo zhongde jidian tihui]," *People's Drama* 1 (1981) 17-21.

order to highlight such a political theme, Zhang had to abbreviate those plots concerning the religious and racial conflicts (Christian vs. Jew) in *The Merchant of Venice* — which, according to her judgment, "were too unfamiliar cultural backgrounds for the Chinese audiences to fully appreciate anyway" — so that the "major" class contradictions "could be foregrounded between Antonio, the rising bourgeois, and Shylock, the feudalist exploiter."[19]

To further strengthen such a politicized theme, both Portia and Jessica were beautifully portrayed for the purpose of representing "the humanist spirit of the renaissance period," which strives for individuality, human rights, and freedom against a feudalist autocracy."[20] Such an appropriation of Shakespearean themes for an extended political allegory was naturally questioned by Chinese drama critics and Shakespeare scholars. Zhou Peitong argued that a culturally and racially oppressed Shylock is crucial to the integrity and complexities of the Shakespearean play, whose power lies precisely in "the tragic fate of a *Jewish* Shylock."[21] Yet, such a deviation from the "original" text did not bother the members of the Chinese audiences, who loved the play for its very relevance to their own Cultural-Revolutionary experiences during which they encountered too many "heartless" and "selfish" Shylocks. The "kind" and "honest" Portia thus became their new cultural model for a freer and better life. The setting of Venice as a harsh and morally bankrupt city embodied for them a "realistic significance," as Director Zhang Qihong has rightly claimed.[22]

Others, however, enjoyed the play simply because it was produced as a romantic comedy that had deviated from the prevailing mode of "social problem plays" in the early days of post-Mao China. Yang Tiancun, for instance, has testified that, in contrast to the predominant serious plays that merely invited one to think about the social concerns, the joyful and humorous events in *The Merchant of Venice* somehow made him forget everyday reality and a painful past so that he could more fully enjoy the happy moments in his theatrical experience. This effect of the theater, Yang asserts, should be viewed as an important function of literature and art, which encourages one's

[19] Zhang 18.
[20] Zhang 18.
[21] Peitong Zhou, "We Need Both Daring Innovations and Faithful Representations — On China Youth Theater's Production of *The Merchant of Venice* [Jiyao dadan chuxin, yeyao zhongshi yuanzuo — ping Zhongguo Qingnian Yishu Juyuan yanchude Weinisi Shangren], *People's Drama* 1 (1981) 19-21.
[22] Zhang 17.

new vision in and a persistent pursuit for a better future.[23] Yet it is important to note that Yang's remarks were made in 1981 when the majority of the Chinese audiences were tired of a highly political — and politicized — everyday life and an indigenous theater that was always intended as part of a political education, either to fully support the Maoist regime as had happened during the Cultural Revolution in a promotion of the "eight revolutionary model plays," or to denunciate Maoist art only to valorize the new official ideology of a Dengist de-Maolization. Thus, a defamiliarized stage representing life and love in a remote Occident offered a welcoming dose of relief and recreation.

Yet, however much one attempts to disassociate himself/herself from the political aspects of the theater, it is still common to find, for instance, readings of *The Merchant of Venice* that link it to topical subjects such as the economic reform of post-Mao China, as was demonstrated in an article entitled "A Song of an Enterprising Spirit: On the True Meaning of *The Merchant of Venice*." In this article, Hao Yin emphasized the title of the play, which, according to him, pointed to the important role of the merchant class in the historical site of Venice, which was then the cradle of commercialism and capitalism in the West. Thus, he claimed, with the very title of the play, Shakespeare already affirmed the positive and heroic status of Antonio, who represents courage, virtue, and spirit of the rising class of bourgeoisie, a class that had taken the lead in the industrial revolution of England. Traditionally in Chinese Shakespearean criticism, Hao further argued, Shylock has always been inappropriately singled out as the most negative character in the play since he, in contrast to Antonio, is a bad and heartless business man. Hao observed, however, that this Chinese degradation of Shylock had a great deal to do with traditional Chinese culture, which looked down upon merchants in favor of farmers, who were believed to be engaged in honest and productive activities. Yet, the argument continues, this antimerchant mentality is rapidly changing in the current economic reform. Thanks to the correct party policies at present, Hao argued, peasants and farmers are now increasingly proud of becoming successful business men and women and, in some cases, even "millenaries." Inevitably, then, Shylock could be seen in a new and more positive light.

---

[23] Tianchun Yang, "Watching *The Merchant of Venice* [Kan Weinisi Shangren]," *Drama and Film* [Xiju yu dianying] 7 (1981) 28-31.

After interpreting *The Merchant of Venice* as a play that was immediately related to contemporary Chinese reality, Hao Yin went on to give a long Marxist recounting of the age of Queen Elizabeth, during which "capital was being accumulated through world trade at the highest speed." As if this sociological and cultural background were not enough to support his thesis, Hao surprisingly presented a biographical account of Shakespeare himself, who had left home at the age of sixteen, leaving behind his wife and two children. Despite the conventional explanation of "a deer incident," Hao argued, the "real reason" for the English Bard's home-leaving was that he "was no exception from the rest of the young people of his own generation, who had chosen to travel extensively to the outside world to seek for an adventure and a career in order to find his own fortune" (22-23). Seen in this light, then, Hao believed that "the Shakespearean characters and themes in this play were indeed products of a hurricane of enterprising developments in all walks of life that had swept Shakespeare away from his hometown and landed him squarely in London, the center of economic development in England at that time. This is, indeed, the central theme of *The Merchant of Venice.*"[24] In Hao's view, then, *The Merchant of Venice* presented "a miniature world of competition in a market economy" and "promoted the idea of economic efficiency." In the last analysis, therefore, Shakespeare "provided the merchant class with a living picture of how to liberate itself from conventional modes of thinking and behavior," thus leaving behind a precious lesson for his readers and audiences in the many years to come (Hao 20).[25]

In this episode of Shakespearean reception, the evocation of an economic reform seems to support Deng Xiaoping's regime which, at that time, attempted to differentiate itself from its radical predecessors of the Cultural Revolution, predecessors who repelled the West and its social and economic structure alike. In the case of Hao Yin's interpretation of the Shakespearean play, we see a complicated phenomenon in which the intellectual's appeal to the Occident as a

[24] Yin Hao, "A Song of an Enterprising Spirit: On the True Meaning of *The Merchant of Venice* [Yiqu dui xinshen jinquzhe de zange: lun Weinisi Shangren de zhenti]," *Journal of Nanyang Normal College,* [Nanyang shizhuan xuebao, shekeban] 1 (1986) 20-27.

[25] For a more detailed account of the reception of *The Merchant of Venice* in China since the beginning of the twentieth century, see Fan Shen, "Shakespeare in China: *The Merchant of Venice*," *Asian Theater Journal* 5.2 (1988) 23-37.

complementary Other to change Chinese society for the better seems temporarily to coincide with the Dengist official ideology. Deng's regime had a history of a love-and-hate relationship with the Occident, for it attempted to experiment with an Occident-like economy without, paradoxically, introducing the Western social and ideological system. Seen from another angle, one may also argue that the image of the West was explored not only by the Chinese intellectuals as a powerful weapon against the ruling ideology; it has also been skillfully used, from time to time, by the Dengist reformers as a political weapon against the Maoist conservatives who resisted even an economic reform. It is thus ironic to note that when the Chinese people followed the call to duty by the Communist Party to push for a political reform — a reform that was also initiated by Deng Xiaoping himself — their historic pro-Western drama was eventually oppressed by the Dengist regime itself during the 1989 Tian'anmen student demonstration when the Statue of Liberty was transformed into the Goddess of Democracy. Here, the image of the West was once again repelled and rejected by Deng Xiaoping since this image was now endowed with a political statement against Deng himself. Here we see a typical example of how the West has become the signifier of a set of value systems, imagined and fictionalized, that are used to create a cultural and ideological message put forth in opposition to the Chinese official Other. In some instances, the West is also used as a powerful image against the official conservative Other by the official radical Self, who, as recent history has ironically proven, eventually allied itself with the conservative Other in their suppression of the Chinese people. Here we see a full implication of the problematic and paradoxical function of an Occidental Other in contemporary Chinese society.

In 1988, with the benefit of a few years' hindsight, Zhang Xiaoyang came to offer a fuller explanation of what he termed a "metamorphosis of Shakespeare on Chinese stage." Commenting on the tremendous success and popularity of the 1986 "China Shakespeare Festival," during which many Shakespearean plays were produced both in modern theaters and in diverse traditional operatic theaters such as *kunqu* (Jiangsu and Zhejiang opera) and *huangmeixi* (Anhui opera), Zhang Xiaoyang believed that contemporary Chinese society had "the best cultural and historical conditions" to "perfectly understand" and "completely receive" the dramas of the English Bard since the unique positions of the two peoples in their own histories provided them with "the best opportunity to apprehend each other's values, experiences, and emotions."[26] To further elaborate these "shared historical conditions," Zhang Xiaoyang emphasized the fact that both post-renaissance Elizabethan and post-Cultural-Revolutionary Chinese society experienced the same transitional period from a dark, ascetic, feudalist monarchy to an open, precapitalist, and premodern era. Just as the Elizabethan emphasis on humanism attempted to challenge the centrality of God in the universe, the post-Mao restoration of the "self" rejected the Maoist principle of a "revolutionary," "heroic," and "collective spirit." These cultural, sociopolitical, and ideological conditions contributed, among other things, to a formation of a "historical aesthetic consciousness" ("shidai shenmei yishi") on the part of both the "producing subject" ("chuangzuo zhuti") and the "receiving subject" ("jieshou zhuti") in contemporary China.[27] Both subjects found in Shakespearean plays a liberation by means of art from political dominations. This art "reflects reality and personal feelings, thus combining poetry, history, and philosophy most harmoniously."[28] Based on these claims, Zhang Xiaoyang reached a dramatic and perhaps even shocking conclusion, a conclusion that paradoxically celebrates the "values" of the original texts in spite of his earlier emphasis on the historical difference that separated the different cultures: "the Shakespearean workers in the China of the 1980s should thus try to interpret and produce Shakespearean plays according to the dramatic principles advocated by Shakespeare himself, since this is the only way which will allow us to conform, in the same breath, to the aesthetic consciousness of both the producing and receiving subjects in our own society."[29] Strange as such a claim may sound, a claim that connects the peculiar Chinese historical conditions with an "authentic" Shakespeare, Zhang's observation at least reveals the popularity of the English Bard at that time and the Chinese critics' readiness to justify his popularity in conventional — and sometimes not so conventional — ways. It also demonstrates how the image of the West — quintessentialized by Shakespeare and his fabricated dramatic tradition — has been utilized as "cultural capital" with which the accumu-

---

[26] Xiaoyang Zhang, "Shakespearean Production and Aesthetic Consciousness of Contemporary Times [Shaju yanchu yu shidai shenmei yishi]," *Foreign Literature Studies* [Waiguo wenxue yanjiu] 3 (1988) 68-74.

[27] Zhang 68.

[28] Zhang 72.

[29] Zhang 72.

lated power and prestige associated with the West became immediately appropriated into assess of Chinese "heritage" for the purpose of changing Chinese reality.

Yet the English Bard alone did not monopolize the post-Mao Chinese stage. Other Western plays, too, were successfully performed and received precisely because of the ahistorical Chinese reception that had nothing to do with an "accurate" historical understanding of the original Occidental plays. Ibsen's *Peer Gynt*, for example, has been almost universally regarded by Western critics as one of the most difficult plays to produce on stage. Peter Watts, in his introduction to Ibsen's *Peer Gynt*, has pointed out that "in England, ironically enough, *Peer Gynt* is much better known from Grieg's incidental music than from Ibsen's text. Ibsen had never meant *Peer Gynt* for the stage, any more than Hardy meant *The Dynasts* or Browning *Pippa* [for theatrical production]."[30] Watts also tells us that "it was not until 1874, seven years after its publication," that Ibsen thought about asking Grieg to provide music in anticipation of a possible production. *Peer Gynt* was finally performed in Norway in February 1876, and in the English-speaking countries, "there has never been," according to Watts, "a professional production of the full text."[31]

Whatever its difficulties on the English-speaking stage, *Peer Gynt* [Pei'er jinte] turned out to be a major success in Beijing, when it was performed by the Central Drama College in 1983 and 1984. It was warmly received not because the audiences "understood" the play in its "original" Norwegian terms, but rather because it evoked for the contemporary Chinese audiences their own immediate Cultural-Revolutionary reality. The twentieth-century Chinese theatergoers could not help but recall in Gynt's character individuals frequently encountered during the Cultural Revolution who were afraid of being their true selves and of expressing their genuine feelings toward the people around them. During the Cultural Revolution, in order to survive politically dangerous situations, lovers, husbands, wives, parents, and children were forced to criticize and otherwise betray each other in public. People preferred to play it safe, or to "go round about" — Peer Gynt's motto throughout his life — to avoid difficulties and conflicts. To "go round about," or in Ziao Qian's Chinese

---

[30] See Peter Watts's "Introduction" to Henrik Ibsen's *Peer Gynt: A Dramatic Poem*, tr. and intro. Peter Watts (New York: Penguin Books, 1966) 15.
[31] Watts 17.

translation, "yushi raodaozou," was a familiar phrase for most of the
Chinese who survived the unnerving experiences of the Cultural Revolution.[32] Chinese audiences bringing such experiences with them inevitably saw in Peer Gynt reflections of their own recent past. The
play reminded them of their own problematic and fractured identities and of their own ambiguous feelings about the unsolvable conflict
between personal happiness and "revolutionary" goals, conflicts that
were highly intensified during the ten years of the Cultural Revolution.

It was such cultural experience that almost everyone in the Chinese audience would recall when he or she was confronted with Peer
Gynt's question at the end of the production: "Where was I? Myself
— complete and whole? / Where? With God's seal upon my brow?"
It was, therefore, no surprise that Xu Xiaozhong, director of *Peer Gynt*,
viewed the question of "how to live one's life" as the central psychological conflict in the divided self of Peer Gynt" (Xu 45).[33] This question seemed to be addressed not to Peer Gynt, but to the Chinese
audiences themselves who looked for an answer in their "posthumous"
questionings arising out of their previous, traumatic experiences. It
was thus inevitable that they were deeply touched by Solveig's answer to Gynt's question: "In my faith, in my hope, and in my love."[34]
Solveig does not here just solve a riddle for Gynt, she answers in her
own terms many of the unanswered and (even for a time unanswer-
able) questions of many Chinese, especially that of the young who
constituted the majority of the audience for this production. Having
grown up in the abnormal days of the Cultural Revolution, the young
people of the early 1980s had been taught little about personal values,
identity, and least of all, about love. When the play ends in Solveig's
singing "in the sunshine": "I will cradle you, I will guard you; / sleep

[32] Xiao Qian's Chinese translation of *Peer Gynt* was published in *Foreign Drama* [Wai-
guo xiju] 4 (1981).
[33] Xiaozhong Xu, "Representing Ibsen: Thoughts on Directing *Peer Gynt* [Zaixian
Yipusheng — daoyan Pi'er Jite de sikao]," *Drama Journal* 3 (1983) 44-49. In this essay, Director Xu presented an interesting reading of this play: "not only is Peer Gynt
an epitome of the nineteenth-century Norwegian petty bourgeoisie, but he also em-
bodies the specific characteristics of the nineteenth-century adventurer in the capitalist world. Not only does he represent the negative traits of a Norwegian citizen,
he above all else stands for a stereotype of 'a citizen of the world.'" As for the play's
"universal appeal," Xu observes that the symbolic and perhaps even grotesque style
of a play ultimately expresses a philosophical concept of "how one should live his
life" (Xu 44, 45).
[34] Henrik Ibsen, *Peer Gynt: A Dramatic Poem*, tr. and intro. Peter Watts (New York:
Penguin Books, 1966) 222.

and dream, dearest son of mine," playing at once the role of "mother," "wife," and "purest of women," it provided an education in beauty, faith, truth, and love for most members of the post-Mao audience.[35] Those who say the play were enraptured not because of its Norwegianness or its "Romanticism," but because of what they perceived as its relevance to their situation. Watching the production of *Peer Gynt* thus became a dramatic dialogue in which the audiences were transformed into the characters of the play, waiting for an answer from opposing characters who offered a view of life different from that of their own. Similar to the Polish dramatist Jan Kott, who interpreted Shakespeare's *Macbeth* as the Stalinist machine of murder and blood, the Chinese audiences in 1983 recreated their own plots, characters, and dramatic scenes from their personal Cultural-Revolutionary experience while watching Gynt's "going round about" his problems and difficulties.[36] The Chinese audiences had no choice except to confront their own problems even when Gynt tells them not to do so.

In addition to Shakespeare and Ibsen, Brecht was another popular Western playwright who, in the late twentieth century, appealed to the Chinese imagination as a counter Other. Brecht's *Life of Galileo* [Jialilue zhuan] produced in 1979 by China Youth Theater in Beijing was so popular among the post-Cultural-Revolutionary Chinese audience that it ran for eighty productions, all with a full house. According to Chen Yong, codirector of *Life of Galileo*, foreigners who saw their play often wondered how the Chinese audience "would accept Brecht," who was too "progressive" even for the Western audience.[37] Chen believed, however, that the popularity of the play was due to its meaning and message the production team tried to deliver. For her, Brecht's play is about the coming into being of a new age, the dawn of which is "necessarily accompanied by countless difficulties, setbacks, sharp contradictions and violent conflicts and even betrayals among the vanguard." Chen reassured us that such an understanding in 1979 "is particularly revealing after the crushing of the Gang of Four and as we face the reality of the Four Modernis[sic]ations and their huge tasks, and also educates us in a general way."[38]

---

[35] Ibsen 222-23.

[36] See Jan Kott, *Shakespeare: Our Contemporary*, tr. Bolesław Taborski (Garden city: Doubleday, 1966).

[37] Yong Chen, "The Beijing Production of *The Life of Galileo*," *Brecht and East Asian Theater: The Proceedings of a Conference on Brecht in East Asian Theater*, ed. Antony Tatlow and Tak-wai Wong (Hong Kong University Press, 1982) 88-95.

[38] Chen 90.

Yet, if Chen's interpretation of *Life of Galileo* spoke only for the production crew's "good will," Lin Kehuan voiced a similar view from the spectrum of literary reception. As if to back up Chen Yong's claim, Lin explored, in a more detailed manner, how and why *Life of Galileo* would be read as if written with the 1979 contemporary Chinese audiences in mind. For Lin Kehuan, Galileo represented an image of "a new man," a term he quoted from Brecht as the authorial intention underlying the message of the play. Yet, Lin Kehuan emphasized the fact that Galileo challenged the established religious "truth" in the seventeenth century with scientific evidence; with this courageous stance, he indicated "the dawn of a new era" — a popular metaphor used by the Chinese people to allude to the end of the Maoist age and the beginning of a period of renaissance. Galileo's line that "thinking for oneself is the greatest happiness of one's life" became for Lin Kehuan a motto of a new man — he was able to doubt and question the culturally dominant "truth" at that time. He constantly strove to reunderstand and reevaluate not only the world around him but his own self and his own position in the universe.

Due to the historical circumstances of 1979 China, when Mao Zedong's mistakes during the Cultural Revolution had not yet been officially admitted by the Party apparatus, Lin Kehuan had no choice but to leave his commentary implicit. Yet, anyone familiar with the 1979 Chinese society can readily apprehend the clearly implied understatement — Galileo's story of another time and place has a particular significance for the Chinese people who were constantly told what to think during the Cultural Revolution. More critically, Brecht's play brought back the painful memory of one's own cowardice of not standing up for their principles against Maoist excesses. In this connection, Lin Kehuan argued that Galileo was truly "a great man" whose magnanimity resided precisely in his open admission that he was *not* that "great." Western readers may find such a view cowardly, but according to Lin Kehuan, the play emphasizes this view when Galileo tells Anthony that the real reason for the betrayal of his scientific principles was that he could not bear the painful torture imposed by the church, not because of his clever strategy to bide his time, as Anthony wanted to make him believe. By admitting that he *was* weak, Lin Kehuan explained with a clearly implied message, Galileo proved himself a "greater man" than Anthony, who merely pretended to be "great" by "attempting to claim a laurel to cover up a cowardly act."[39] In 1979

---

[39] Lin Kehuan, "A Dialectical Dramatic Image: On the Characterization of Galileo [Bianzhengde xiju xingxiang]," *Dramatic Art* [Xiju yishu] 2 (1979) 218-28.

China, this image of a "new man" with a "true" "greatness" could po-
lemically be compared to the much-too-familiar image of the "old man"
Mao, who was worshipped as "flawless," "forever correct," and, hence,
"the great helmsman of revolution both in China and in the whole
world."

One of the greatest assets of Brecht's *Life of Galileo*, Lin Kehuan
further argued, was that Galileo was characterized as at once "a hero
and a criminal." "If we regard Galileo as a hero, he is only a weak
one; if we argue that he is a criminal, he has nonetheless contributed
a great deal to Mankind."[40] Quoting from Marxist theory of dialectical materialism and its corresponding aesthetic principles, Lin claims
that Brecht created "a dialectical character," one which radically depart-
ed from one-dimensional stereotypes who have to be either perfectly
heroic or completely evil. Lin's comment on Brecht's play, of course,
rejects the prevailing theory of literature and art during the Cultural
Revolution, which demanded that the so-called "main heroic characters of worker, peasants, and soldiers" ("gongnongbing zhuyao jing-
xiong renwu") be exclusively portrayed as "grand and tall in stature
and perfect and complete in characterization ("gaodaquan").[41] It is
in the depiction of Galileo as embodying a contradictory self or a split
personality, Lin Kehuan told us, that Brecht rendered a vivid, be-
lievable, and true-to-life "giant of science" during the renaissance period. This understanding of the play may, or perhaps may not, have
surprised Brecht or his more recent Occidental interpreters. Yet, it
is obviously a different, Chinese reading that is made possible only
in the cultural and social milieu in contemporary China at the conclusion of Mao Zedong's "old age."

Moreover, it is clear that Brecht's play was for the post-Cultural-
Revolutionary audiences first and foremost a familiar story of scientists and intellectuals who had frequently been purged during various political movements for openly expressing their antiofficial voice.
This view is supported by codirector Chen Rong's testimony that the
response to the performance was "unusually strong and positive" in
literary circles and among the intelligentsia, "especially the scientists."[42]
Indeed, viewing the reception of Brecht's play in the retrospect of more

[40] Lin 223.
[41] For a detailed description in English of the Cultural-Revolutionary theory of literature and art as promoted by Mao Zedong's wife Jiang Qing, see Ellen R. Judd,
"Prescriptive Dramatic Theory of the Cultural Revolution," *Drama in the People's Republic of China*, ed. Constantine Tung and Colin MacKerras (Albany: State University
of New York Press, 1987) 95-118.
[42] Chen 94-95.

than a decade, it now seems likely that both the Chinese producers and receivers in 1979 perhaps had already perceived the defense of science and democracy as its basic theme, a theme that had been demanded by the Chinese intellectuals since the beginning of the century during the May Fourth Movement, and most importantly, was once again evoked during the 1989 student demonstration in Tian'anmen Square.

In fact, one can well imagine that the 1979 Chinese production of *Life of Galileo* was only made possible after Mao's death and before Deng Xiaoping ceased to be popular among the Chinese people. In this atmosphere it could be — and was allowed to be — understood at least partially as a limited protest against Mao's reign of terror and as an affirmation of Deng's newer "age" of science and democracy, which the latter "sincerely" promised at that time. If the play were to be performed again after the crackdown of the 1989 student movement, however, the plot in which Galileo was forbidden by the Church authorities to point out a black spot in the sun — an exclusive symbol of Mao and the Party's omnipotent power in contemporary China — could easily have been denounced again as blaspheming against Deng Xiaoping. The Chinese audience, indeed, would have no other choice but to reinterpret the persecution of Galileo as being imposed not by the Inquisition, but by Deng's regime, which had mercilessly rounded up student and intellectual leaders who demanded nothing but science and democracy. Once again, it is the various social and cultural milieux of different historical moments that create an Occidental Other whom one can personally and politically relate to in everyday reality.

This trend of producing Western plays or Westernized-Chinese plays culminated in the First Chinese Shakespeare Festival held simultaneously in Beijing and Shanghai from April 10 through April 23, 1986, on the occasion of celebrating the 422nd anniversary of Shakespeare's birthday. This festival was cosponsored by Shanghai Drama College, China Central Drama College, Chinese Research Association of Spoken Drama, and Chinese Shakespearean Association. According to a review article by Zhou Peitong, twenty-six Shakespearean plays were produced during this festival in diverse dialects and dramatic subgenres such as modern spoken drama and local operas, with more than seventy different productions, including both professional and amateur theaters. In addition to scholarly exchanges between Shakespearean scholars from China, America, Italy, West Germany, and other countries, some of the plays were also performed on university campuses and in factories, where the audiences from grass roots organizations received the English Bard with warmth and enthusiasm.[43] Some of these plays, such as *Richard III*, *Titus Andronicus*, *The Merry Wives of Windsor*, *All's Well That Ends Well*, *Timon of Athens*, and *Antony and Cleopatra*, had never been performed in China before and are, in fact, only rarely seen even on the Western stage.

Part of the impetus for this great outpouring of Shakespearean production was the claim that Shakespeare, above all others, is an artist who transcends cultural boundaries. For this reason, the drama critic Kong Genghong claimed, Chinese dramatists were justified in presenting at least four of the English Bard's plays in the style of traditional Chinese operas: *King Lear* as Beijing opera, *Macbeth* as *kunqu* opera of Jiangsu and Zhejiang Provinces, *Much Ado about Nothing* as *huangmei* opera of Anhui Province, and *The Winter's Tale* and *Twelfth Night* as *yueju* opera of Zhejiang Province. These productions were thus hailed by Kong Genghong as "pioneering undertakings" of a "Chinesization" of Shakespearean drama, which, he claimed, enriched both the Western tradition of Shakespeare and that of Chinese operatic theaters.[44] It was also reported that, in view of the drama crisis of the late 1980s, when Chinese theater had been increasingly threatened by the television and movie industries, it was to be hoped that a combination of the Shakespearean heritage with that of the Chinese indigenous theaters would revive the faltering modern Chinese stage.[45]

Indeed, perhaps no other modern country has witnessed such a great number of foreign plays passing into its national dramatic repertory in such a short period of a few years. Yet, through these successful productions of Western plays, the Chinese people were by no means self-inflicting a European colonialism upon themselves. On the contrary, it is the Orient that "anti-imperialistically" used the Occident

[43] Peitong Zhou, "Shakespearean Plays in China," *Observer* [Liaowang] 15 (1986) 39-41.

[44] Genghong Kong, "Shakespeare: Review, Production, and Chinesization [Shashibiya: pinglun, yanchu jiqi 'zhongguohua']," *Foreign Language Studies* 4 (1986) 92-95. For a more detailed account of Chinese operatic adaptations of Shakespearean plays, see Ruru Li's report, "Chinese Traditional Theater and Shakespeare," *Asian Theater Journal* 5.1 (1988) 38-48.

[45] Zhou, "Shakespearean Plays" 339-41.

to achieve its own political aims at home through deliberate acts of "misunderstanding." It is for such a political end that the Chinese dramatists, critics, and audiences can rightly justify their "anti-imperialistic" means, with which they have successfully fragmented the official culture and the Maoist ideological superstructure in the very representation and dramatization of a Western Other. Indeed, one can perhaps even argue that Modern Chinese history and its problematic and paradoxical relationship with a Western Other can be seen as a highly theatrical event in which the Chinese people play the roles of the Occidental Others — be they characters in Shakespearean, Ibsenique, or Brechtian drama. The Chinese actors and actresses have undertaken dramatic dialogues with Chinese audiences, which are drawn into the Occidental plots precisely because they see in these very plots the stark reality of contemporary China. Thus, such recent dramatic history that makes prominent a presence of Occidentalist stage in a postcolonialist country such as contemporary China should not be slighted as a mere incident of a self-infliction of colonialism by the colonialized people themselves. Rather, it should be appreciated as an intricate event in which the East and the West are brought together by their own specific cultural and historical conditions in which neither the East nor the West are — or should be — fundamentally privileged over its Other.

Having thus argued for the complicated positive implications of "Occidentalism" in contemporary Chinese theater, however, I would like to conclude this essay by offering a brief consideration of the issue of voice in the Chinese representation of the Western Other. It is important to point out that when I talk about the production and reception of the Western plays in Chinese theater, I have been concerned with only a small section of Chinese urban society, in which only a limited number of Chinese intellectuals are actively engaged in theater activities. This limitation holds true despite the fact that some of the dramatic productions discussed here were broadcast as national television programs and were thus available to a broader and diversified national audience. Therefore, the voices of the Chinese people evoked in this essay certainly do not in all cases embrace the totality of different voices from various divisions of Chinese society; the voices of the Subaltern, or the barely literate workers and peasants laboring through their lives at assembly lines and in the remote countryside seem especially in danger of being overlooked, if only because they have been largely mute in the discourses discussed here.

The voice of "the Chinese people" — which intellectuals have often claimed to express in their writings — may on further inspection turn out to be merely a device by which these same intellectuals have addressed their own peculiar grievances against the status quo. Furthermore, the production and reception of the Western plays can sometimes properly be viewed as the result of a collaboration of representatives of the status quo with intellectual elites who thereby become their spokesmen. As we have seen, Hao Yin's interpretation of *The Merchant of Venice* as a play promoting a Chinese economic reform provides a striking example of such a collaboration.

These caveats become all the more important if we keep in mind the fact that the majority of the Western plays produced on the Chinese stage were performed by professional theaters in urban China, theaters that were financially sponsored and subsidized by the Chinese government. Unlike theater professionals in the West, the Chinese theaters and their personnel are, without exception, underwritten by different levels of governmental institutions. The China Youth Theater and the Central Drama College, for example, are directly attached to the Ministry of Art and Culture, while the Beijing People's Art theater is financially supported by the office of the Beijing Municipal Government. One must always keep in mind this official dimension of the Chinese theater, which helps account for the frequent and much-expected calls to duty by the government and for the presence of official censors at all levels of control. But acknowledging the absence of certain voices in recent Chinese dramatic events as well as the pervasive presence of the official state apparatus in the theatrical institutions of present day China in no way justifies a view of the Chinese theater which denies its politically liberating function. As I hope this essay has made clear, the contemporary Chinese theater has, for the most part at least, successfully played within the limited space between the official ideology and a variety of antiofficial discourses. With startling ingenuity, its ideological heteroglossia towers over stereotypical ideologies of both East and West, and deserves far more serious attention than it has thus far received.

Streams out of Control: The Latin American Plot

CARLOS RINCÓN

> Now more than ever, and in the future more than
> now, everybody's personal identity, and every col-
> lective hope, depend on complex mediation between
> the local and the global.
>
> Marshall Berman

I

Booksellers in front of the University of Teheran hawk their wares
heaped on tables in a bazaar-like atmosphere: "*One Hundred Years of
Solitude* / one hundred pages for one hundred *tuman*." In the vast spaces
of what used to be the Soviet Union, in Samarkanda and in Yerivan,
in Tiblisi and in Alma Ata, Gabriel García Márquez's novel circulated in *magnitisdat*, clandestine recorded cassettes that were the oral
version of the written *samisdat*, unofficial, counter-official. This occurred at a time when scarcely anyone was noticing that the Soviet
Union, with its noncapitalist version of modernity, was a multiple
and extremely varied conglomerate of different peoples, ethnic groups,
and civilizations in the Euro-Asiatic space. Before Perestroika came
on the scene, when the incompatibility between political "opening"
and a one-party system, between the modernizing process of economic
reform and the structures of real socialism became somewhat apparent, the texts of García Márquez had a special destiny in Moscow
itself. Transformed by the *magnitisdat* into a multiplicity of voices, they
occupied their own space for half a decade, outside the opposition
between hagiography and demonology, shielded from the tumultu-
ous process of decanonization and the end of personality cults. In spite

179

of millions of official editions, the *magnitisdat* copies commanded the same hefty price as the cassettes of the legendary poet-singer Vladimir Vysorsky.

Under the predominance of the Russian tongue, what symbolic demands and necessities could lead to the intercultural transfer of such a highly specialized written product to its oral restoration to a community (read out loud or recited from memory), thanks to chromium dioxide tape and electronic acoustic reproduction? And, after the Iranian Revolution and its overwhelming consequences, would it be legitimate to enter into this calculation economic resources, techniques of printing, the logic of a book's internal organization (title, number of pages, chapter divisions) as part of a will to dialogue, a recognition of the non-Islamic (i.e., something distinct from the inability for self-representation, self-understanding, and self-awareness that is the key theme of Orientalist discourse?[1] The possibilities of appropriating these texts according to the specific codes of perception and deciphering of the postcolonial Muslim world and those of a multiethnic and multinational state whose collapse no one foresaw present a decisive fact. These dissimilar recipients possessed cultural and symbolic resources that would be revalued and activated, thanks to a great transfer of South-South cultural capital. Questions of working-in-representation come into play in this transference, in postcolonial images and languages, as Gayatri Chakravorty Spivak formulates in her question: "Can the Subaltern Speak?" Because of this relationship, local cultures that depend on the historical condition of place and find themselves included in and marked by the process of cultural globalization have their own authority over that very process.

The presence of Jorge de Burgos in the epistemological-detective novel *The Name of the Rose*, and just a few years later as a blind man named "Borges" in the postcolonial fiction of Magrheb author Tahar ben Jalloun, evinces a double process: the delegitimization of the master-code parallel to the proliferation of *petit histoire* that accompanies the crisis of metanarratives and the role of Latin American fiction in articulating these phenomena in the context of the literature of the 1980s. The reception of the texts of García Márquez in the United States is a crucial index to the fragmentation, dissociation, dislocation, and cultural decentralization that crystallize in this reception, and that are detectable in books ranging from Williams Kennedy's *Ironweed*, Alice Walker's *The Color Purple*, Toni Morrison's *Song of Solo-*

---

[1] Edward Said, *Orientalism* (London: Routledge & Kegan Paul, 1978).

mon, to John Nichol's *The Milagro Beanfield War* and the visible bor-
rowings from the Colombian novelist in Ann Tyler's *Dinner at the Homesick Restaurant*, to Paul Theroux's *The Mosquito Coast*, or even John
Updike's *The Coup*. America's supreme metafictionists Robert Coover,
John Barth, and, most especially, Thomas Pynchon (*Vineland*) have
notably appropriated García Márquez's texts. With this appropriation, the metaphorical-topological images of the position of margi-
nality obtain their own dynamic, which appears as an imaginative
strategy demonstrating what the universal system represses — a strategy for putting the margins into the center. The principles of renar-
rativizing texts to construct new tales and rewriting known and highly
codified genres form an element of the streams of cultural capital that
also have been direct, in spite of a secular relationship of inequality,
toward a South-North flow.

Recent Latin American narrative has become an integral part of
the permanent stock and prospective programming of the main European and U.S. publishing houses. Something similar occurs with
the more specific product of Latin American television, the *telenovela*,
the spread of which in Western Europe coincides with the deregula-
tion of television channels. The Brazilian productions have also obtained popularity in Asia and in Africa south of the Sahara. In 1985,
Polish television viewers considered *A escrava Isaura* the best television program of the last decade, in Beijing, during the period when
Deng Xiaoping tried "opening up" the country to the outside world,
television owners rented out seats in their houses to those wanting
to watch *The Tale of the White Slave*.

In the past twenty years, emigration from the countryside to the
cities has been much more accelerated in Latin America than in other continents. Seventy percent of Latin America's population now live
in cities, and capital cities house between a third and a quarter of
the population of their country. Under these conditions, in Latin
America the phenomenon of greatest cultural relevance in the 1980s
was the change in social life that came with the introduction of new
electronic technologies in mass media as part of the general cultural
consequences of the technical transformation of social communication. At the same time, Latin American societies also were gradually
perceived as part of a cultural market in the process of industrialization and globalization. One of the basic characteristics of this process was the rise of urban cultures without territorial memory, now
directly linked to the audiovisual media. This lack of a point of territorial reference is a phenomenon generated in the criss-crossing of

action of new technologies and their products, a phenomenon of their influence even when not in use.[2]

The accelerated and amplified expansion of the cities; the drastic change in urban political culture visible at the end of the populist movements; the appearance of television presidents; the transformation of communication and the social imaginary under the action of the media; the ungovernable scenes of catastrophe (ecological disasters, rampant insecurity, epidemics, and the breakdown of public services, etc.); the changes in the use of urban space are among the many items on the agenda of the recent urban processes on the subcontinent. Here I am particularly interested in the cultural sphere in the complex, flexible strategies that were negotiated in this decade-long process: the incorporation of large social groups, whose basic cultural capital is so-called *cultura popular*,[3] into the structures of urban life with its implicity access to forms of internationalized consumption. Such strategies and models can basically be characterized as inconsistent with the hierarchical binarism of center versus margin characteristic of the ideological universe of the 1970s, that of Manichean absolute opposites.

Certainly, recent tactics for the selection, adaptation, and refunctionalization of certain products and practices in the international globalization culture provide a substratum of cultural memory. This substratum consists of secular and discontinuous cultural codes characteristic of a heterogeneous cultural tradition of the subcontinent's colonial and national societies. But in the midst of eclectic transactional strategies and mechanism that incorporate, tame, and adapt heterogeneous fragments of the dominant global cultural regime to the new urban culture of the actual Latin American societies, a specifically contemporaneous mutation can be substantiated. This mutation is related to an aesthetic of excess, discontinuity, and bricolage that manages a mass culture with its ideology of consumption and planned obsolescence.

There are certain ironic and parodic traits of a recycling nature with this new urban culture — multiple manifestations of the politics of diversity in its style of appropriation (decoded and recorded) and

---

[2] Jesús Martín Barbero, *De los medios a las mediaciones* (México: Gustavo Gili, 1987).
[3] Jean Franco, "What's in a Name? Popular Culture Theories and Their Limitations," *Studies in Latin American Popular Culture* 1.1 (1982) 5-14; William Rowe and Vivian Schelling, *Memory and Modernity: Popular Culture in Latin America* (London and New York: Verso, 1991) 49-150.

in the operations of resemantization that are carried out within this context. This leads to carnavalesque combinations, to some degree democratized in overstimulating pastiches of elements, icons, and even complete sectors of the mass media industry, and more generally to the contemporary capitalist culture with its profit structure. This playful characteristic, with which supposedly fossilized single-cultural identities become unfrozen, expresses the simultaneous heterogeneous Latin American cultural experience of, premodern underdevelopment of modernity and of the reality of postmodernism as a social, political, and cultural configuration.

It is worth emphasizing that this definitory element of jocular disruptive cultural practice, appropriate to today's Latin American urban centers, is also found in the new mixed cultures that have risen from the immigration of "Latinos" to the United States. It is well known that this massive emigration, which has resulted in the Latinamericanization of the United States, particular in the regions of California, Texas, and New York, has led to the creation of the Chicano and Nuyorican cultures. Referring to this type of phenomena, Tzvetan Todorov notes that "the constant interaction of the cultures [leads to] the formation of hybrid cultures."[4] In addition to this formation of mixed cultures, there are extremely varied forms of cultural practices by emigrants for whom neither the ghetto nor the melting pot provides a cultural solution. For them the answer is not legitimization by inclusion or identification with dominant cultural norms, nor a recalcitrant cultural resistance through complicity counter-identification. Instead, a spectrum of responses to the power of institutions and discourses are invoked that constitute an ambivalently positioned "Latin" subject. This spectrum puts the romance of the Latin-marginal parodically on the scene.

The memories of Esperanza's childhood in the fiction of Sandra Cisneros is an illustration of this key element, also characteristic of a specific cultural form like the Chicano version of rock in its stylistic multiplicity. In rock music, the aesthetic of the cover-version has been considered as a democratic principle of intertextuality. In this way it does not express a "single cultural identity," but the "negotiation of mixed or transitional cultural identities."[5] In order to constitute

---

[4] Tzvetan Todorov, "Le croisement des cultures," *Communications* 43 (1986) 22.
[5] Angela MacRobbie, "Postmodernism and Popular Culture," *Postmodernism*: ICA Documents, ed. Lisa Appagnanesi (London: ICA, 1986) 5:57.

provisional interrelational identities, Chicano rock and roll music (with its mixture of rhythms and Latin American instruments, Mexican songs with blues and rock melody) treats ethnicity "as plastic and open-ended. For [Chicano rock musicians], ethnicity is as much a dynamic construct as an inherited fact, as much a strategic response to the present as an immutable series of practices and beliefs derived from the past."[6] This form of ethnic minority culture formation plays a crucial role in developing a photo from the unprinted negative of the technoculture, because inclusion of Chicano musicians from the technoculture leads them "to cultivate a sophisticated capacity for ambiguity, juxtaposition and irony."[7]

Because the question of streams of cultural capital in Latin American societies includes such diverse processes as the South-South transference of symbolic products, and the massive and permanent presence of the media in daily Latin American life (with its imagistic construction of the real, its forms of perception, speech patterns, categories of thought coined by the vast proliferation of images and the transformation of social communication), and because the consideration of these streams demands at least two perspectives (to understand the character of the direction in which it moves and the exchange and negotiations between cultures that it creates), I am going to attempt to map out the situation. One must take into account the demand to escape the subordination of one language, cultural experience, and identity to another.[8] In sections two and three, I will concern myself with the transference and reception of literature in the South and in the North; Latin American *telenovelas* are the subject of the fourth section. In section five, I will reconstruct some of the principal strands of the Latin American urban culture of the 1980s.

In discussing these currents of cultural capital, one must understand that this process has taken place in the course of ten "lost" years characterized by processes of democratization at a time when all existing models of economic development were bankrupt; the exaggerated growth of the informal economy sector; the propagation of neoliberal corrective measures, and attempts to join the world market and embrace its new forms of capital accumulation.

---

[6] Georg Lipsitz, "Cruising around the Historical Bloc: Postmodernism and Popular Music in East Los Angeles," *Cultural Critique* 5 (1986-1987) 169-70.

[7] Lipsitz 159.

[8] Jean-François Lyotard, *Le postmodernisme expliqué aux enfants* (Paris: Galilée, 1986) 43-64.

II

There are two writers whose texts determined, and continue to determine, the image of Latin American fiction projected beyond all geographical, political, and intellectual frontiers: Gabriel García Márquez and Jorge Luis Borges. Having to condense a bit, and considering the enormous amount of cultural resources that have led to a reevaluation of his work, I will limit my comments to García Márquez whose *One Hundred Years of Solitude*,[9] like other pivotal works of recent international literature such as Thomas Pynchon's *V*[10] or Italo Calvino's *If on a Winter's Night a Traveler*,[11] pays tribute to the Lord of the Labyrinth.

Pierre Bourdieu has stressed that "work" of art only exists as a symbolic object given value if it is received by spectators "capable of recognizing and knowing it as such."[12] At the same time, he distances himself from those who use the notion of literary "institution" to do away with one of the most significant characteristics of the functioning of the literary field: its very low level of institutionality. As shown by the reception of *One Hundred Years of Solitude* in such far-flung and diverse corners of the world as the People's Republic of China or the Arab-Muslim world, the first thing that must be captured in this reception, at the level of the experience of reading, is an operation of direct or oblique self-recognition by readers. In this manner, after the appearance of the Lebanese translation from the French of *One Hundred Years of Solitude*, in 1981, Abdelkader Rabia wrote:

> To open the pages of the novel in the Arab language is to discover a captivating world, and for the Arab reader, an easy rediscover of the atmosphere of *A Thousand and One Nights*, an admitted source of inspiration for García Márquez is today, in this second half of the twentieth century, one of the giants of world literature.[13]

[9] García Márquez, *Cien años de soledad* (Buenos Aires: Editorial Sudamericana, 1969); English translation: *One Hundred Years of Solitude*, 1st ed. (New York: Harper & Row, 1970).

[10] Thomas Pynchon, *V*, 1st Perennial Fiction Library (New York: Harper & Row, 1986, c1963).

[11] Italo Calvino, *Se una notte d'inverno un viaggiatore* (Turin: Einaudi, 1979); English translation: *If on a Winter's Night a Traveler* (New York: Harcourt Brace Jovanovich, 1981).

[12] Pierre Bourdieus, "Le champ littéraire: préables critiques et principes de méthode," *Lendemains* 10.36 (1985) 7.

[13] Abdelkader Rabia, "Gabriel García Márquez et sa fortune dans les pays arabes," *Recherches et Etudes Comparatistes Ibero-Françaises de la Sorbonne* 3 (1981) 96.

The role of the texts of García Márquez in Deng Xiaopings's China in the period of "opening up," as well as their welcome reception in the peripheral Soviet republics and in Japan, show that this effect of emotive and situational self-recognition is repeated in the most unexpected latitudes, constantly adjusting itself to extremely varied conceptions of ego, beliefs, morality, and reality. The program initiated by Deng in 1978 had as its point of departure a tacit verification of the economic disaster and the failure of the social transformation attempted by a Stalinist-line party that understood itself as "the only organization capable of centralizing the leadership of the struggle of the proletariat" and which, according to Lui Shaogi, described its character as determined by "our party's political struggle and political life, its ideological education and political leadership."[14] Deng's reform, with its emphasis on economic efficiency and managerial competence, marked the beginning of the end of the Marxism-Leninism-Mao Zedong Party as the only instrument capable of channeling the great torrent of the Chinese people. In this context, after the devastation of Mao's Cultural Revolution, since the beginning of the 1980s until the events at Tiananmen Square in which the army upheld the power of the Party, the cultural movement *Xungen Wenxue* (scar literature) proposed as its goal a type of present-day archeology: the establishment of a plurality of identities corresponding to the heterogeneity of the times and spaces of the diverse ethnic groups, peoples, and cultures of that immense country. The intellectuals of *Xungen Wenxue*, and especially its writers as Mo Yan and Liu Zhenyun with their hallucinatory and frequently eroticized fiction and chronicles, had as their model the text of García Márquez.

As far as readers and writers in Japan, a country where a culture of traditional behavior is coupled with a postmodern concept of reality, the reception of García Márquez's functions as the reflection of their own abundant narrative resources. This presupposes a challenge that leads the West to both a self-conscious declaration of its rationality in the garb of modernity and its dependence on the forms of the Other to mark its own boundaries of rationality. Thus, Macondo is in Kikirikij, the village that proclaims its independence from the Empire of the Rising Sun in the celebrated satirical-marvelous utopian book of the same name by Inoue Hisashi. Moreover, two elements of Japanese cultural and literary tradition, ignored by the West,

---

[14] Stalin, *Leninism* (Moscow: International Publishers, 1933) 78; Lui Shaoqui, *Three Essays on Party-Building* (Beijing: Foreign Languages Press, 1980) 181.

facilitated Japanese readers' reception of García Márquez. Buddhism includes the concept of *mujo*, which can be roughly paraphrased as uncertainty, immanence of change, mutability of forms within the human condition. Second, the combination of the marvelous with the everyday, the display of encyclopedic knowledge about the life of ghosts, of the uninterrupted chaos of civil wars, characterize the great parodic, episodic, and self-referential fiction of *Gesaku* prose. *Gesaku*, unlike the other great cultural form of the Edo period, *Kabuki* drama, could never be correlated with the narrow modern European concept of *Weltliteratur*. In contrast, Japanese readers could easily see García Márquez as the most prestigious of narrators in the *Gesaku* tradition, as a Japanese narrator *avant la lettre*.

The figure of a triangle helps one to understand the activation of both repressed narrative sources and resources in the peripheral regions of the Soviet Union that accompanied the appropriation of the texts of García Márquez. One side of this figure is constituted by the liberation of a new epic attitude capable of both including myth and of mythologizing, as demonstrated in the work of masters such as Fazil Iskander, Yuri Rytieu, Yuvan Shestalov, and Bulat Okudshava, who read *One Hundred Years of Solitude* as a synthesis of the novel and epos under the sign of myth. The second side of the triangle is made up of texts written on the periphery of the former Soviet Union, such as the novels of the Siberian Valentín Rasputin, Armenians such as Shabua Amiredzhibi and Grant Matevosian, or Baltic narrators such as Youzas Bultushis, which neither opposed nor supported the Russian hegemony. Their attitude is one of nonidentification. This second side plays with the demands for verisimilitude and the borders of official censorship and self-censorship. The two sides of this triangle rest on a common base that is made up of the great discovery by Tschingis Aitmatov and Vazil Zemliak: the signification of Macondo as a compressed space and an organizing point of the world, a topological entity foreign to the West, that is, *omphalos*, center of the universe.

The search with the aid of fiction for identities of class, ethnicity, gender, religion, and culture in the midst of processes of modernization is a visible characteristic of the reception of García Márquez in the peripheral regions of the former Soviet Union.[15] This can be seen

---

[15] This is also true of the Chinese reception of García Márquez (Jiang Yuanlun, "Chutu. Dangai xiaoushuo zhong de yizhong wenhua xianxiang," *Dushu* 10 [1986] 85).

in films such as Nikita Michalkov's *Urga* (1990), a fairy tale about the friendship between a Mongol shepherd and a Russian truckdriver, which combines Gengis Khan, plastic, fifty different types of green, and the deafening sounds of discotheques. Michalkov playfully winks at the spectator with his recognizable allusion to the fictions of García Márquez, in the same manner that Polanski, in his nostalgic film *Chinatown* (1973), names the hotel "Macondo," and thereby gives a clue to his reading of the modernization of Los Angeles.

These texts and films, as well as the films of magic realism such as *Urga* or the realistic magic in the prose of Hisashi (which laughingly questions Japanese modernity), Mo Yan's or Zulfikar Ghose's, are evidence that since the beginning of the 1980s the handling of magic realism had ceased to be the privilege of Latin Americans. Devices of narrative theme and organization (such as the multiplication of hyperbolic action, character, and the marvelously narrated world, of the writing process and the splitting of the narrative subject into diverse instances) that appear as characteristic of recent Latin American narrative are no longer exclusive to their fiction. At the beginning of the decade, we find three novels that allow us to measure the enrichment brought by the currents of Latin American cultural capital. Two of these novels are by well-known authors of that period, Günther Grass and Aitmatov, while the other is by a writer unknown at that time — Salman Rushdie.

In the introduction to his 1980 novel *I kolsche weka dlitsja den*, Aitmatov, whose ethnic group Kirghis still maintains some nomadic characteristics, invokes *expresis verbis* from García Márquez and emulates as well Gogol and Bulgakov (who until then did not form part of the "[multi]national heritage" of the Soviet Union), as cultivators of "fantastic realism." Into this retrospective fiction of memory about the landscape of the Kazakhstan steppes, a science fiction tale is interjected. This subgenre, which crystallized as a complement to the modern, and which in postmodern literature had a role similar to that of the detective story in modern literature, is united with a Central Asian legend about a man who is turned into a slave because he lost the memory of his culture. In novels like this, using living oral culture as a resource, the articulation of ethnic and cultural identities gives rise to an ethical reflection on the history of the century.

Beside the dramatic events in Yugoslavia and the former Soviet Union, the evolution in the 1980s of postcolonial India reconfirms the growing impression that the nation, sustained by the idea of unity, is a social model that simply does not fit at the dawn of the twenty-first century. Accounts of the military assault on the Golden Temple in Amritsar, the riots in Ayodhya, the assassinations of Indira and Rajiv Gandhi, and the bellicose declarations of the high castes of Hindus in the face of the short-lived intentions of Prime Minister Singh to take into account the demands for separate lands by Muslims in Kashmir, Sikhs in Punjab, and the United Liberation Front of Assam, showed how illusory the desires of the British imperialists were to "unify India," and the fantasy of the "Raj."

At the beginning of the 1980s, Salman Rushdie, storyteller of Bombay and Cambridge, narrated the history of the 1001 children born during the night of August 15, 1947, by the same forceps as the modern state of India. *Midnight's Children* recounts the impossible world of the 581 who survived, even though some possessed the gift of infallible memory, the clairvoyance and telepathic vision to handle the midnight conference that was supposed to bring them together. They divide into groups according to their ethnic, religious, linguistic, social, and ideological interests, and Indira Gandhi takes up the task of undermining the entire conference. In this network of fiction and familiar history, Macondo shines through in the hyperreal image of Calcutta, and García Márquez's patriarch is reincarnated in the form of the terrible widow with hair parted in the middle. But it is in the power of the self-representational fable and the treatment of the question of nation that one can best measure the extent of the postcolonial reception of García Márquez's texts. The distance between Salman Rushdie's first novel, *Grimis* (1975) and *Midnight's Children* (1981) shows that with the transference of cultural capital South-South the question of self-representation of cultural difference comes into play in a specific way. Its very heterogeneous collection of fractured local solutions is integrated into globalizing structures that are engendering new forms of social life, economic orders, and communities of readership. From these aspects, *The Autumn of the Patriarch* appears as the text that contributes decisively to the revalorization by narrators in what was then known as the Third World of their own cultural resources in order to confront postcolonial challenges. This revalorization is confirmed in the fiction about demented patriarchal dictators constructed by Congolese novelist Soni Labou Tansi or the fiction of the Benghali writer Amitav Ghosh.

III

In a situation one supposes was understandable in metaphorical-topological terms of space and territory, in the imagery of metropol and periphery, center and margin, position and boundary, inside and outside, the reception of the text of García Márquez contributed decisively to the deconstruction of the very structures of the antique-seeming map of the world of political and cultural relations evoked by this system of metaphors. The great carnavalesque fictions of García Márquez affected the hierarchies prevalent in the processes of writing as symbolic-cultural remodelings. In the South-South transfer, they not only helped put into question the usurpation of signifying and representing functions but also, by activating uncultivated self-represantational resources, stimulated the production of texts, which, by adopting a marginal place for themselves, brought the margins into the center by applying a deconstructive critique to the dominant self-historism of the West. In the South-North transfer, the results are parallel, as demonstrated by the reception of García Márquez in the Islamic-Arabic and Northern countries.

Said has pointed out that the Orient has not been an interlocutor for Europe, but its silent Other. Since the Enlightenment, "Oriental" history was considered a stage that should be left behind in the dialects of spirit, the emancipation of the rational subject, the hermeneutic of meaning. Historians of literature even resorted to Keats or Hölderlin to put forward the thesis that the Orient surrendered its historical relevance.[16] In order to put into perspective the present situation of Arab narrators, with their changes in literary paradigms and the disappearance of the aura of modern metropolitan classics, Jamel Eddine Bencheik notes: "Latin American literature — and, above all, that of García Márquez — has transformed the 'new novel,' or, perhaps better said, the contemporary novel. García Márquez is a kind of guide in the new quest for fiction."[17] It is within this proliferating network of the margins that Farazdak, Omar Ibn Ali Rubia, Abu Navas, Ibn Haldunly, and another dozen classics of the pre-Islamic era and of the Abadidas become tied to García Márquez with the use of intertextual strategies in *Les 1001 années de la Nostalgie* by Rachid Bodjedra.

[16] Edward Said, "Orientalism Reconsidered," *Literature, Politics and Theory: Papers from the Essex Conference 1976-1984*, ed. Francis Baker, Peter Hulme, Margaret Iversen, and Diana Lonley (London and New York: Methuen, 1986) 215-18.
[17] Rabia 96.

With regard to the reception of García Márquez in the North, the change of orientations brought about by this reception encouraged writers to find their own particular voice and actually to begin writing. This phenomenon occurred across America and Europe, from Jayne Anne Philipps and Angela Carter to Patrik Süskind. The curious and significant self-designation involved in the new versions of the "history of the world," which Günter Grass, Burnes, or T. Coraghessan Boyle put forth in a carnavalesque form, reveal a change. If the modernist aesthetic project in a sense constituted a critique of modernity and a refusal to endorse its celebratory grand narratives, contemporary fiction assumes and practices an incredulity with regard to metanarratives, those universal guiding mythologies and principles, accepting instead the inevitability of a plurality of perspectives and the dissolution of various older aesthetic and ideological polarities and boundaries. The attentive and reflective readings of García Márquez's fiction stabilized a set of key aesthetic strategies. Combined, these textual objects and practices can be seen as definitory in contemporary fiction. Barth designated it as "postmodernist fiction" in his second manifesto. Larry McCaffery observes:

> If a single work may be said to have provided a model for the direction of postmodern fiction of the 1970s and 1980s, it is probably García Márquez's *One Hundred Years of Solitude*, a work that admirably and brilliantly combines experimental impulses with a powerful sense of political and social reality. Indeed, García Márquez's masterpiece perfectly embodies a tendency found in much of the best recent fiction — that is, it uses experimental strategies to discover new methods of reconnecting with the world outside the page, outside of language.[18]

With this common denominator, one can legitimately correlate Barth's *LETTERS*, William Gaddi's *JR*, William Kennedy's *Ironweed*, and Rushdie's *Midnight's Children*; similarly with the *Macondo* of García Márquez, a new topography takes shape, mapped out in works such as Pynchon's *Vineland*, or Aitmatov's *Buranny*, Rachid Boudjedra's *Manama*, Beat Starchy's *Innerwald*, and the Japanese master Hisashi's *Kikirikij*, articulating the contemporary polarity between globality and local cultures.

---

[18] Larry McCaffery, *Postmodern Fiction: A Bio-Bibliographical Guide* (New York, Westport, London: Greenwood, 1985) xxv–xxvi.

IV

In the 1980s, through their mass media Brazil and Mexico began to have a voice in the bustling hubbub of the world information order previously dominated by the North. Brazilian entrepreneurs expanded toward Europe and entered the world audiovisual market with a product without which it would be difficult to imagine the world today: the *telenovelas*. In Mexican media, the same epochal turning point had taken place, and President Carlos Salinas de Gortari sought to include Mexico in the trade agreement that had just been negotiated between the United States and Canada. *Rede Globo*, the fourth largest network in the world, obtained control of the Italian affiliate of the French company *Telemontecarlo*. *Televisa* of Mexico, the second largest Latin American media consortium, fomented the establishment of radio and television stations in the United States, a lucrative and promising future market that the Monterrey Group today controls as a monopoly.

The Latin Americans have been very successful in marketing their own distinct production of *telenovelas*. Both *Rede Globo* of Brazil and *Televisa* of Mexico have found that the *telenovelas* are one of the most profitable components of their exportable products. With the need for television companies to guarantee revenue for several years at the lowest cost possible within the framework of deregularization, the know-how of the program production industry in Mexico and Brazil, as well as the *telenovelas*, had its impact on the industrial rhythms of production and the structure of programming. The production cost of a *telenovela* is less than thirty thousand dollars an hour, less than half the production cost of a single soap opera in the United States. "It is an essentially Latin American genre, because it characterized us, it identifies us," as *telenovela* author Ignacio Cabrujas has declared.[19] Furthermore, the genre has developed significant variants resulting from an encounter between form and memory, between the lift of the countries and their cultural heterogeneity.

Several theorists see television as constituting the postmodern psychocultural condition — a world of simulations detached from any reference to the "real," circulating and performing exchanges in centerless flows. Ann Kaplan uses rock videoclips and Lawrence Grossber's *Miami Vice* as examples of this phenomenon. Grossberg describes the series in this fashion:

[19] José Ignacio Cabrujas, "Telenovela nuestra de cada día," *Communicación* 47 (1984) 11.

Miami Vice is... all on the surface. And the surface is nothing but a collection of quotations from our own collective historical debris, a mobile game of Trivia... The narrative is less important than the images... Narrative closure becomes a mere convenience of the medium. And the spectator as subject all but disappears in the rapid editing and rather uncomfortable camera angles.[20]

Kaplan distinguished five types of video clips, couching her argument in negative terms:

What characterized the postmodernist video is its refusal to take a clear position vis-à-vis its images, its habit of hedging along the line of not communicating a clear signified. In postmodernist videos, as not in the other specific types, each element of a text is undercut by others: narrative is undercut by pastiche, signifying is undercut by images that do not line up in a coherent chain, the text is flattened out creating a two-dimensional effect and the refusal of a clear position for the spectator within the filmic world.[21]

These unstable determinations in a negative light almost always represent a constant. For example, in his analysis of the cult video "Road to Nowhere," Dick Hebdige stresses that the video creates "a space of subliminal narrative *suggestions* which is neither 'realist' nor 'modernist'... encouraging neither identification nor critical reflection."[22]

There cannot be a sharper contrast within the actual development of cultural production, marketing, and consumption on a global scale than between the characteristic aesthetics of these cultural artifacts and the symbolic order of the *telenovelas*. The revealing paradox of change in contemporary culture, as a passage from modernity to postmodernity, resides here in the international success of the *telenovela*, wherein signs are the *function* of a reference to the world, which can only be explained as a result of a product emerging from this terrain of transformation. Because of this, the *telenovela* is defined by the cultural matrices that function within it, rather than by its codes or content. More than the texts themselves or the daily rites of reception, attention is focused on two other factors: One is the social actors who intervene in the circulation of the *telenovela*, possessing abilities and

[20] Lawrence Grossberg, "The In-Difference of Television," *Screen* 28.2 (1987).
[21] Ann Kaplan, *Rocking around the Clock, Music, Television: Postmodernism and Popular Culture* (London and New York: Methuen, 1987) 6.
[22] Dick Hebdige, *Hiding in the Light: On Images and Things* (London: Comedia, 1988) 237.

knowledge which, constituted in memory, become a prism for the reading that different social groups, sexes, ethnic, regional, or national groups carry out. The second factor is the existence of a collective imaginary from which these groups project their identity.[23] As media theoretician Jesús Martín Barbero has shown, social demand and cultural dynamics are tangled up in the logic of the market, giving rise to re-elaborations and recuperation of *Ungleichzeitigkeiten* within a discourse that combines the new audiovisual technologies with a slide show of narration and archaic recognition.[24]

The newspaper serial as a narrative genre that corresponds to deep layers of a collective imaginary, only through which it obtains entry into the historical memory of the Latin American societies, has its present-day version in the *telenovela*. In the genre of newspaper serials, conflict, and dramaturgy, action, and narrative language are interwoven, and "the dramatic effects" result in the "expression of a moral exigency."[25] The mixture of temporalities and of extremely varied discourses in the *telenovela* assumes the techno-perceptive transformation of the new urban masses carried along by the electronic audiovisual media. But at the same time, mechanisms of recognition, united with a symbolic weave of interpellation and the sensation of feeling oneself interpellated (and because of this, related in a specific way to the constitution of subjectivity) supposes another class of realities. To recognize oneself in the newspaper serial-*telenovela* presupposes a psychosocial substratum: to participate in a primordial sociability in

---

[23] See Gladys Daza Hernández, *TV Cultura: los jóvenes en el proceso de enculturación* (Bogotá: Nueva América, 1989); Renato Ortiz, et al. *Telenovela: história e produção* (Petropolis: Vozes, 1989); José Marquez de Melo, *Produçâo e exportaçâo da fiçâo televisual brasileira* (Sâo Paulo: UNESCO, 1987); M. Wilton de Sousa, *A rosa púrpura de cada día: trajetoria de vida e cotidiano de receptores de telenovela* (Sâo Paulo: USP, 1986).

[24] See Jesús Martín Barbero, *De los medios a las mediaciones* (México: Gustavo Gili, 1987); "Televisión, melodrama y vida cotidiana," *Diálogos de la comunicación* 17 (1987); "Matrices culturales de las telenovelas," *Estudios sobre culturas contemporáneas* 4-5 (1988). Michael Dobbs of the *Washington Post* indicates that the airing of Mexican *telenovelas* has been the salvation of former Soviet state television, and comments: "When *The Rich Also Weep* is aired on Ostanki Television, dubbed in Russian, life in the former Soviet Union slows to a standstill. Wars are suspended as soap-obsessed fighters flop down in front of TV sets. The water pressure goes up. The number of burglaries goes down. Fields are abandoned" ("Age of TV Dawns in Russia; Fans Swoon over Mexican Soap Opera," *International Herald Tribune*, Paris, September 9, 1992).

[25] Peter Brooks, "Une esthétique de l'étonnement: le mélodrame," *Poétique* 19 (1974) 356. See Marlyse Meyer, *De Folhetins* (Rio de Janeiro: Centro Interdisciplinar de

which the determinate factor is kinship, the neighborhood, the place of origin and friendships, with all their fidelities.

Within specific explorations of the discrepancies of temporality, power, and development between the anthropologist and his constructed object, Johannes Fabian hypothesizes a concept of culture that is primarily a conglomerate of matrices and practices of knowledge and behavior.[26] Jean Franco has similarly given new dimensions to the category of the *popular*, understanding it as a specification of a particular *cultura popular* on the basis of the existence and handling of cultural competencies different from those of the hegemonic.[27] High culture and popular culture, as well as industrial culture and forms of mass communication, appear today as parts of a structuring and destructuring matrix eminently appropriate to the time-space-money experience of urban life in contemporary societies of Latin America. It is worth repeating that today the traditional and the modern are not found in opposition to each other, and that the division among high culture, *cultura popular* and the industrial culture (as exclusive and closed categories) is meaningless. Therefore, forms of mass communication have resulted in new processes for the production and distribution of culture, a result that cannot be accounted for by simple-minded technological determinism, the mobilization of desire and fantasy in the context of a politics of distraction, or the promotion of a culture of consumerism. The *telenovela*, upon activating these matrices of *cultura popular*, with its archaic narrative typical of newspaper serials and the visual tale of publicity as discourse, manages to interpellate millions of people on every continent who are now included in processes of such an accelerated modernization that it has reached the status of a historical transition. The *telenovela* has thus become an interstitial receptacle for strategies of transforming negotiations around socially constituted subjectivities.

V

In the last decade, Medellín became the world capital of illegal narcotraffic. Among the multiple strategies employed by cocaine businessmen was that of violence as a device of defense and pressure. Within

Estudos Contemporâneos, 1990); Silvia Oroz, *O Cinema de lágrimas da América Latina* (Rio de Janeiro: Rio Fundo Editorial, 1992).

[26] Johannes Fabian, *Time and the Other: How Anthropology Makes Its Object* (New York: Columbia University Press, 1983).

[27] Franco 10-14.

this context, new forms of rendering services came into existence, including those of young *sicarios* "hired assassins."[28] From the point of view of the multitemporal heterogeneity that characterizes the cultural modernity of Latin American societies, Medellín and its *sicarios* had almost an emblematic significance. In this case, the processes of economic and symbolic reconversion, which peasants were undergoing in their adaptation to urban life, were the objects of an intense compression of time. New cultural forms and products of modernization could not substitute for what *sicarios* considered traditional or for what they took to be their own identity. Rather, there was a knitting together of distinct modalities of symbolic development. It did not involve a superimposition, but a fluid elaboration of definitions of identity and culture. An investigation of participatory sociology among the *sicarios* is the multitemporal heterogeneity characteristic of the cultures they make up and which gives its own particular stamp to modernity within its limits in Latin America.

Alonso Salazar's study distinguishes the first layer, that of traditional culture oriented by the mythology of the not-so-distant mining and agricultural colonialization of the region. The Catholic popular religiosity and a strong sense of profit and retaliation are derived from that experience. The second layer he distinguishes has to do with the processes of urbanization in the first part of the century and, at the same time, with more recent forms of population scattering: the *malevo* culture and the salsa. That is, the world of the tango and the barrio, together with the cult of the Argentine singer Carlos Gardel, killed in an airplane accident in Medellín. With this *machista* and aescetic culture is joined a culture of the body and an enjoyment of libidinal discharge arriving from the Caribbean with its salsa music. Finally, and as revealed in the discourse of the *sicarios*, there is a uniquely modern culture. This is defined by the values of consumption as a source of enjoyment of creature comforts and prestige, a sense of the ephemeral and a language corresponding to the norms of the audiovisual dominated by discontinuous images.[29] With the redefinition thus accomplished within a modernizing perspective, the (traditional) cult and the (traditionally) popular (with its authentication and ritualization of identity) and the culture of the mass media (with its industrialization of cultural production), a new crossbreeding or syn-

---

[28] Ciro Krauthausen and Luis Fernando Sarmiento, *Cocaina & Co* (Bogotá: Tercer Mundo, 1991) 85-90.

[29] Alonso Salazar, *No nacimos pa' semilla* (Bogotá: CINEP, 1990) 183-212.

cretic synthesis does not arise. Rather, a simultaneous mixture and a cultural hodgepodge are the determinant results. With these new mixed cultures and their transitional cultural identities, the mass media become the access channel to modernity.

Another of the strong currents that give tension to the new urban cultures is deterritorialization, which spawns new cultural forms, above all among youth. A key sector of the unbalanced national demographic pyramids has as its experience an audiovisual culture (television, music, videoclips, game machines), not tied to any territory, with the use made of the culture being its decisive element. In a broad sense, one could even talk about strategies of reterritorialization, of forms of recycling, recuperation, and resignification, and of an attempt to come to grips with the elements, components, and icons of global culture offered by the media. Here, as in the case of rock music and audiotechnology, the relationship between two or more codes is carried out with the help of modes of connotation that give them added meaning. The social recourse to multiple codes, the ironic play of the signs with televised spectacularity is, to mention an example, the regulating strategy of the emergence of the figure of *Superbarrio* after the 1985 earthquake in Mexico City. The Mexican-masked icon comes from a world that makes spectacles of the good and evil of wrestling, and to the degree that the encoding and decoding of the world exists in a parodic fashion through its Superheroes (Superman, Batman), it adopts a double-voiced or culturally hybrid form permitting it, in the everyday reality of the megapolis, to put itself at the service of the needy.

This process of hybridization not only escapes the scheme of an intercultural mixing of heterogeneous elements into a synthesis of theories of *mestizaje*, it also puts into question the cultural politics giving hegemonic groups or their elites a modern character and reduces the traditional to the popular sectors, at the same time putting forth the massification of the consumption of cultural goods as a step toward cultural development. The modernization of the sector would be in this form a task of private capital, while the State has to concentrate on conservation of patrimony. Néstor García Canclini makes this clear in his study on forms, in which borders between the *popular*, the high culture, and the mass media have been moved with the obsolescence of the old repertories, encyclopedias, and mental cultural maps. The empirical analysis of these processes, especially in the borders themselves, as in the case of Tijuana, in which there has resulted a space of exchange, fusion, and transformation of cultural identities that are always related, demonstrates the character of the far-reaching process from the point of view of the flows of cultural capital it accomplishes.[30] Under conditions of uneven and combined development, as different as the historical-cultural processes are in the various Latin American countries and regions, these cultures are today the rule, rather than the exception.

[30] Néstor García Canclini, *Culturas híbridas. Estrategias para entrar y salir de la modernidad* (México: Grijalbo, 1989) 263-328.

A Sort of Homecoming: An Archeology of Disneyland

BRAD PRAGER AND MICHAEL RICHARDSON

Angered by American agricultural trade policies, tractor-driving French farmers blockaded the entrance to the new Euro Disneyland outside Paris on Friday, preventing several hundred families and busloads of schoolchildren from entering the park... As one farmer manning the roadblock outside the $4-billion Euro Disneyland told a reporter from the British news agency Reuters: "The other day we blocked a motor-way, causing a 15-mile traffic jam, and the news didn't even mention us. This way, we are sure of being talked about."[1]

The global significance of the Disney corporation should not be underestimated. Its name has become an emblem of family values and financial success worldwide, emerging as the single most profit-able film studio, purchasing television networks, running the single largest tourist attraction in America (Epcot Center/Walt Disneyland in Orlando), and expanding its empire into Japan and France. Dis-ney speaks to the contemporary consumer-family — its mark on com-modities is the equivalent of a "Good Houskeeping" stamp of fun and freedom. The peanut butter with the all-too-familiar Mickey seal[2] is assuredly the one to feed your children. The Disneyland theme park relates to the parent who visits with his or her family as the mirror in Snow White relates to the queen, repeating back to the parent that he or she is the most virtuous parent of all, who by bringing his or

---

[1] Rone Tempest, "Protesters Block Euro Disneyland," *Los Angeles Times*, June 27, 1992:A8.

[2] The whole phenomenon surrounding the fascination with the Mickey Mouse im-age, although not discussed here, deserves further investigation. Mickey Mouse has

her family to Disneyland, exposes them to "The Happiest Place on Earth." Disneyland is exactly the festival that its visitors expect the future to be.

Disneyland grew out of other forms of amusement, eliminating them by virtue of its superior adaptability and unlimited commercial potential. This American corporation has, more successsfully than any other, systematically filtered out the less popular elements of amusement and preserved that which sells, leaving other amusement parks and relics such as zoos and circuses fighting to survive. Zoos and circuses find themselves chained to live animal displays complete with, horror of horrors, excretory and digestive functions beyond the control of their trainers. The unpredictable nature of animals, as well as their inability to conform to the modern imperative of constantly offering something new markedly diminishes their commercial potential.[3] Watered-down scientific amusement equivalents such as the San Francisco Exploratorium are tied to the relatively dull, and again, easily exhausted, educational motif; the effort to make science "fun and interesting" to the general populace falls short of the technological wonders that Disneyland consistently generates.

The Disney corporation, however, presently finds itself at a crossroads. With the arrival of Euro Disney onto the European cultural scene, European intellectuals have come to view Disney as an unwelcome visitor. The French writer Jean Cau calls the theme park "a horror made of cardboard, plastic and appalling colors, and construction of hardened chewing-gum and idiotic folklore taken straight out of comic books written for obese Americans."[4] Novelist Jean-Marie Rouart exclaims, "If we do not resist it, the kingdom of profit will create a world that will have all the appearance of civilization and

---

transcended mere advertisement status to become a cultural icon, capable of demanding entire art exhibitions devoted to "Mickey Art": historical and cross-cultural comparisons of renditions of the mouse.

[3] In a bizarre incident several years ago, Ringling Brothers, Barnum, and Bailey circus, in an attempt to provide a new and exotic animal to its tired collection of lions and white tigers, unveiled what it called the world's only existing unicorn: a small, passive goat with an anomalous looking horn in the middle of its forehead.. The circus came under serious critical attack when animal rights activists charged the circus with fraudulently grafting a horn onto an ordinary goat. Needless to say, the unicorn soon disappeared from the show's repertoire.

[4] Alan Riding, "Only the French Elite Scorn Mickey's Debut," *The New York Times*, April 13, 1992: A1:2.

all the savage reality of barbarism."[5] One must be careful to note, however, that the French in particular have always had an ambiguous relationship with U.S. culture. To anyone paying attention, the French *publique* appears to enjoy American culture. Mickey Rourke enjoys a superstar status that he does not have even in his own country, and American football jackets are as popular there as anywhere else. As the French philosopher Michel Serres notes, "It is not America that is invading us, it is we who adore it, who adopt its fashions and above all its words."[6] Despite the disagreement, all agree the cultural clash has caused a stir to say the least. One must assume that there is a specific character to the park that makes the clash so heated. In a much quoted rejection, now attributed simply to "one French official," Euro Disney was called a "cultural Chernobyl" and, ironically enough, François Mitterand called it "not my cup of tea."

Yet this criticism on the part of the French intellectuals seems to amount to no more than a (trans)cultural conservatism, which offers an inadequate solution to the problem of how to deal with intellectually unpopular elements of popular culture. The question "to amuse or not to amuse," which French intellectuals are answering compulsively in the negative, is misguided at best. One can never rid oneself of the evils of culture and preserve the remainder. Such an attitude of overall nastiness is often attributed to theoretician cum sociologist, Theodor Adorno. It is a mistake, however, to assume that Adorno believed the elimination of mass culture to be some manner of universal corrective; he makes no such claim.[7] Such puritanical gestures, Adorno asserted, characterized the misguided Thornstein Veblen, who recommended in his *Theory of the Leisure Class* an elimination of all *kitsch*. In his discussion of Veblen, Adorno recounted Veblen's attack. Veblen's theory of the leisure class was a manifesto written in favor

[5] Alan Riding, A13:1.

[6] Alan Riding, A13:1. Additionally, it should be noted that Professor Serres spends a good part of his year in California.

[7] Although Adorno is often characterized as a curmudgeon who called for the abolition of amusement, such an approach to Adorno's thought is a misunderstanding. To be sure, the "Culture Industry" chapter of *Dialectic of Enlightenment*, written by Adorno together with Max Horkheimer during their exile in California, critiqued much of popular entertainment culture. While in California, Adorno also wrote polemics against Jitterbugging and the Astrology column of the *Los Angeles Times*. For Adorno, the problem was not merely that there were a bunch of regressed Californians participating in the occult via the *Los Angeles Times*; rather, this manifestation of occultism was symptomatic of a larger problem of capitalism that would not have been readily solved by the elimination of popular culture.

of "causal thinking,"[8] a result of his close association with the social Darwinists of the period. Veblen claimed that society should leave regressive and barbaric thinking behind, to be replaced by the rationality of the industrial revolution. In this respect, he viewed kitsch as a jump backward into barbarism. Even sports were not immune: "According to Veblen, the passion for sports is of a regressive nature: 'The ground of an addiction to sports is of an archaic spiritual constitution.' ... athletic events were the models of totalitarian mass rallies" (80). Kitsch also took the form of architectural ornamentation. Such ornamentation was, for him, not only incompatible with his functionalist view of dwelling, but also "represented relics of past epochs or indications of the regression of those who were not producing anything, those exempt from participation in the industrial labour-process" (79). Adorno summarized Veblen's general position:

> Those characteristics of culture in which greed, the search for personal advantage, and confinement in mere immediacy appear to have been overcome, are nothing but residues of objectively obsolete forms of greed, personal ambition, and bad immediacy. They originate in the need to prove... that one can spend one's time on the useless in order to improve one's position in the social hierarchy, increase one's social honor, and strengthen one's power over others. (75-76)

Veblen was concerned with the ability of the human species to adapt to the natural and historical conditions imposed upon them. "Veblen," Adorno wrote, "would like to make a clean slate, to wipe away the rubble of culture and get to the bottom of things" (84). Veblen fails, however, to grasp what Adorno calls the interdependence of the useful and the useless. Neither the theorist, nor the boldest of economists, in an effort to trim fat from the cultural budget, can save what he or she likes about society and dismiss the rest. Culture and kitsch are parts of a whole: "To reject appearance is to fall completely under its sway, since truth is abandoned with the rubble without which it can not appear" (84). Moreover, an analysis of just such rubble produces the greatest insights. Adorno's interest in the rubble that was popular culture was guided by his theoretical fascination with the particular in relation to the whole. Susan Buck-Morss explains:

---

[8] "Causal thinking is for *Veblen* the triumph of objective, quantitative relations, patterned after industrial production, over personalistic and anthropomorphic conceptions" (Theodor W. Adorno, "Veblen's Attack on Culture," *Prisms*, tr. Samuel and Shierry Weber [Cambridge: MIT Press, 1981] 77).

"What distinguished Adorno's approach was not only his Hegelian assertion of the dialectical relation between the particular and the general, but the fact that, unlike Hegel, he found the general within the very surface characteristics of the particular, and indeed, within those that were seemingly insignificant, atypical or extreme."[9] Buck-Morss makes the connection between this approach, and that of Walter Benjamin: "There can be no doubt that it was Walter Benjamin who convinced Adorno of the validity of this approach."[10] Benjamin explained the plan of the Arcades Project as "to erect the large constructions out of the smallest architectural segments that have been sharply and cuttingly manufactured. Indeed, to discover the crystal of the total event in the analysis of the small, particular moments."[11]

What follows is an effort to locate the Disney phenomenon historically as that which exists in the present moment. Theme parks are the particular of the "total event" that is society, and as such are fruitful objects for analysis. The Disney parks constitute the visions of utopia particular to this era, and any such vision of Utopia tells more about the present than the future; the utopia always carries with it the aporias of the culture out of which it emerged.[12] An examination of Disneyland as the apogee of American amusement culture provides insights into the prevailing American social and cultural ideologies, and the relationship that Disneyland as amusement holds toward them.

This very relationship, however, is one that was born in Europe, not in the U.S. While no amount of propaganda on the part of the Disney corporation can hide the fact that Disney is primarily an American phenomenon, there is a connection between Disneyland and Europe. This connection runs much deeper than the Disney corporation's somewhat superficial attempts at locating the origins of particular fairy tales in European folklore, taking pains to recite publicly the history of the tale of *La Belle au bois dormant* [Sleeping Beauty], whose castle is the central point of the new theme park,[13] and Walt Disney's own

---

[9] Susan Buck-Morss, *The Origin of Negative Dialectics* (New York: Free Press, 1977) 74.
[10] Buck-Morss, *The Origin of Negative Dialectics* 74.
[11] Walter Benjamin, as cited in Susan Buck-Morss, *The Dialectics of Seeing* (Cambridge: MIT Press, 1989) 74.
[12] Examples are too numerous to laundry list — from the utopia of Thomas More to the distopias of George Orwell and Aldous Huxley.
[13] The other fairytales have European origins as well: *Cinderella* (also French) as well as *Snow White* (German), *Pinoccio* (Italian) and *The Little Mermaid* (Dutch) (Jenny Rees, *The Mouse that Ate France, The National Review*, May 11, 1992: 58).

French ancestry.[14] Both the structure of the modern amusement park and the ideological underpinnings of Disneyland have their origins in Europe. It is not the blood of the d'Isigny family that was the export of Europe, but the blood of the Enlightenment. Disneyland offers its patrons a variety of temporal and spatial displacements that coincide in a vision of a harmonious and homogeneous society made possible by capitalism and technology. At Disneyland nothing is beyond the reach of humankind; in the Enlightenment tradition, it successfully bends nature to its will. In doing so, Disneyland not only reinforces the ideological status quo but also, by virtue of its totalizing and homogenizing program, eliminates resistance by leveling differences. As Europe exported the Enlightenment and capitalism to the new world, what it now meets with is its own product. Whether in Disneyland, Disney World, or Euro Disney, Disney reinforces the principles critiqued by the pair of transplanted Germans Horkheimer and Adorno: the principle that nature is to be dominated to meet human ends, the corresponding faith in technology and progress, and the subsequent levelling of difference. Seen in this way, the Godzilla, which has emerged from the Atlantic to gobble Paris, was born in Europe itself. It follows that an exploration of the Disney phenomenon is an exploration of late capitalism,[15] and a study of Euro Disney is a study of the American brand of late capitalism's confrontation with Europe.

The notion that a theme park in its very conception is inherently complicit in the reinforcement of the dominant cultural ideologies can be supported by an examination of the European origins of the con-

---

[14] Walt Disney himself found his origins in Normandy from the island of Isigny-sur-Mer: his ancestors, including Hughes d'Isigny, invaded England in 1066. This is a somewhat graceless reminder, since it is dubious how flattering it is to the French that Disney himself was originally a cultural export. Rone Tempest, "Eeque! A Mouse!" *Los Angeles Times Magazine*, April 5, 1992:27.

[15] Here, by the term "late capitalism," we do not mean that capitalism has recently passed away. Rather, we mean it in Jameson's sense of the term, as the stage in which "no one particularly notices the expansion of the state sector and bureaucratization any longer: it seems a simple, 'natural' fact of life. What marks the development of the new concept over the older one is not merely an emphasis on the emergence of new forms of business organization beyond the monopoly stage but, above all, the vision of a world capitalist system fundamentally distinct from the older imperialism that was little more than a rivalry between the various colonial powers" (Fredric Jameson, *The Cultural Logic of Late Capitalism* [Durham: Duke University Press, 1991] xviii-xix).

temporary amusement park. Europe's World Expositions of the mid-ninteenth century represent the organized and highly structured ur-form of the theme park. Herman Lotze called these expositions "the first actually modern festivals."[16] The Crystal palace of the first World Exposition in London in 1851 was some 1500 feet in length and 112 feet high. A blend of ornamental gardens, statues, and fountains, the palace contained palm trees as well as pumps and pistons. The subsequent exhibitions in Paris were on an even grander scale: the 1889 Paris Exhibition left the Eiffel Tower as a permanent trace on the city landscape. The blend of technology, art, and capitalism had an enormous regulatory function:

> A phantasmagoria of politics had its source in the World Expositions no less than a phantasmagoria of merchandise, wherein industry and technology were presented as mythic powers capable of producing out of themselves a future world of peace, class harmony, and abundance. The message of the World Expositions as fairylands has the promise of social progress for the masses without revolution. Indeed the fairs denied the very existence of class antagonisms.[17]

The concept of phantasmagoria lies at the center of Benjamin's analysis of the World Expositions. Rolf Tiedemann explains Benjamin's use of the concept: "Phantasmagoria: a *Blendwerk*, a deceptive image designed to dazzle: [it] is the whole capitalist production process, which constitutes itself as a natural force against the people who carry it out."[18] For Benjamin, the phantasmagoria consisted of "the blend of machine technologies and art galleries, military cannons and fashion costumes, business and pleasure, synthesized into one dazzling experience."[19] In their movement to America, the World Expositions not only retained their phantasmagoric quality, but provided the ground for the development of the American amusement industry. The World Columbia Exposition of 1893 in Chicago, while taking its form from the earlier European expositions, set the American standard for such world fairs. Judith Adams writes:

---

[16] Herman Lotze, as cited by Benjamin in Buck-Morss, *The Dialectics of Seeing*. The discussion that follows of the European World Exhibitions is paraphrased from Buck-Morss's elaboration of Benjamin (85-88).

[17] Buck-Morss, *The Dialectics of Seeing* 86.

[18] Rolf Tiedemann, "Dialectics at a Standstill," tr. Gary Smith and André Lefevre, *On Walter Benjamin* (Cambridge: MIT Press, 1988) 276.

[19] Buck-Morss, *The Dialectics of Seeing* 85.

It also introduced the essential elements of American amusement parks from Coney Island to Disney's EPCOT Center. It gave us the midway and the Ferris wheel, but more importantly it created a material Elysium within an enclosed site by means of city planning, architecture, and technology. Its successful merger of entertainment, engineering, and education within a clearly sectored landscape provided a model for Disneyland and theme park designers.[20]

Like the expositions before it and Disneyland after it, the Chicago Exposition was built on a vision of a utopia made possible by the "mythic powers" of capitalism and technology. Like its historical counterparts, it sought to deflect difference by presenting a homogeneous society, in which "blacks and American Indians *were* quasi-ethnological entertainment." The exposition ignored "the horrible effects of capitalism, that is, the growing number of people living in poverty, unemployment, and the spread of slums in urban areas" (Adams 20).

The very structure and layout of the amusement park has additional European roots. William Mangels, in his study, *The Outdoor Amusement Industry*, comments that "for more than three hundred years elaborate outdoor amusement centers have existed in several European countries. Known usually as 'pleasure gardens,' they were remarkably similar to those of today in their general layout and variety of entertainment."[21] Some of the earliest gardens were located in England — Vauxhall Gardens was the first English resort to become internationally famous (6). The Gardens, featuring such amusements as fireworks, rope dancers, and ultimately, parachute drops and balloon ascensions, remained open for nearly two hundred years before closing in 1850 (6-7). Interestingly enough, Mangels notes that "in France, enterprising showmen also promoted amusement parks of unprecedented magnitude during the eighteenth and nineteenth centuries... some of the devices in vogue were rediscovered at a later date in the United States" (10). The "bold undertakings of Gallic Showmen," who founded France's Ruggieri Gardens in 1766, included a fireworks display (a current Disney trademark) to close the evening's entertainments, and "Sau du Niagara," the arche-Log Flume ride, a staple of modern amusement parks (10-11). The English Victorian

---

[20] Judith A. Adams, *The American Amusement Park Industry* (Boston: G. K. Hall, 1991) 19.
[21] William F. Mangels, *The Outdoor Amusement Industry* (New York: Vantage Press, 1952) 4.

pleasure fairs provided yet another model for American forms of amusement. Like the World Expositions, these fairgrounds were the site for unveiling new technologies to the public. "Just as steam had revolutionized mining, manufacture and transport, so did it revolutionize the fairground in a way that was both sudden and spectacular."[22] The new technologies were integrated into the park's very structure: larger rides were propelled by portable steam engines mounted on horse-drawn wagons, and, later, steam was replaced by electric current as that which propelled larger and more elaborate rides such as mechanical organs, waterfalls, and scenic railways.[23] While some of these gardens and fairs lasted longer than others, they all can be characterized by an effort to stay *à la mode* — their success or failure depended largely on their ability to consistently provide the public with something new and exciting, a lesson not lost on Disney.

Another crucial component of these fairs, the display of freaks and geeks in the sideshow format, has disappeared from the modern amusement park. However, one should not assume that their function has faded away. "Wombwell's Menagerie," as well as the "Pig-faced Lady," the "Fat Boy and Fat Girl," and the "Scotch Giant" (Beaver 58-59) levelled differences between park-goers by reassuring them that they were part of the set of "normal" persons in contrast to the "abnormal" attractions. Disney parks adopt the feature of levelling differences in a somewhat less obvious and more updated fashion. Additionally, the sideshows lent a pseudoscientific atmosphere to the parks that made patrons feel as though they were on the cutting edge of the natural sciences.

The westward migration of the amusement machine saw an intermediate step in New York's Coney Island. At Coney Island the first round-trip roller coaster ride was unveiled in 1884. The park preserved the relationship that characterized the Victorian fairs between the rides and their social function as that which introduced the public to the

[22] Patrick Beaver, *The Spice of Life — Pleasures of the Victorian Age* (London: Elm Tree Books, 1979) 66.

[23] Beaver's rhapsodic prose belies the magnitude of the impact of the steam engine on the fairs: "There it stood with its burnished, gleaming brasswork, its swift and quietly moving piston and valve rods, its 'quarreling eccentrics,' its flapping belts, spinning governour and fly-wheel; a whole, complex unit of concentrated energy rocking gently to and fro on massive iron wheels... providing fun, thrills, music and light and, almost like a playmate, joining in the merriment and the laughter with the exciting 'whoop-whoopwhooooop' of its siren" (Beaver 68-70).

new technology by making technology appear fun and friendly. The new coasters "allowed the public to intimately experience the industrial revolution's new technologies of gears, steel, and dazzling electric lights" (Adams 15). Another aspect of Coney Island, which plays upon the interdependence of amusement and culture, was its Steeplechase Park, opened in 1897. Adams observes that Tilyou's Steeplechase Park was conceived of with the knowledge that "Coney revelers were young, single, and seeking a brief release from repressive sexual mores" (43). Through the park's use of "outrageous blowholes" the fairground offered "the opportunity to see shapely legs never glimpsed on a city street."[24]

Luna Park, another Coney Island venture, like its European predecessors, featured spectacular and elaborate displays. Its opening night in 1903 consisted of "swirling pinwheels and crescents, blazing spires and turrets, and shows depicting strange lands and people, all incredibly ablaze with 250,000 electric lights" (Adams 47-48). Here the transition was made from the Steeplechase's sexual orientation to a more wholesome technological orientation. Adams notes that while Steeplechase Park encouraged sexual titillation and exhibitionism, Luna Park "set out to appeal to desires for unrestrained extravagance, the magnetic wonder of the fantastic, the vitality of ceaseless motion, and lush illumination" (48). Luna Park included a "Trip to the Moon" ride and a "Twenty Thousand Leagues Under the Sea" ride.

While the sexual motif of Steeplechase Park was doomed to failure because of its limited appeal, Coney Island's later cultivation of a larger target audience, particularly the family unit, represented an important and decisive evolutionary turn for the amusement park industry. By providing its patrons with physical and visual excitement, by playing upon the seducing notion of the spectacle, and by allowing a first-hand look at the future, the park provided the model for parks to come. The insight of Coney Island's many different proprietors regarding what did and did not "sell," forced the shift into an amusement format which, while retaining the ideas and ideological implications of the World Expositions, also worked successfully to exploit its patrons' desires for physical and visual stimulation. It is this synthesis of these two elements that Disneyland has adopted and turned into the standard for amusement in the era of late capitalism.

---

[24] The blowholes consisted of bursts of air from random, hidden locations that lifted up the skirts of unsuspecting female park visitors (Adams 43).

Above the gates through which one enters Disneyland stands the inscription: "Here you leave today, and enter the world of yesterday, tomorrow, and fantasy." Although a somewhat more jovial inscription than that which introduced Dante's descent into hell, the two resonate eerily. What links the various "lands" in Disneyland is that they are all displacements: into the past, the present, and the fantastical. Despite what appear as radical temporal jumps into the old West, the twenty-first century, or an Animal Farm-esque world in which bears laze about, drinking moonshine and playing banjos, each are not-so-different variations on a flawed original. Not-so-different in that they cannot disguise the one bad stench that pervades the park: against its best efforts, the park reeks of the present. Disneyland fails to make good on its promise to leave behind "today." To be sure, they make every effort in this direction: Disney baby strollers (each identical and wearing the Disney stamp) are available, while ticket vendors encourage patrons to exchange their hard currency for Disney Dollars, each bill replacing the image of Jefferson, Lincoln, and Washington with Mickey, Goofy, and, in a telling gesture, Scrooge McDuck. The dollars are, of course, "legal tender" throughout the park.[25] Disney would encourage you to leave your money behind, but this is the one connection to "todayness" without which Disneyland cannot function. On this most obvious level, Disneyland bears the mark of the capitalist economies from which it emerged. More subtly, the mythologies of the present (the domination of nature, an axiomatic faith in technology and progress, and an uncritical acceptance of the free enterprise system) inform the park's utopian vision so greatly that the Mickey-Mouse shaped balloon that promises to lift the patron far above the present is filled not with helium, but rather with lead.

The idea of the domination of nature first manifests itself in the taboo on live animals within the park. Ironically, this park, populated by larger-than-life mice, ducks, bears and an ambiguous orange animal known simply as Goofy, forbids patrons from including pets from home in their Disneyland experience. Nature as it appears in

---

[25] The separation between the cold and desolate parking lot and Walt Disney World in Orlando, Florida, is greater than the gate which separates them in Annaheim, California. The Orlando Disney World is separated from the parking lot by a man-made (Disney-made) lake that serves to highlight the radical break from "the real world."

the park is anything but natural. Disneyland solves the problem of nature's unpredictability by eliminating nature per se and replacing it with an altogether fabricated version. In lieu of live animals, Disney offers costumed figures of humanized animals, distorted into slightly smaller than human proportions and neatly clad. Interestingly enough, these animals inspire fear rather than fascination in the children with whom they interact. Up close, the frozen smiles of the Disney characters are the stuff which children's nightmares, not their dreams, are made of. Mysteriously, these animals are mute. This voicelessness allows these figures to walk the line between animal and human. Silent, they avoid the difficult problem of replicating animal sounds and simultaneously also avoid breaking their illusion of animality by not employing human voices. This is the happy harmony with nature: animals purged of their more unseemly qualities. In fact, the appearance of a "real" animal sends the attendants into a frenzy of activity in an attempt to suppress this outburst of nature. The appearance of a small rodent in front of the "Matterhorn" ride, aside from generating the obvious ironic commentary from park patrons, results in the amusement park equivalent of Defcon-3. Other animals are merely replaced by machines, or even immobile plastic figures. The fish that populate the undersea world of the "Submarine Voyage" are astonishingly un-lifelike plastic replicas. The unspoken motto of Disneyland is that the fabricated is better than the real. In Umberto Eco's formulation, "A real crocodile can be found in the zoo, and as a rule it is dozing or hiding, but Disneyland tells us that faked nature corresponds much more to our daydream demands."[26] If one were to take a real trip down the Mississippi, he continues, "where the captain of the paddlewheel steamer says it is possible to see alligators on the banks of the river, and then you don't see any, you risk feeling homesick for Disneyland, where the wild animals don't have to be coaxed" (44).

Disney's reshaping of nature is not limited to animals. The Lagoon that surrounds the "Submarine Voyage" ride, containing six million gallons of water, is said to be twenty-five times as clean as drinking water, since any bit of grease or dirt would distort viewing of the "underwater show" — even its water remains unviolated by, good heavens, dirt. The supposedly wondrous "Swiss Family Robinson Tree House"

[26] Umberto Eco, *Travels in Hyperreality* (San Diego: Harcourt, Brace, Jovanovich, 1983) 44.

tree is made of steel and plastic.[27] The entire Matterhorn mountain "consists of 2,175 pieces of steel of varying lengths and widths. The contours were moulded and shaped using a second skeleton of 3/8 inch steel wire topped with a layer of metal mesh and layers of plaster — two of them sprayed on and the third one applied with a trowel form maximum verisimilitude."[28] An exact replica of the true Matterhorn (though at 1/100th the size), the mountain even faces in the correct direction. Disney takes from nature what is attractive and useful and discards the rest. Every rock and every animal sound heard throughout the park is a mechanical reproduction coordinated by Disney that leaves absolutely nothing to the patron's imagination. What it expects to hear from nature, it does.

The park shares the almost religious faith in technology and technological progress that Benjamin found characteristic of the post-industrial revolution era. Benjamin stated fearfully, "progress becomes the signature of the course of history *in its totality*," identifiying with "uncritical assumptions of actuality rather than with a critical position of questioning."[29] Almost all of the rides in *Tomorrowland*, Disney's vision of the future, follow the same basic pattern. In each of the rides there occurs a "crisis," and it is only the invisible hand of technology that snatches the families from the jaws of death. In the "Mission to Mars," when a freak meteor storm threatens the ship, the completely mechanical mission control mannequins act quickly to engage the ship's lightspeed engines to engineer a safe retreat. Similar circumstances prevail in the "Submarine Voyage" (during which a huge mechanical squid threatens the well-being of the passengers). Finally, in "Star Tours," the most recent (and the most technologically advanced) ride in *Tomorrowland*, it is up to the robot pilot to navigate the way through not just a meteor storm, but a space dogfight as well. The message is always the same: technology will overcome in the end any problems that it may face, no matter how outrageous.

An interesting development to observe is the evolution of *Tomorrowland*. The very continued existence of the "Mission to Mars" ride

---

[27] The story itself, of a family left stranded on a deserted island, is a Robinson Crusoe story of the overcoming and domination of nature. The extent to which the family replicates the society from which it came is complete, down to the tea service in the "dining room" of the tree house.

[28] Steve Birnbaum, *Steve Birnbaum's Guide to Disneyland* (Hearst Professional Magazines, 1989) 84.

[29] Buck-Morss, *The Dialectics of Seeing* 80.

attests to the historically contingent view of the future. Historically dated (especially in light of President Bush's approval of manned flights to Mars), and technologically unimpressive,[30] there is some talk of sectioning it off from the rest of *Tomorrowland*, referring to it as a *Tomorrowland of the Past*. In order to satisfy the demand for the "new," *Tomorrowland* must stay current, constantly shifting its facades. The spell Disneyland hopes to create through its displays of technology is broken when the technology is neither new, nor in conformity with everyone's expectations of the future. Disneyland conspires to perpetuate the spell within its confines. According to Benjamin, the postindustrial world had become reenchanted, and its inhabitants lived as if in a dream. Benjamin saw amid the collection of images and objects within the Paris Arcades, the potential for awakening. The only way of emerging from the dream in which they were enveloped was the "dialectical image." He wrote: "In the dialectical image the past of a particular epoch... appears before the eyes of... [a particular, present epoch] in which humanity, rubbing its eyes, recognizes precisely this dream *as* a dream."[31] Disneyland prevents the awakening on two levels. Disney systematizes and hence concretizes mythologies which were otherwise transitory. "Not the presence of the gods is to be deplored, not their return to walk the earth, but the attempt to build them a permanent home."[32] Impressively, Disneyland also seeks to keep as clean from historical "trash" as it keeps its *Main Street* free of garbage. In the new Euro Disney, they have dispensed with the troublesome *Tomorrowland*, which continually failed to keep up with the real "tomorrow," and replaced it with the less problematic *Discoveryland*. The "Mission to Mars" ride is conspicuously absent, replaced by "Le Visionarium."

As one waits to board the "Mission to Mars" in Anaheim, one is given a glimpse of what Disneyland pretends is the technology behind the ride, but as Benjamin cautioned in his *Work of Art* essay, technology generates only an aura, and helps the patron become the "expert" not at all. There is nothing but the flash of NASA screens, which in the age of "Star Tours" becomes the "Droid repair station."

[30] Birnbaum notes that both the obsolescence of the ride and its lack of sensual excitement: "The vibrating and heaving of the seats and the terrific roars and hisses that play over the big sound system are fine, but there is also something of the sensation of being inside a giant washing machine" (Birnbaum 90).

[31] Benjamin cited in Buck-Morss, *The Dialectics of Seeing* 261.

[32] Buck-Morss, *The Dialectics of Seeing* 256.

The naked steel girders in the "Space Dock" make one feel as though they are a part of technology and the future, but in reality, having learned very little, they are more on the outside than before. United only under the merchandising campaign of the *Star Wars* film series, and M&M/Mars Bars corporation, who sponsors the ride and whose cartoon figures decorate the walls of the exit hallway, the success of the rides of *Tomorrowland* stems from the uncritical acceptance of new technologies and the promise they bring for a trouble-free future.

The facades of the new change, but the underlying program is always the same. The visions of the 50s and of the 90s have much in common. As Benjamin remarked, "The illusion of novelty is reflected, like one mirror in another, in the illusion of perpetual sameness."[33]

The final element in the Disneyland "phantasmagoria" is the integration of capitalist and industrial paradigms as the final ingredient necessary to a vision of future harmony. This third "mythic power" irrevocably grounds the park historically in the present era of late capitalism. An "authentic" turn-of-the-century *Main Street*, one of Disneyland's "past" worlds, is transmogrified into something better: a large outdoor shopping mall. On *Main Street* one can purchase just about anything bearing the Disney stamp: T-shirts, mugs, jewelry, porcelain figures, and even Disney cooking appliances such as a Mickey Mouse toast stamp and a Mickey and Minnie shaped waffle iron.[34]

Patrons can stop on *Main Street* and share "Great Moments with Mr. Lincoln" in which a mechanized Abe Lincoln delivers a speech composed of fragments of Lincoln's actual speeches. Naturally it is a mechanized Abe (because a human could never be a part of the show), and historical fact is better presented by technology that will long outlive the humans who generated it. That Lincoln's speech consists only of fragments is precisely the problem with the display. The account of the Civil War somehow neglects mentioning slavery. As a result, the text compilers have put together little more than a mishmosh of jingoism that provides, ironically, a ludicrous explanation of both cause and effect of the Civil War.

[33] Walter Benjamin, "Paris, Capital of the Nineteenth Century," *Reflections*, tr. Edmund Jephcott (New York: Schocken Books, 1978) 158.

[34] The only items that are not sold with the Disney stamp are cigarette lighters and shot glasses. Store clerks are trained to respond with indignant reproaches which suggest that Disney does not put its logo on just anything. Cigarettes and cigars are also nearly impossible to purchase at the park, being sold at only one convenience store.

Even more interesting than the Lincoln display itself is the exhibit hall at its exit. The exhibit hall is a mural devoted to "The Fifth Freedom: Free Enterprise."[35] The wall makes it clear that without free enterprise, nothing worthwhile in America, including Disneyland itself, would exist. Out of the same logical wellspring from which came Lincoln's account of the Civil War, the mural reconstructs American history through the rubric of free enterprise. The mural connects such unlikely bedfellows as Louis Brandeis, Thomas Edison, Andrew Carnegie, Albert Einstein, Thomas Wolfe and, of course, Walt Disney. While Carnegie's remarks on the importance of private property and the law of accumulation of wealth are obviously quite in keeping with the theme of the mural, the remarks of some of the other "honorees" require some fairly extensive mental gymnastics to be considered as exhortations for free enterprise. Pearl Buck, the only woman and one of two minorities to appear in the mural, is quoted: "If any person believes in freedom and in human equality, he is a good American and I will trust him." Not exactly an appeal for capitalism, but indelicately woven into the mural's attempt to present a seemingly universal mandate for the free enterprise system. Edison's remarks are even more distant from the subject at hand: "The three great essentials to achieve anything worthwhile are first, hard work, second, stick-to-itiveness, and third, common sense." Aside from the quotations and portraits of "defenders" of the free enterprise system, the mural presents a montage of all of Disneyland's ideological underpinnings: a happy mix of science, progress, and capitalism. A black child selling lemonade stands next to a rocket ship taking off into space, while the steel mills surrounding Andrew Carnegie are followed by Pearl Buck amid laughing, smiling children reading books, which might as well be titled "The Joy of Capitalism." This fusion of elements recalls the panoramas that figured so prominently in the *Passagenwerk*. "There is, of course, another use of montage that creates illusion by fusing the elements so artfully that all evidence of incompatibility and contradiction, indeed, all evidence of artifice, is eliminated... This was the principle... of the 'panoramas.'"[36] Benjamin criticized the panoramas for not making clear the gap between sign and referent, but instead fusing them "in a deceptive totality so that the caption merely duplicates the semiotic content of the image in-

[35] The first four "freedoms," as articulated by Franklin D. Roosevelt in a famous speech, were freedom of speech, freedom of worship, freedom from fear, and freedom from want.

[36] Buck-Morss, *The Dialectics of Seeing* 67.

stead of setting it into question."[37] The most important maneuver in the totalization of the Disney vision is the exclusion of the present. By tantalizing park patrons with a utopian future always just beyond their reach, and replacing their memories with a fabricated past, Disneyland precludes the possibility and necessity for social change in the present time period. The promise of Disneyland is that the patrons themselves will have to do nothing to bring this utopia about except let capitalism and technology carry on unimpeded. No radical restructuring of society is necessary, no proletarian (or even bourgeois) revolution is needed — just sit back and enjoy the ride.

To further foreshorten the possibility of dissent and conflict, Disneyland suppresses ethnic, racial, and sexual differences. The "It's a Small World" ride presents a vast array of mechanical figures in a variety of ethnic and national settings, which suspiciously all look alike save for mock differences in skin tone and clothing. All the while the "It's a Small World After All" song is piped in through hidden speakers in a sort of hypnotic suggestion that maybe people are not so different "after all." Perhaps Adorno had this song in his head as he wrote in *Minima Moralia* "that all men are alike is exactly what society would like to hear. It considers actual or imagined differences as stigmas indicating that not enough has been done; that something has still been left outside its machinery, not quite determined by its totality."[38] The Disney totality involves a shrinking of the world — just as the "It's A Small World" ride offers a microcosm of the world as filtered through the Disney lens, the entire park is set up so as to bring Europe and the rest of the world within arm's reach. In the span of several hours, one can take a jungle cruise through Africa, visit with the "Pirates of the Carribean," ascend the Matterhorn, and return in time to have a mint julep in New Orleans — no bothersome customs officials here. The success of Disney in this regard can be seen in concrete numbers. In 1990, Disney World attracted more tourists than Great Britian: "Many vacationers figure they can escape pollution, if not the crowds, yet get an enriching experience in Disney's ersatz foreign lands."[39] Far from presenting a thick cultural description, however, Disney represents each of these foreign cultures with the same plastic automatons and the same bland food.

---

[37] Buck-Morss, *The Dialectics of Seeing* 68.
[38] Adorno, "Mélange" in *Minima Moralia* (New York: Verso, 1980) 102-03.
[39] Peter C.T. Elsworth, "Too Many People and Not Enough Places to Go," *New York Times*, May 26, 1991: 3:4.

Throughout the park, Disneyland's representations repeat this theme, constantly narrowing and refining their scope. Having eliminated global differences, the park next targets America. The film *Circlevision 360* offers a distorted vision of America in which Native Americans are heard and not seen, and Afro-Americans are seen and not heard. The rest of the film portrays smiling, happy white families merely transposed in a variety of locales. The *Hometown Parade* offers trite cultural stereotypes — the overweight, undershirt-clad husband vegetating in front of a television while a grotesquely distorted "housewife" sings about the joys of cooking and cleaning, smartly dressed yuppies marching obediently to the urgings of the Big Bad Wolf who commands them to make money for him, and the traditional figures of suburbia including a pot-bellied, donut-eating cop and a somewhat reckless freckle-faced paper boy. The parade offers a narrow and homogeneous view of a "Hometown," which comes closer to *Leave It to Beaver* than a California that is seeing the elimination of whites as a majority of the population. Minorities exist only in token form, and even then are either impotent in the society, as in the *Circlevision* film, or entirely disregarded.

Even sexual differences are levelled in Disneyland. Most of the animals are androgynous in appearance, and those that do represent "couples" in the traditional, i.e., male-female, sense never appear together. Snow White is never seen with the Handsome Prince, and Mickey never appears with Minnie. Lawrence Rickels notes that familial relations are conspicuously absent from Walt Disney's creations. "D. [Walt Disney] turned to the animation of *Bambi* at the time of his father's death; but the guilty commemoration was held back until its delayed (controlled) release in 1943 alongside Dumbo (where the father, already beating a retreat in *Bambi*, can only be found missing). D. compulsively rewatched *Bambi*, which he favored above all his other productions (each time unreservedly weeping)."[40] The closest thing to a "family" is Donald Duck and his three nephews — a secondary bond that exists only in thought and not in action.

This effort to level all difference extends even further, to the point that Disneyland attempts to eliminate subjectivity, and hence resistance, absolutely. The rides in *Tomorrowland*, the most updated rides of the park, are structured so that the enjoyment of the ride is confirmed through group experience. *Circle Vision 360* caters to more

---

[40] Lawrence Rickels, *The Case of California* (Baltimore: The Johns Hopkins University Press, 1991) 248.

than 200 viewers at once, and the "Star Tours" ride puts the passenger in a cabin with at least thirty other people. Everyone at Disneyland is put through the mill of sameness, as Eco notes:

> Disneyland is a place of total passivity. Its visitors must agree to behave like robots. Access to each attraction is regulated by a maze of metal railings which discourages any individual initiative. The number of vistors obviously sets the pace of the line; the officials of the dream, properly dressed in the uniforms suited to each specific attraction, not only admit the visitor to the threshold of the chosen sector, but in successive phases, regulate his every move ("Now wait here please, go up now, sit down please, wait before standing up," always in a polite tone, impersonal, imperious, over the microphone). (48)

This is not to be taken to mean that all shared experiences are "bad," rather that in Disneyland, the identities of each of the participants is subordinated to an undifferentiated collective. The only freedom at the park is, in Adorno's phrasing, "the freedom to choose what is always the same."[41] The vision of utopia is that of homogeneity. In the future, *Tomorrowland* tells us, everyone will be the same. Even the employees must appear well-groomed, freshly washed and clean-shaven. Disneyland provides the "guest" with the mood, and as long as the Mickey symbol is on the experience, the mood is going to be a good one. The artists of *Fantasia* write that "in making *Fantasia* the music has suggested the mood, the coloring, the design, the speed, the character of motion of what is seen on the screen. Disney and all of us who work with him believe that for every beautiful musical composition there are beautiful pictures."[42] The German playwright Heiner Müller identifies the real impact of such a film:

> What was so barbaric about this film, something I learned later, was that every American school child between the ages of six and eight gets to view it. Which means that for the rest of their lives these children will never again be able to hear certain music without seeing those Disney figures and images. The horrifying thing for me in this is the occupation of the imagination by clichés which will never go away. The use of images to prevent experiences, to prevent the having of experiences.[43]

[41] Adorno, *Dialectic of Enlightenment*, tr. John Cumming (1972; New York: Continuum, 1989) 167.

[42] E. Taylor, *Walt Disney's Fantasia* (Los Angeles: Walt Disney Productions, 1940) Introduction.

[43] Heiner Müller, "Intellegence Without Experience — an Interview with Harun Farocki," *Germania* (New York: Semiotext[e], 1990) 165.

The freedom of a day at Disneyland is that it is a day spent denying the one activity that constitutes freedom: the interpretation of one's own experience.

With all this in mind, we must then return to the original conflict — Disney's attempt to (re)integrate itself into Europe. Given the extent to which Europe has influenced Disneyland, both structurally and ideologically, and its popularity among European visitors to the United States, it would seem a simple matter to bring Disney into Europe. What then is the problem?

One could argue that the smaller cultural differences have caused the most trouble. These have included, among others, the ban on wine and spirits in the park, which some maintain is an insult to France, the dress code for employees,[44] or the prohibition on employee smoking while on duty. As a response to these complaints, the corporation has made some modifications in the park to lessen the feeling that the ugly American is back in town: French is the offical language, Gérard Depardieu narrates the film based on Jules Verne's undersea voyage at "Le Visionarium," and some (though not many) of the strict dress code restrictions have been relaxed. Even the French would agree, these issues pose no great threat to French culture. As Robert Fitzpatrick, president of Euro Disney points out: "This is a culture with several thousand years of history. It has successfully resisted multiple invasions. If it really feels threatened by the arrival of a mouse, then the culture is in much greater danger than you think."[45] The question is really altogether different. If all the aforementioned differences are truly reconcilable, what remains as essentially "American," and thus alien, in this apparently universal entertainment?

America has dominated the market of the world capitalist system insofar as it has flooded it with the products of its culture industry; it has perfected the packaging and selling of entertainment worldwide.[46] Disney is essentially American in the sense that it is the form of amusement perfected for the moment of late capitalism: it is a prod-

---

[44] Of course these regulations have been much disputed by the new Parisian employees, who claim to have no intention of changing their habits. The most recently disputed clause in the contract included a controversial rule that all workers should wear "proper underwear."

[45] Rone Tempest, "Eeque! A Mouse!" 27.

[46] While the current economic situation in the United States may call into question its status as the leading producer of goods in general, the claim still holds true regarding the entertainment industry.

uct of the country that best represents the latter. Disney's relationship to late capitalism is further reinforced by the fact that Japan, another nation entrenched in late capitalism, not only engages in a wholesale importing of American entertainment, but is the location of Disney's third amusement park, Tokyo Disneyland.[47]

In the French intellectuals' criticism of Euro Disney's arrival, they misunderstand the significance of Disney's American character. What is American about Disney is the way the received idea of an amusement park was refined, packaged, and perfected for an age of global markets. If one is to critique Disney, one must recognize that the park's ideology is a historical development, and the French have more in common with that history than some of their public intellectuals are willing to admit. So long as they do not recognize Disney as part of a much larger context, an elimination of Disney, or American pop culture in general, misses the mark — only a critique and/or restructuring of the late capitalist situation would break Disney's hold on the public. This may or may not be a desideratum: the question remains up for debate. Still, in 1992, no child, not even a French child will accept Zola's Naturalist Amusement Park and Campground or any proposed substitute for that amusement park which is ideologically and structurally compatable with the mythologies of the present.

Douglas Kellner hypothesizes that Jean Baudrillard's short introduction to *America*, "Warning: objects in this mirror may be closer than they appear," can be interpreted to mean that "the processes which he is describing from his observations of the United States will soon be manifest in France and much of the rest of the world."[48] To be sure, Baudrillard had foresight. Yet, while some may continue to complain that "Mickey Mouse and Donald Duck 'are to culture what fast food is to gastronomy,'"[49] it would be a serious misunderstanding to posit Disneyland as the Big Bad Wolf coming to blow down the cultural houses of Europe. Rather, it is Disneyland's inherent connection to the social and cultural situation of late capitalism that insures their mutual and continued reign.

[47] According to 1990 statistics, Tokyo Disneyland had the third largest attendance of the world's theme parks (12 million visitors), behind Disney World, Florida (28.5 million) and Disneyland (12.9 million). Disney seems to have a monopoly (Elsworth 3:4).

[48] Kellner 168.

[49] Associated Press, "Sacrebleu! Disneyland in France," *San Jose Mercury News*, April 7, 1992:2.

Value, Representation and the Discourse of Modernization: Toward a Political Economy of Postindustrial Culture*

ROBERT WEIMANN

For Walter Jens
Undaunted spiritus rector,
grand old/young man of letters

"Cultural capital" is not exactly an inviting phrase, but as a provocative metaphor it may well be taken to suggest that the present space of cultural activity is much less autonomous, much less a derivative of a nucleus of creativity in the fine arts, than seemed to be the case in the circumstances of an earlier, "classical" phase of industrialized society. It was easier a hundred years ago, even thirty years ago, to think of the arts as comfortably remote from the sphere of economics. The worlds of industry, including the applied sciences, technology, and engineering, would more often than not be associated with, in Max Weber's phrase, a specifically modern "rationality of purpose" ("Zweckrationalität") as opposed to a "rationality of value" ("Wertrationalität").[1] The dividing line between the world of high culture and that of mere instrumentality appeared simply to be given and was widely accepted. In fact, the gulf between them deepened to the extent that the world of applied rationality came to be recognized in its historical contingency, as part of that remorseless circuit of appropriation and consumption which has led Western industrial civili-

---

* This essay is the English version of one of my contributions to a study of *Modernity, Value, and Representation*, as projected by a research team in Forschungsschwerpunkt Literatur, Wiss. Neuvorhaben (Berlin-Munich).
[1] Max Weber, *Wirtschaft und Gesellschaft*, 4th ed. (Tübingen: Mohr, 1956) 12f.

zation on a problematic path, into an unprecedented crisis for itself and in relation to the underprivileged rest of the world.

However, as we now look back upon it, the alliance, not to say symbiosis, between modernity and "rationality" began to crumble at a remarkably early stage. For Max Weber, such alliance was central to, indeed constitutive of, his definition of modernization as an ensemble of progressively rational developments in culture, economy, and administration. But as early as the forties, the presuppositions of a progressive concept of modernity were profoundly challenged: In Adorno and Horkheimer's *Dialektik der Aufklärung*,[2] Enlightenment reason and myth are redefined as mutually complicitous; reason is contaminated by the unreasonable functions to which it is put, if not entirely usurped by irrational uses of power. If anywhere the modernists' disaffection from their own intellectual legacy crystallizes into a profound gesture of revaluation, it is in Adorno and Horkheimer: in their essay the alliance of modernization and modernity, progress and reason breaks up — the Enlightenment discourse of modernism is revisited as "the failed attempt to take off from the forces of destiny."[3]

Along these lines, distinctions between culture and industry were extended to those between high culture and *Kulturindustrie*, implicating an ever widening spectrum of incongruities, as between traditional premises of rational thought and social value and what, in the context of modern mass culture, had resulted from it. Now the link between production and "interaction" (as civilized relations of social give and take), first outlined by Hegel in his Jenenser Lectures, definitely seemed to be a matter of the past. That is, the economic exchange of material values was one thing, worlds apart from reciprocal action as a potent paradigm of civilized exchange in the enlightened sense of Hegel. After all, such reciprocity demanded norms and standards (which, of course, it did not have), above all, as against unenlightened encroachments by force and constraint. Under these circumstances, the workaday world of "interaction," as a world once considered as perfectly compatible with cultural values, was written off, and the enlightened principle of reciprocity was relegated to a finer mode of communication through symbols. Symbolic action, and

[2] Theodor W. Adorno and Max Horkheimer, *Dialektik der Aufklärung* [Dialectics of Enlightenment] (1947; New York: Continuum, 1983, c1973).

[3] In Habermas's pregnant phrase: "als den misslingenden Versuch, den Schicksalsmächten zu ent-springen." See Jürgen Habermas, *Der philosophische Diskurs der Moderne* (Frankfurt: Suhrkamp, 1985) 139.

the arts in particular, advanced to become the epitome of cultural exchange.

At this conjuncture, notions of culture had to be renegotiated at the point of intersection (and opposition) between the discourse of modernism and the aims of modernization. As areas of compatibility between exchange value and cultural value were eroded, communicative "interaction" had to relocate itself in a more confined space, so as to defend an unconsummated modern project of emancipation. Whenever this "project of modernity" was viewed as a failed one, theoreticians turned away from the attempt to realign in one representation those dichotomous areas of value, cultural and economic. If, at this date, it is too late (or perhaps too early) to make entirely acceptable suggestions toward a new approach to the divisions (and realignments) in the political economy of values economic and cultural, perhaps the time has come at least to take stock of some of the problems and perspectives on our way (from) there.

Culture and Technology: Con-Versions of Circulation

This brief introduction to the intellectual background of the problematic should at least partially assist in the present attempt to redefine value and representation at a point where they confront both the (modern) gaps and the (nonmodern) links between technology and culture. In our time, to quote again the editors of this journal, it appears to make sense to talk, if not of interaction, at least of "streams" and "circulation." Circulation, which is conducive to both exchange and communication, challenges and transgresses the boundary between cultural discourse and political economy. Straddling the two, this language appears designed to help view in conjunction such highly differentiated spaces and activities as have been consistently disconnected from one another by modern ideas of autonomy and related concepts in neoclassical and romantic aesthetics.

For transgressive projects such as these, the place and moment in time are no doubt propitious. While there is no end to ever more powerful uses of "instrumental reason," the political economy of rationality itself is rapidly changing and in urgent need of redefinition. In fact, it is no exaggeration to say that the convergent forms and pressures of circulation, thriving on technological innovation, have more and more come to serve as a catalyst of a new type of modernization process. In the past, increasing productivity and continuous growth had generally resulted from the dynamic of machines and energies pumped into the production process, as at the center of the rationalization drive of industrial capitalism. But today the impetus to increase productivity results not primarily from improved machinery and an increased demand for industrial output but from a technologically developed system of media and devices that store and process information and exponentially enhance its uses. It is this computerized, digital apparatus circulating information, data, signs, pictures, and texts that today is the main means of increased productivity, without which even the more traditional energetic-machinetic instrumentarium of industry could scarcely hope to remain competitive.

In this situation, which scarcely needs to be outlined in detail, the political economy of value in postindustrial technologies has strangely come to be realigned with a new cultural potential of the same. This, surely, comes as a surprise to many of us. At any rate, this was in no way anticipated by those who in the past had grappled with the problem: Adam Smith's definitions of value (and, in this tradition, some important premises in Marx's approach to it) were entirely innocent. Nor was Hegel, or the French utopian socialists, prepared even to contemplate such perspectives. And the most ambitious sociology of modern art in our own time, that of the Frankfurt School, recoiled from, rather than helped explore, the perspective of economic-cultural convergence. But today there is, if no convergence, at least a new unprecedented area of complicity between the technological uses of rationality and some of the most widely received symbolically structured systems of cultural interaction and communication. More than anything, this area is in each respective case marked by an overriding set of reactions against the traditional fixtures (political, semantic, historical) of representation. Such reaction appears especially strong where symbolic forms themselves surrender their representational function in favor of a new political economy of the sign.

Despite the undiminished or even expanding operation of the energetic-machinetic foundations of modern industry, the underlying change in the sources of societal productivity seems important enough to be emphasized more strongly. Classical industrial productivity had assumed a relative balance in the availability of labor force, capital, natural resources, and technology. In postindustrial society, production for obvious reasons cannot dispense with any of these factors; even so, productivity is predominantly stimulated to the greatest degree possible by electronically accessible, scientifically based information, by what Daniel Bell, abstracting from its material means of mediation, calls "theoretical knowledge."[4]

Today, the organization, the accessibility, and the communication of this knowledge serve as decisive catalysts for what can no longer quite be called "industrial" growth. Owing to the new technology behind the processing of this knowledge, the labor force, the available quality and quantity of natural resources, and even disposable capital itself have begun to shrink as an impetus for modernization. As against these, the achieved rate of multiplication, the sheer scope of the availability of data, signs, and information can scarcely be exaggerated. Suffice it to recall that in the twentieth century alone over eighty percent of all of mankind's inventions and discoveries were witnessed, two-thirds of these since the Second World War. Approximately sixty to seventy percent of all scientists and scholars who have up to now lived on earth are still alive; that is, to a considerable extent, they continue to be involved in the establishment, communication, reception, and utilization of scientific data. Since the turn of the century, the amount of technical knowledge has increased annually by thirteen percent. This represents a doubling every five and one-half years. Recent estimates suggest an even more dramatic growth rate. Although his figures have thus far not quite been confirmed, in 1982 John Naisbitt suggested that future growth rates of information to about forty percent annually would lead to a doubling of data in only twenty months.[5]

It is in view of developments such as these that the circumstances in which new constellations of value defy traditional divisions (mostly in representational forms) between aesthetic and economic discourses need to be examined more closely. These constellations are not entirely new: as Jacques Derrida has shown in his essay "Economi-

---

[4] Daniel Bell, *The Coming of Post-Industrial Society* (New York: Basic Books, 1973) 18. In *The Cultural Contradictions of Capitalism* (New York: Basic Books, 1976) 14, Bell discusses the "disjunction of realms," that is, the increasing differentiation among cultural, "techno-economic" and "socio-political systems," but in doing so he follows a characteristically modern definition of culture as the "realm of symbolic forms" (12). Such definition — in this case, Ernst Cassirer's — would seem always already to prescribe "the radical disjunction between the social structure (the techno-economic order) and the culture" (37), even when today this disjunction needs to be reexamined and modified.

[5] John Naisbitt, *Megatrends: Ten New Directions Transforming Our Lives* (New York: Warner Books, 1982) 24.

mésis," the barriers between these discourses can be put into question even as deep demarcations between them were inscribed and, of course, fortified within the Kantian text.[6] There is, even at its inception, no strict line of separation between the poetics of representation and the discourse of economic production and value. The emergence of the claim on aesthetic autonomy itself is not isolated from the workings of instrumental reasoning, no matter how much the classical text seeks to conceal its own complicity. If this is so in an eighteenth-century context, we should not be surprised to trace some deliberate rehearsal of the same alliance, albeit in radically different form, in the thought of the leading theoretician of the modern aesthetic. Note how Theodor W. Adorno in his *Ästhetische Theorie* seeks to bypass, or at least to neutralize, an a priori dichotomy that his own modernist aesthetics elsewhere tends emphatically to vindicate:

> The antagonism in the concept of technology as something that is inneraesthetically determined and as something developed outside of the work of art is not to be thought of as absolute. It came about historically and can disappear. Today it is possible to produce something artistic electronically from the specific nature of extra-artistically developed media.[7]

Today such "antagonism" in the uses of technology is, of course, quite fundamental still, especially when compared with what in ancient Greece was comprehended by a radically encompassing concept of *techne*, the etymological root of *technik*, or "technique." Here we can only remind ourselves of the gradual process of differentiation among the *technai*, as first established with any consistency by Aristotle: it was his line of distinction between the fine arts and the useful arts according to which "the spheres of use and beauty came in practice to be dissevered," so much so that "the useful object ceased to be decorative."[8]

In revisiting the relationship between economic technology and aesthetic production, we are today at least more wary of (un)necessary complications in a broad spectrum of relationships — a spectrum that extends from continuing antagonism to a new kind of convergence.

---

[6] Sylviane Agacinski, Jacques Derrida, et al., *Mimésis des articulations* (Paris: Aubier-Flammarion, 1975) 57-93.

[7] Theodor W. Adorno, *Ästhetische Theorie*, 3rd ed. (Frankfurt a.M.: Suhrkamp, 1977) 56.

[8] See *Aristotle's Theory of Poetry and Fine Art*, ed. Samuel H. Butcher, 4th ed. (New York: Dover, 1951) 115.

But by and large, the traditional opposition between the rationality of purpose in economic production and the supposed freedom from purpose in aesthetic communication appears flawed or at least highly relative. Today there is little doubt that reproduction and communication in the arts (as, for example, in music, theater, design, entertainment) are availing themselves more and more of the technological instrumentarium of sign-transporting media, just as, in its turn, technology in the economic-scientific area stands and falls with the range of exchange and communicability of signs and sign systems.

New Conjunctures of Value

What in our context appears especially important is the fact that, in the one case as in the other, information is not used up and is not emptied out by its reception. Its consumption may lead to obsolescence and a limited degree of exhaustion, but hardly to an elimination of the materiality of the related signs and signals. Since no shortage of material resources is to be expected for the micro-electronic circulation of these signs, its source of production may well be considered inexhaustible. Nor is the information process limited by the traditional need to conserve resources, as are the basic elements of mass and energy which underlie the more strictly industrial mode of expansion. This alone is of huge consequence for the dynamic of current modernization processes; for the range of innovation and increase in the productivity of economically viable information technologies (as compared to the limited availability of labor or capital) appears virtually unlimited.

At this point it is difficult to resist the conclusion that all this must have certain implications for the political economy of value. Information, accessible to the extreme and supplied through a material that is abundantly available, is to a certain extent able to resist an object form. This is in no way to suggest that information cannot be treated as a commodity. On the contrary, we all know that certain kinds of information can be bought and sold like properties on the market, and that its price can be correlated with the conditions of supply and demand. Yet the marketability of electronic information depends on an economic value that is not (as in traditional political economy) measured in man-hours. In this respect, even the commercial exchange of information is relatively independent of the value attributed to labor, including the labor invested in producing the material means and media of circulation itself. Again, the point is that it is not simply the product, i.e., the data processed by information technology, but the *processing itself* which has become reproducible. Hence, ability to disseminate information is much greater than the possibility of letting it stagnate in unused form.

However, if the political economy of signs, signals, and data, along with their interactive processes of circulation and reception, do not stand and fall with their exchange value, we need to ask, on what grounds can the question of value in postindustrial societies be reopened? As an answer to this question, it surely would be rash to reject Bell's notion of a "radical disjunction" between technology and culture only to suspend it in the opposite notion of a radical convergence between the two. There is no doubt whatever that the trend toward convergence between cultural and techno-economic values is relative when what is valuable in the rationality of the mode of information continues to resist representations of value in the field of culture.

Therefore, if a somewhat schematic response to the question may pass muster, it seems safest to ground the trend toward convergence on either side of the relationship in question: on the one hand, communication itself has become one of the constituting functions of a new level of instrumental reason; on the other hand, technology, at the highest level of its instrumentalization, allows for an unprecedented density of potentially valuable cultural communications to be presented to an audience of millions. If, on both sides, it is again circulation that provides a newly encompassing frame of reference, the question may well be asked whether, as against the language of either convergence of disjunction, a more fully adequate notion may not be derived from the figure of circulation itself: for despite continuing differentiation processes between cultural and technological modes of communication, the facilities and media used here and there constitute an overriding circuit of knowledge and power. What we have are circular endeavors of an intellect that is both present (and, to be informed, receiving) *and* absent (or "objectified," in that such absent or past inventiveness has made the apparatus of circulation possible in the first place). It seems difficult categorically to separate these different locations of intellect, one intelligently using the objectifications of the former, when electronically processed signs and messages themselves help to constitute and promote an unprecedented circulation of cultural energies, functions, and activities. Here we have, independent of its quality, more than an extraordinary potential of signs and images realizable in aid of the uses (or abuses) of cultural values: there is a point at which the convergence of these streams of cultural and techno-economic energies, through their circulation, leads to new, compelling ways and strange compounds of interaction.

However, it is one thing to be aware of this potential space of convergence as profoundly changing the economic-cultural landscape of modernity, and quite another to realize that the dynamic of this change implicates modes and configurations of value that radically depart from traditional representational form. In fact, it is the mode of information itself that helps undermine such claims to validity and authority as used to be associated with modern representations of value. What then this new conjuncture of values reiterates (and what our own critical reconstructions need to confront) is a deficit of legitimacy, the crisis of authority in the discourse of modernism itself. This is not the place again to examine the impasse of such concepts of authority as were integral to the predominant representational form of the modern.[9] Suffice it to suggest here that the decline of representational function is correlated with the new technology of information exchange. In fact, the impasse of representation may be said to have an equivalent in the diminishing sensory quality and corresponding uses of subjectivity in the microelectronic channels of communications itself.

As the distance between the mediated sources of information and the subject to be informed has become very considerable, the traditional humanistic links between the production and the reception of knowledge are gravely weakened. The strength of these links resided in a capacity of the subject, celebrated in neoclassical and romantic poetics, for embracing, through the sheer powers of the imagination, the act of creation and that of re-creation: the subject-centered, unified site of insightful knowledge, its legislation, and its affirmation in the mind of the recipient. The trajectory from here to there was collapsed in the imaginative act of (re-)collection and (re-)creation: the knowledge and the knower were inseparable. It is only when the person who knows finds himself at more than two removes from the sources of knowledge itself that its circulation becomes paramount. But to the extent that this circulation relies more and more on the "materiality" of the means of communication, the space for subjectivity shrinks

---

[9] I have pursued this in "(Post)Modernity and Representation: Issues of Authority, Power, Performativity," *New Literary History* 23 (1992) 955-81. This draws on, but goes beyond, my Introduction to *Postmoderne — globale Differenz*, ed. Robert Weimann and Hans Ulrich Gumbrecht (Frankfurt a.M.: Suhrkamp, 1991) 9-53, which I have continued to use in the present essay.

or, as we shall see, is more and more confined to the sphere of reception and the act of selection.[10]

Value as Representation

Further complications in the uses of subjectivity come into the picture as soon as we realize that labor in its classical definition cannot remain a valid norm in the political economy of value in our own time. Adam Smith, in *The Wealth of Nations*, did not for a moment hesitate to define the value of a product in relation to the amount of work used to manufacture it:

> The value of any commodity, therefore, to the person who possesses it, and who means not to use or consume it himself, but to exchange it for other commodities, is equal to the quantity of labour which it enables him to purchase or command. Labour, therefore, is the real measure of the exchangeable value of all commodities.[11]

And, even more emphatic:

> Labour alone, therefore, never varying in its own value, is alone the ultimate and real standard by which the value of all commodities can at all times and places be estimated and compared. (51)

From premises such as these, widely accepted down to Karl Marx and beyond, the value of a product or a commodity was viewed as a representation of the work and time invested therein. But in the face of microelectronically processed innovation and productivity, the question needs to be asked whether the entire modality of value determination can still adequately be defined in representational terms, as *aliquid stat pro quo*. The value of a product (not to mention a given productivity) made available through information technology does not *represent* the inherent cost invested in terms of any equivalent amount of "societal labor, measured by its duration."[12]

The representational structure of value in its information form (as, for instance, the value of computerized data, signs, texts) is in question as soon as the physical intellectual expense of the labor of living

---

[10] See *Materialität der Kommunikation*, ed. Hans Ulrich Gumbrecht and K. Ludwig Pfeiffer (Frankfurt a.M.: Suhrkamp, 1988).

[11] Adam Smith, *An Inquiry into the Nature and Causes of the Wealth of Nations*, ed. R. H. Campbell and A. S. Skinner (Oxford: Clarendon Press, 1976) 1:47.

[12] This is from the traditional definition of "Wert" ("value") in *Philosophisches Wörterbuch*, ed. Georg Klaus and Manfred Buhr (Leipzig: Enzyklopädie, 1969) 2:1150.

beings tends to be more and more removed from the actual site of processing and distributing their "products" and the productivity in question. At such a remove, the exchange value of signs follows a different order of correspondence, where, in Baudrillard's phrase, "the economic (quantitative) is converted into sign-difference." Even so, this order is much closer to, and can even collapse in, pure utility or trends prescribed by fashion, taste, or status. As Baudrillard continues to note in *For a Critique of the Political Economy of the Sign*:

> With respect to signs, the use value/exchange value distinction is virtually obliterated. If "sign use value" is defined as differential satisfaction, a sort of qualitative surplus value anticipated through a choice, a preference, a semiological calculation; and if sign exchange value is defined as the general form (the code) that regulates the interplay of models; then it becomes clear the extent to which use value issues directly from the functioning of the code and exchange value system.[13]

Although it may appear questionable whether the "exchange value" of technologically processed signs can *tout court* be identified with "the general form (the code)," both utility and exchange value cannot be abstracted from circulation as their prime prerequisite. Circulation, providing the coordinates of realization for both cultural and economic sign values, also helps constitute the postmodern context in which (for science, politics, services, advertisements) economic value increasingly submits to the order of signs.

As a consequence, nonsymbolic modes of exchange are privileged as against the more traditional representation of value in terms of a direct human investment of labor. As Baudrillard notes, "parallel to the ascension of economic exchange value into sign value, there is a reduction of symbolic value into sign value."[14] The repression of symbolic modes of exchange is vitally connected to, in fact is part of, the decline of representation.

Once the order of equivalence collapses, there is no need for representing value in what serves to substitute for it or what, originally, helps to delegate it. But if economic value is to be measured by nonrepresentational standards, the whole dialectic of utility value

---

[13] Jean Baudrillard, *For a Critique of the Political Economy of the Sign*, tr. Charles Levin (St. Louis: Telos Press, 1981) 205.
[14] Baudrillard 120. See 128: "symbolic exchange finds itself expelled from the field of value (or the field of general political economy)... And the logical organization of this entire system denies, represses and reduces symbolic exchange."

and exchange value appears undermined. As Baudrillard suggests, the next step would be to go "beyond use value," insofar as, in its classical conception, use value may be said to represent "a kind of moral law at the heart of the object — and it is inscribed there as the finality of the 'need' of the subject" — according to which "law" the "circulation of value is regulated by a providential code that watches over the correlation of the object with the needs of the subject."[15]

While Baudrillard's suspicion of teleology may appear somewhat excessive, he does not address the question, as formulated by Michel Foucault, whether or to what extent "the irreducibility of labour and its primary character" would not by itself preclude a providential or, for that matter, a representational scheme of reference. Writing on "The Limits of Representation" (as his chapter heading has it), Foucault at once seems to question "labor" as "an irreducible, absolute unit of measurement":

> How can labour be a fixed measure of the natural price of things when it has itself a price — and a variable price? How can labour be an absolute unit when it changes its form, and when industrial progress is constantly making it more productive by introducing more and more divisions into it?[16]

Working under a self-imposed need for running abreast, after the end of the "classical age," a three-tiered decline in the representations of labor, life, and language, Foucault contents himself by noting that while the "unit" of labor "is not a fixed one," it "is not really the labour itself that has changed; it is the relation of the labour to the production of which it is capable" (223). In these circumstances, it is possible for him to ignore that, in fact, long after the end of the "classical age," labor continues to be represented in concepts of value or in uses of wealth, even when — a point as important as it is valid — labor "is based upon conditions that are... exterior to its representation" (225).

However, reviewing changes in parameters of value between industrial society and the new mode of information, we need to establish a broader perspective on the changeful relationships of labor and culture, work time and spare time, the production of cultural goods and their "meanings." If, in this context, the orthodox Marxist definition of value appears problematic precisely because of its represen-

---

[15] Baudrillard 130, 133.
[16] Michel Foucault, *The Order of Things: An Archaeology of the Human Sciences* (New York: Vintage Books, 1973) 223.